# About the Author

Richie Fitzgerald is Ireland's first pro surfer. He competed at both European and World Championship level, and was the first European invited to the world's most prestigious big-wave event, the Eddie Aiku Invitational in Hawaii. Born in Bundoran, Co. Donegal, he was the founder of Ireland's first and largest surf shop, Surfworld. He has two children with his wife, Briohny, and chases the summer by splitting his time between Ireland and Australia.

*Prologue*

# In the Eye of a Storm: Part 1

On a cold, gusty, pre-dawn morning in December 2007, I sat in the back of my van with the fan heaters on full blast. My teeth chattering with anxious anticipation more than the biting winter cold that was whipping in and penetrating though every available cavity in the vehicle. My nostrils filling on each intake of breath with the sharp, sea-salty, overpoweringly fresh aroma of fishy seaweed that only a sea in full storm can produce. Gulls screaming overhead as they soared and dived without beating a wing in the ferocious gale. I was parked at the top of the harbour in Mullaghmore, Co. Sligo, on Ireland's northwest coast. Sitting alongside me in the passenger seat was my long-time big-wave surfing partner, Gabe Davies. We both desperately needed a moment of solitude, a personal calm before the storm. So, with that in mind I closed and locked the van's sliding side door, banishing all the film crew, line producers, onlookers and the health and safety officers from our immediate orbit.

The day was just starting to get bright with streaks of pale, wintery dawn light making their first appearance. The weak illuminations gave us the necessary chink of light that we needed to take stock of Mother Nature's full rage in the monstrously churning charcoal-grey and white-capped sea. Within moments the silvery treads of struggling low light that characterise the depth of winter had finally broken over Donegal Bay. The new December day stretching from the southwest brought into sharp focus the true extent of the furious cold saltwater arena we were about to step into.

Neither Gabe nor I had slept a wink the night before, both of us suffering from the duality of expectations and pressure mixed with excitement, fear and a healthy slice of ambivalence for the coming hours. I climbed into the driver's seat, turned on the engine and slowly rolled out of the car park. Our creeping exit caused dismay among the production and camera crew visible in my rear-view mirror – their hands on their heads, arms waving in anguished disapproval – as we drove off in the direction of the headland hoping for a private moment to address our age-old predicament of 'to go or not to go'. The former had always emerged victorious, but today was unequalled in the intensity of that decision making. The knowledge that we could be risking it all, life and limb, and for what? Certainly, it wasn't for fame or financial reward. To us, it was for something that ran much deeper than that: it was personal, private even, with a strong sense of ownership of the waves at Mullaghmore for us both. The most powerful desire for us that morning was eclipsing everything else. It was something on a more primal level, pressing and critical as tide, time and opportunity weren't going to wait no matter how much we willed them to. That unflinching power of nature blasting in the face of our physical human fragility. Inside of us, it was exposing every doubt we had, laying bare all our fears. It was a day we knew would come around eventually, whether we wanted it to or not.

I'm not a believer in destiny. It's too strong a word in its neatness for me. It's only applicable when you are talking about important stuff like royal succession and George McFly. In many ways, that day was what Gabe and I had been working towards for most of our lives. We had led the way in Irish big-wave surfing; now we were ready to meet the moment head on. Stars weren't aligned but we were the right surfers in the right place at the right time. We had manufactured this moment for ourselves, ready for a coming together of all the necessary human and natural elements. The enormous potential of what could be achieved that morning became shockingly clear. We had put in countless years of hard work to be ready for a day like this, with no big-wave surfing roadmap to follow. For me, I've always believed you put in the time, ride your luck as best you can, and when the chances come you need to be ready to grasp them with both hands. This day was one of those moments. The potential apex of our careers was now tantalisingly within our reach. We were ready for it, or as ready as you can be facing into what was for both of us a no mistakes, no second chances game of Russian roulette at dawn. Only one winner could emerge when the dust settled. It would either be us or the gigantic waves.

That morning, the northwest coast of Ireland was under the influence of a massive, unprecedented 50-foot swell. Waves were well in excess of 40 feet high all along the coastline. A coastline, I might add, that is no stranger to some of the world's most violent storms and enormous waves capable of sinking a Spanish Armada. A heaving mass of treacherous white water extended for miles out to sea. The incoming walls of triple-storey milk-coloured white water tumbled forward, licking the coastline like giant tongues of fiery flames that fizzed and roared before exploding off the cliffs. The crescendos of white water were being mercilessly flung hundreds of feet into the air, drenching and inundating everything in their path, creating a hanging salty mist that shrouded the immediate coastline and everything on it.

The one exception to this chaos in Donegal Bay was Mullaghmore Head, the famous big-wave spot that is just tucked into the westerly reach of the north Sligo harbour town. The headland was somehow holding its shape. The intricate and deceptively delicate balance of wave size, swell direction, tide movement, wind, headland formation, bottom contour and water depth were all in play that morning. The combined result wasn't exactly nature's smooth symphony; it was more an almighty power struggle between all the elements. Mullaghmore Head offered a fleeting fusion for these clashing, attritional elements. Here, the biggest waves the Atlantic could throw at the coast would peel and break with colossal size and unimaginable power beyond the bluff. The key component for us that morning among the mayhem of the maelstrom was looking for any basic uniformity to the tossed seascape and waves. As massive and windswept as they were, the waves at Mullaghmore Head looked surfable. That's the silver bullet in these situations. A tiny window of opportunity that requires a short, uneasy entente cordiale between the dexterous, warring natural elements. This second of ceasefire could in theory allow us just enough time for the briefest of moments to exploit it. Each moving mountain of water that morning offered some semblance of shape and open face that could give us permission to launch. A promising setting to us, which to everyone else looked an extremely unfeasible one at best or suicidally life-threatening at worst.

Our understanding of storms heading for Ireland had progressed beyond 'the night of the big wind', but it was still an era before big winter depressions and damaging storms were christened with innocuous names like 'Steven' - without the PH - or 'Patricia'. So, this storm was a nameless monster covering what was most of the North Atlantic, from Nova Scotia to Iceland to Ireland and back again. Between chirpy morning radio show skits and the big hits of that year from Leona Lewis and Mika, the early news bulletins from national broadcasters came across crystal clear on the van's speakers. Every station was warning people to stay off the coast. Severe code red weather warnings were on repeat from Malin Head to Mizen Head and everywhere in between. The headlines were of record high seas and damaging storm-force winds to be expected all day along the Atlantic seaboard as the deepening area of low pressure enveloped the whole country. The storm front was inducing a nightmare before Christmas scenario for our entire coastal waters.

As Gabe and I crested the small hill that cloaks the final approach to Mullaghmore Head, I noticed my knuckles were gripped white to the steering wheel. 'I'll need a crowbar to pry them free,' I said to myself with my whispered words unconsciously leeching from my loose lips. 'Talking to yourself again, Rich,' Gabe responded as we both cracked a nervous smile that broke the silent tension. As we drew near, the entire headland gradually unfurled in front of us. If you believed in old man of the sea superstitions or long-held sailors' omens, well then, they were all present and pointing at the shore screaming at us to stay on land. The leaden sky, grey storm-tossed sea and giant, inky-black slabs of treacherously blasted wet rock that categorise the bluff were in sharp contrast to the relative safety of the sodden but deeply green verge we parked up on. Our sleepy, early-morning monotone responses were replaced in an instant with a hyper-sensitive awareness, that we had reached the point of no return.

Immense building-sized chunks of storm-whipped ocean came

thundering in, each liquid fist smashing the coast square in the jaw with a relentless flurry of blows. Set after bigger set of waves detonated out to sea, making the swells seem like something out of a cartoon. Nothing of this size or even close to it had been surfed in Ireland before, or anywhere in Europe for that matter.

There is nothing more sobering than the feeling of insignificance that you register when pitting yourself against such staggering forces of nature. That morning for both of us was the culmination of 15 years of joint big-wave dedication that had already yielded many successes and a few character-building failures. Most importantly, the last decade and a half had proven that together we were much stronger and more capable than the sum of our individual parts.

We were eagerly looking to add our names and the Irish coastline to that most exclusive list of the world's biggest and best waves. We had surfed Mullaghmore plenty of times before, but not at this size and intensity. Was it possible for an Irishman and Englishman to buck the world order of global big-wave surfing? Would it be possible by day's end to sit alongside the achievements previously only seen in places like Hawaii and Northern California? Most important for us that morning was to see whether we were up to the task at hand. Were we good enough? Could we successfully stand in and fill those big international shoes? Passing the toughest of surfing tests was the prize. Crumbling at the altar was just as possible a reality.

The likelihood that my life would lead to such a dramatic, pressurised and momentous morning in Mullaghmore was not a foregone conclusion or the pinnacle of some predetermined surfing destiny. The real story of how I reached that moment would have seemed unimaginable to that young schoolboy taking his first cautious steps in the sea at Bundoran.

# 1

# Bundoran

My father's idea of going for a swim – like so many Irishmen of his generation – was to take off his socks and shoes and roll his trousers up to just below the knee, accessorise himself with an off-white hanky tied over his head in four knots, and stand in ankle-deep water reluctantly directing traffic in a sea world that was many light years beyond his comfort zone. My mother, being an inlander herself, was only marginally better. She also hated to get her face or hair wet while swimming. The result of this was that she rarely went out into the sea or a swimming pool. When an opportunity presented itself and she did go for a swim she had pursed lips and only breaststroked within her depth from point to point.

So, for me, my brother and my sisters, our love of the water was most definitely a product of our coastal environment and proximity to the beach and surf, rather than genetically handed down. My oldest sister Frances set the pace and tempo of the Fitzgerald kids. She absolutely loved the sea, and would go for a swim around Bundoran's challenging Rougey Point at the drop of a hat. She was a real ocean person. She could surf too, before I could, even in the depths of winter in the early 1980s when it was way too cold to go for a dip. She would go for a brisk walk or run around the seashore just to feel the salt air on her face as much as anything. Her enthusiasm for the sea was infectious, infusing an early curiosity, fascination and love for the ocean in me.

I was born in Sligo town on New Year's Eve 1974, the youngest of five siblings – with three sisters and one brother – but I grew up in the bustling seaside town of Bundoran, 22 miles north of Sligo. The town sits just over the Leitrim-Sligo county border, marking Donegal's most southerly point. I was very much a product of and shaped by my family. In saying that, I was also just as much a product of the unique coastal community and environment I grew up in. Neither of my parents were born in Bundoran. My dad, also Richard, was born in 1931 to Irish emigrant parents in the blue-collar, working-class Irish neighbourhood of Elizabeth, New Jersey, USA. My mum was born in 1936 in Co. Cavan, where she was raised on her parents' small family farm near the Leitrim-Cavan border. My dad returned to Ireland at a young age when my grandparents decided to raise their young family in Ireland, choosing Bundoran as their new hometown. It was extremely rare in those years for any Irish emigrant families to return home to Ireland from America. It was all one-way traffic, so their decision was very much the exception. They established Fitzgerald's boarding house, which is still in town today but now the much more luxurious Fitzgerald's Hotel. My dad's family were famous for their music. My grandfather, another Richard (I'm the fifth Richard Fitzgerald in a row) was a very talented musician, establishing himself as a respected and in-demand violinist on both sides of the Atlantic. He was a native of Killenaule, Co. Tipperary, the ancestral homeland of the Fitzgerald name in Ireland. My grandfather passed on his musical knowledge to his children, especially my father, his sister Kathleen and brother Barney. The three siblings together eventually formed and remained the nucleus of the Richard Fitzgerald Ceili Band in Bundoran. For much of my life, especially during my younger years, I have memories of my dad being away constantly on tour overseas or gigging away at night all over Ireland.

My mum, Margaret 'Peggy' Martin, like my dad, came from a big Catholic family deep-rooted in Ireland for countless generations. With only a primary school education she emigrated to the UK at age 15. As her older sister Emily was already living and working in Luton, my mother took a production line job working at a ball bearing factory for Vauxhall cars. She later spent time working in New York, for the *New York Times* and then the British Overseas Airways Corporation (BOAC). She met my dad on a visit home to Ireland and shortly after her return to New York she decided that she was going to move back home to Ireland permanently.

When Mum and Dad got married it was a bit of a celebrity affair: an Irish music star marrying a beauty queen (my mum was Miss Ireland in the 1950s, though she would kill me for saying so here). I suppose their marriage was the reason our house always had a bit of a showbiz feel to it when I was growing up. It became commonplace to have Irish celebrities and entertainers constantly in our house. Our home was like a train station for musicians and entertainers of every sort. We would have Paul Brady pop in for a cup of tea in the morning and Ronnie Drew at the dinner table at teatime. I remember sitting on Ronnie's knee as a wee cub; the Dubliner was a lovely man as far as my memory serves me, beard and all. After bedtime, the front door would nearly be knocked off its hinges as Big Tom would have broken a string or blown an amp next door in the Hollyrood ballroom. Castleblayney's finest would be standing in our porch in a state of panic, talking to my dad and looking for a lend of equipment to save his Mainliners gig from disaster. Which of course my dad always obliged. It was only much later in life that I realised this wasn't the norm in every household and how cool it was to have constant visitors like this through our front door. At the time though it was a regular occurrence for us Fitzgerald children growing up in that musical atmosphere and we didn't know any different.

My parents' decision to make Bundoran their home, the place where they wanted to put down their roots and start a family, really cast the die in the sea for all of us. Especially for me, with the most enticing of all playgrounds – the broad Atlantic – filling my view of our western skyline.

In 1972, two years before I was born, *Time* magazine named Bundoran a 'favourite frontier sanctuary of republican paramilitary gunmen', while at the same time British government intelligence sources documented and identified the town as having an 'active service unit'. This was the infamous IRA unit responsible for so much bloodshed while operating in Fermanagh and south Donegal. For some, this is a shocking indictment of the town at the time; for others it is quite the opposite. How you perceived the rights and wrongs, the religious divide, the violence and the hardball politics depended on how and where you were brought up, your family experience, history and the views you subscribed to. Derry, a city that has always had close ties to Bundoran, was reeling from the Bloody Sunday massacre of 14 civilians in January that year. It was a brutal benchmark in the escalating horror of the troubles that had the whole country in its gruesome grasp.

It was this politically charged and religiously entrenched atmosphere, of one person's freedom fighter and another person's terrorist, that permeated everything where I grew up. For most of my younger life, my hometown had illustrated a harsh contradiction for me. On the surface, it was and still is one of Ireland's most popular traditional seaside towns replete with beach blankets, candy floss and Ferris wheel attractions and trappings. It was to this ocean-minded Bundoran that I fixed my gaze and instinctively gravitated towards. My hometown, as I came to discover, was a place of breathtakingly good surf of a global standard, a bracing coastline, golden beaches and the boundless cerulean-blue Atlantic. For many though, Bundoran characterised something completely different. It was a town at the time overflowing as a militant republican stronghold due mostly to its stone's throw proximity to the border with the north of Ireland. The town acted as an important staging post in the subversive armed republican struggle, a place deeply indoctrinated in the republican cause and the political ideology whose proponents openly promoted the gun barrel.

The disconnect between the town's two personalities was stark and ill-fitting to me as I was growing up. At a very young age, I had no real grasp of what it all meant: the reasons, the history, the ideology and legitimacy of causes of the opposing sides. Like any child, my world was narrow and revolved around our family unit, our house, *Star Wars*, Action Man and going to the beach with my friends. Unlike in the movies, I never knew who the good guys in Northern Ireland were supposed to be: there was no good side and no winners.

Although we enjoyed a degree of separation from the north, many of the direct and indirect consequences of the troubles spilled across the border, affecting life in Bundoran. My parents, to my eternal gratitude, had brought us up to be well rounded and about as neutral and open minded as it was possible to be in those days. We were encouraged to be proud to be Irish, and a love for Ireland was instilled in us from early on.

Bundoran had a powerful attraction for republicans north of the border. I never developed any affinity to this militant 'West Belfast by the Sea' version of my hometown. For me, it was totally out of step and not reflective of the real town. On any given summer's weekend, you would have been forgiven for presuming the atmosphere in town served as an incubator for paramilitary involvement more than a Irish holiday favourite. The town in many respects didn't shy away or try to disguise its republican label; it embraced it for economic reasons more than political ones. The effect of this public image severely restricted and marginalised the demographics of the people coming to town that only served to stifle its public image for many years to come.

~

Our house – the Fitzgerald home house – was very much in the middle of our street. In fact, it was in the middle of everyone's street. If X marked the middle of Bundoran then our house was the bullseye centre.

Not many families live in urban town centres or high streets anymore. It's a way of living and family life that has almost vanished from the Irish societal landscape. Most families now live in single dwellings or new housing estates on the outskirts or approaches to towns and cities. That was not the case when I was young. Up until the year I finished school, there were still several families living in the middle of town. The main street, its footpaths and roads were our bike track, football pitch, meeting-up spots and gossip corners.

Although we were in rural coastal Ireland, we were very much town kids. It was also an era where moving house was a rarity, with multiple generations of family living in the same house. Houses and streets became synonymous with family names. Our Atlantic Way and the main street was full of Fitzgeralds, McEniffs and McHughs. Combining the kids from the three families, we could have easily turned out two mixed football teams. Mostly we rode bikes and played football around parked cars on the knee-skinning loose-chip tarmac covering the Hamilton car park. Getting an over-inflated, yellow plastic 'Super Tele' football full throttle in your face was puke inducing for you and laughter inducing for everyone else, while suffering from a shot square in the goolies was just par for the course. Our garage door at the back of the music shop acted as the unofficial goalposts that shuddered under the impact of every huffed deflection and blasted shot.

A house of course doesn't make a home; families do. With all of us living there the house felt much more than just a building to me. It was a big part of the family and took on its own character, looming large in my childhood memories, especially my early surfing ones. It features strongly in my recollections as our first surfing HQ in Bundoran, with the nerve centre of that HQ being our kitchen and sitting room. It was here that the tiny but enthusiastic first generation of Bundoran local surfers would congregate. The group was populated by my brother, sisters, me and all our friends that had any interest in surfing and the sea. Before a surf, we would group together to get changed – or togged out, as we called it – which meant we all arrived down to the water's edge at the same time.

This was a critical factor for us, as there was safety in numbers in surfing's early days. How different that ethos is now, with everyone looking to evade the crowds rather than purposely

attracting one. Getting to the beach en masse was the only way
to assess wind, tide and wave conditions with communal input.
This huddle also gave us the crucial chance to take stock of our
combined inventory. Our scant stockpile of boards and wetsuits
was always sparse and inadequate for the small number who
wanted to surf on any given day. As we decided who was going
first and who got to use which surfboard and wetsuit, we always
kept one eye on the sea; mind surfing the breaking waves, or
how we imagined we could, before we took to the water. If
the surf was bad – and it had to be terrible or blowing a hurricane for us not to surf – we would reluctantly retreat to our
house. Instead of catching waves, we would watch a recorded
clip of surfing on the TV. Everyone's favourite was the only surf
film we owned, which was a pirated VHS copy of George
Greenough's 1973 trippy, psychedelic movie, *Crystal Voyager*. This
featured the archetypal southern Californian hippy vibe, which
was about as non-compatible to us as it was possible to be.
What's more, the film's anti-establishment and anti-Vietnam war
subtext was completely lost on us. We were, however, musically
astute, and debated the merits of its soundtrack by Pink Floyd,
imagining ourselves surfing to their prog rock classics.

Our house had a character all of its own that accommodated
our first ventures into the waves and the wider world of surfing.
The building crossed the line from being just a pile of antiquated
bricks held together with lime mortar into something much
more essential and indispensable to us. It's a cliché but it was
our castle in many respects. It was a refuge, a see you back home
in the 'Alamo', and we loved it. As important as our house was
to us, it is unequalled as a location in the story of local surfing.
Inside those walls saw the very beginning of the surf industry
when we opened the region's first surf shop in 1990, followed
by the formation and incorporation of the town's first surf club

in 1991. It's incredible to me now thinking of all those surfing firsts that took place under our roof.

In the middle of all this surf awakening was our family home. A house that was full of all the fun, drama and hectic family life of five children growing up. School, holy communions, confirmations, the minefield transformation into teenagers, aspirations, first relationships, heartbreak, moving out, getting older, weddings, funerals and new additions all running alongside our journey from surfing green shoots to the national surfing scene.

Outside of our family and away from the burgeoning surf scene, our house was a social meeting point due to its central location and the convenient off-footpath shelter it offered. You would often overhear groups of people who you didn't know from Adam saying, 'OK, we'll see you outside Fitzgerald's after lunch at say 2 p.m.' Even the local football team congregated at the adjacent wall outside our house on weekend mornings, giddily smoking Silk Cut and drinking bottles of Coke and Club Orange while waiting for their car convoy of lifts to arrive and whisk them away. I would always stop and have a chat to the team, especially if it was classmates on the underage boys' teams.

The house itself was a big, rambling Georgian townhouse with three sets of staircases. It was roomy, but all the family action took place in the kitchen and sitting room. The rest of the house was mostly populated by the odd yawning dog or guilty-looking cat skulking about. It sounds idyllic, and in some ways it was. Perfect for five children to run amok with its rabbit warren of interconnected rooms and upstairs-downstairs escapades. The home had its downsides. The most obvious one was that it was permanently attached to my parents' busy 'Fitzgerald's Music Centre' record store that they opened in the late 1960s. The house acted as a storage and distribution depot to the other

seven music shops they owned around the country. The result
of this was similar to so many other families I knew who, like
us, were joined at the hip to their family business 24/7. It was
an upbringing that exposed me from a young age to the world
of business. As much as I disliked many invasive elements of it
at the time, I feel it has stood me well in the long run. Before
I realised it, I was getting an education in the business world
that taught me how to deal with all kinds of people and the
public. Having the constant of a family business from first thing
in the morning until well after the doors closed imbued me
with a strong work ethic, which would help me in my surfing
future. It gave me the courage to pursue my own path in life
while ignoring the naysayers and obstacles that popped up everywhere.

Our house faced the main road and arcades, with the other
three sides being boxed in by the imposing Holyrood Hotel,
the car park behind and takeaways to our right. It was a real
365 degrees of hardnosed make hay when the sun shines seaside
commercialism. Our front door – the most puked on, pissed on
and kicked front door in town – opened directly onto the main
street. Once you opened the front door, you were hit by the
distinctive salty smell of the seaside mixing in with the stale
whiff of grubby litter from passers-by the night before. My
brother and I were dispatched every Saturday and Sunday
morning to clean up the horrendous mess at the front and by
the garage doors. With two yard brushes, a couple of metal
buckets of water and a tin of Jeyes Fluid, we set about the odious
task of clearing smashed glass, blood, vomit and pee mixed with
fag butts, soggy chips, bits of burger, crushed cellophane
containers and endless plastic bags congealed in disgusting piles
from the previous night's revelry. We didn't stop until we had
cleaned the ground, walls and doors and had the place smelling

like disinfectant, always taking great pride in how good a job we managed.

Summer was always crazy in Bundoran. High summer, June to September, was also the time we were off school, when the days were long and the increased water temperature made surfing for hours on end, even in crappy wetsuits, a real possibility. Bundoran was anything but the image of a sleepy seaside hamlet nestled into the Irish coast. The town was loud, garish, brash, busy and a dangerous place to be when the sun went down. It was packed end to end with bars and nightclubs where anything would go and usually did. My overarching memory of Bundoran town in summer as a child and teenager was just how insanely rough it was. It's difficult to express just how belligerent the town got, especially at night; it felt out of control most of the time. I couldn't describe modern Bundoran as being gentrified; it still has an edge today, but it's well blunted in comparison. Most summer evenings now, you are more likely to see a hipster cycling down the packed streets with a scraggy dog in tow and a surfboard under his arm rather than a scrum of bucks in Celtic jerseys thumping the heads off each other outside a chippy. The latter was nothing shocking, being a common everyday sight during the 1980s and most of the 1990s.

Whatever chaos surrounded us in summer or during holiday times, it all faded to black in the background because the over-riding important component for our family was our home's proximity to the sea. It was only a ten-second run up Brighton Terrace before the Atlantic panorama revealed itself right in front of you. As the years went past, my combined footpath sprint and paddle-out travel time – from our kitchen starting line by the heated cream-coloured Stanley oven to the world-class waves of the Peak – was an enviable one minute.

Hot water in the house was never a guarantee, even with

the immersion heater on for eight hours. The immersion heater was the bane of the whole antiquated plumbing and electrical system expanse of households like ours back then. Halfway to Enniskillen there would be groans of despair when the realisation hit that someone had forgot to turn off the immersion heater before leaving. We were never frightened of the imposing British and Irish military, police and customs checkpoint that you had to go through to get to Enniskillen. But absolute despair filled the car at the thought of the immersion heater being left switched on.

With dodgy heating and spotty hot water, our range oven was always on full tilt to cover the building's inadequacies and timeworn failings when it came to utilities and integrity. Sitting eternally on the hob was a once silver but now a faded grey and pockmarked, patinated metal kettle that was freakishly big, always filled to the brim with scalding-hot water in case the heating was bandjaxed, which it was too often. The kettle could be hoisted off and used for baths, my dad's daily shave or dishwashing, before being refilled and returned to the hob with a hissing metallic touchdown of vapourised droplets. The range radiated heat like a black-topped nuclear reactor in a permanent state of imminent meltdown.

As a heat source it can take credit as much as anything for getting us all in the water and surfing over wintertime. Its furnace-like warmth meant it doubled up as a wetsuit drying area, much to my mother's disapproval. If you have ever smelled drying wetsuit boots, you can understand that. Think stagnant rot. We also had two big, beach-crazy Irish Red Setters named Zoom and Rip. When not down on the beach both dogs were plonked in front of the big sitting room fire all night until the last dying black embers of coal collapsed. Our home was always very animal friendly thanks to my mother's influence. We had a revolving door procession of dogs, birds, rabbits and numerous meowing calico cats. Some animals became family pets while others used our house as no more than a handy waystation for food and a dry bed before hitting the road again the next morning, never to be seen again. My sister Karen said of our house, 'If you had a limp, you were in, and if you didn't have one just put one on.' In this, she was referring to stray humans and animals alike.

Our kitchen also housed a huge saltwater fish tank on its gigantic Georgian windowsill above the sink. The tank was full of wonderfully coloured and flamboyantly pompous, cabaret-style tropical fish. One evening, my mother decided to put some rocks and organic material from the beach into the fish tank to make Liberace and friends feel more at home. What she had failed to consider was the water temperature difference between the North Atlantic and our tropical water fish tank. The overnight slow cooker proceeded to blanch the Bundoran beach material, releasing all the ingredients of the dulse seaweed into the tropical tank. The next morning, we were greeted with a fish tank transformed to a mushy, dark brown and black soup. Unfortunately, our fish hadn't survived the night. They were all floating on the surface, grotesquely bloated and bug eyed, the innocent victims of my mother's in-house ecological disaster.

With no animal shelter in town, any injured or abandoned animal (seaside towns seem to attract people who want to just dump or abandon an unwanted pet, and they always do it on weekends) would land on our door, often accompanied by a local good Samaritan saying we found this poor wee dog around the beach and didn't know where else to bring him. My mother never turned away any animal in need of help, love and food. The result of this has left me with a lifelong soft spot for any animal in distress.

Despite all this, I have always felt extremely lucky to have grown up in Bundoran and in that bustling house with the good and bad of its location. It knocked the edges off me from an early age and made me much more worldly than my age suggested. From early life, to navigate your way you had to be socially intelligent, politically aware and possess an ability to read people and situations with radar on, especially at night, to avoid getting caught up in the craziness of it all. In the daytime though, the water was where my real worldly adventures took place.

## 2

# My First Surf

I would love to tell you that my first surf was a life-changing, earth-shattering encounter for me. On paper this inaugural day should have ended in a hazy sunset filled with youthful optimism and an aquatic transcendence. Well, it didn't pan out that way. My first surfing experience was brief, ending in howls of high-pitched torment and the biting chill of numbness.

It's not that the sea and waves were a new realm for me, quite the opposite. In 1983, I had loved the sea for all my nine years of life. I was already a good sea swimmer, confident and curious. I felt comfortable bodysurfing the shore break waves. I adored swimming in summer and rummaging around in the world of deep rock pools, kelp forests, tidal caves and the strange critters that called them home. My favourite of all rockpool dwellers was the rich, red-coloured anemones, which we called bloodsuckers, with their red colour coming from all the blood sucked out of anyone unfortunate to stand in a rock pool with one of them in it, or so we imagined. Only the bravest could touch the rouge jelly bulb of a closed anemone and survive to tell the tale. It was an early initiation to 'go on, touch one, I double dare ya!'

My older brother Joe and sister Frances had taken to surfing just before me. I would watch them on the waves from the shore but showed little initial desire or felt any compulsion to ask for a go, until I was press-ganged into it. Surfing looked to me like a lot of hard work for minimal reward; for starters, having to lug an exceedingly heavy and awkward board down to the beach. A craft I couldn't even get my child-sized arms or cold little fingers around to grasp. Couple this logistical wrestle with the slim likelihood of any piece of adult wetsuit fitting my small size was deterrent enough. I was more than happy in my fantasy world of the Man from Atlantis re-enactments in the shallows. Anyway, adult wetsuits were as rare as hens' teeth in Ireland, while kid-sized wetsuits were unheard of anywhere.

Observing surfing from the shore gave me the impression that it was a pointless exercise. Awkwardly trying to paddle out through stacked walls of white water while being constantly repelled in a backwards tumble. All the while clinging desperately tight like a baby chimpanzee to the lethally cumbersome surfboard into the bedlam of the breaking wave. After a few dozen wave hits, oxygen levels were critically low with all your energy spent, leaving you in a precarious position like a boat without an engine at the mercy of the waves. The exhaustion left you powerless to stop yourself from being dragged semi-submerged in the opposite direction that you desired to go. To add insult to injury, the final humiliation was being unceremoniously deposited back on the sand clutching your board where it had all started just a few minutes before. Back to square one time and time again, day after day, with little or no progress, all the while demanding maximum effort. Surfing, I judged, was an unwinnable war of attrition against the oncoming waves and the power struggle to control your surfboard. I preferred to swim in the surf or glide down the inside of waves on the one flimsy, white polystyrene bodyboard we had. It seemed a better alternative to being smashed across the head by one of the few megatons of heavy surfboards we had access to. If the weight of the board didn't knock you out cold, you entertained the ever-present prospect of being sliced in half by the blade, the sharp 10-inch single fibreglass fin screwed to its underside. The thought of an out-of-control surfboard with its inverted fin hidden under the surface was more ominous than any Amity Island-inspired shark fin nightmare you might have.

The Achilles heel for surfers in Bundoran was the same as for everyone else in Ireland's tiny surfing community. It was owning or being able to get our hands on wave-riding equipment of any description. The simple fact was there were almost no surfboards or wetsuits in town. No surf shops, surf schools, water sports centres, nothing. It was still a few years away from the construction of Ireland's first surf club in Rossnowlagh. In any case that was in another town, granted only a 20-minute drive away but not within walking distance for us anyway. So Rossnowlagh might as well have been in Timbuktu until one of us was old enough to drive. It wasn't that there were any financial restraints; most kids had summer jobs or parents who worked or had their own small businesses in town. One of my favourite teachers in school was the extremely strict but hilariously funny Mrs Connors. On our first day back at school after summer, she would quip to the Bundoran children from the front of the class with a wry smile and the booming voice of a mid-Donegal town crier: 'Welcome children, it's great to see that you have all come back to school for a rest.' The Bundoran kids looked drained after three hectic months of constant summer work. In contrast, the country kids, even though they may have helped on a farm for the summer, were healthy-looking and suntanned from working outdoors. By summer's end, you could have saved the money for a board and wetsuit; you just had nowhere to buy it new or second hand once you had the cash in hand. If a board came up for sale anywhere in the area between Rossnowlagh to Strandhill, you might hear a rumour through word of mouth that 'so and so' in Sligo might be selling a board.

No discussion of suitability, brand, design or size of the surfboard was considered. That was a luxury still many years in the future for us. If you were lucky enough to hear a surfboard was up for sale, you would desperately try and find out the name of the seller and where they lived. If no one knew their telephone number, you would hit the Telecom Éireann phonebook and pester the operator with half an address until they connected you to the right house. Once you got through and found out the address and price, you would beg someone old enough to drive you to Rossnowlagh or Sligo to get the board. All my early surfboards were communally bought with my sister and brother. The purchase was agreed, sight unseen. The surfboards we managed to buy were without exception well used. It would be almost 10 years before I got my first new surfboard and later still before getting a surfboard specifically shaped and made for my own dimensions and requirements.

If a board was for sale, you just bought it. It wasn't that Strandhill or Rossnowlagh had a surplus of equipment. Their local surfing population was also tiny. Crucially, though, they had a head start on us in Bundoran with some local surfing families involved in the sport since the late 1960s. Most importantly this establishment meant equipment better than anything we had in Bundoran. Bundoran had no older generation of surfers to pass down knowledge and equipment to us; we were the first generation. In fairness to the local surfers in both Rossnowlagh and Strandhill, like the Britton brothers, the Lallys, the Byrnes and Burn families, they would always stop you in the street or in the surf if they saw you just to let you know that someone was selling a board or a wetsuit. Early Irish surfing had a unique camaraderie and friendliness among its minute, tight-knit community.

After spending much of the summer of 1983 being a beach rat with my brother and sisters, it would be November before Frances and Joe convinced me to come down and give a surfboard a go. Nothing like waiting for winter's piercing chill as the tonic to try the sport of Hawaiian kings. All was set for the following weekend. Saturday morning was the time and Tullan Strand was the place for my initiation. There was an unbridled innocence and lack of knowledge to our early surfing. It was free of complication and full of a simple ambition that didn't stretch much beyond just standing up on a breaking wave. With little discernible surfing form, we were none too fastidious about an overall plan either. We simply surfed by endless, self-taught trial and error. We would pick a spot either on the Main Beach or Tullan Strand and ride any waves we could catch. We hit the waves with little fanfare and no self-consciousness or awareness of the self-effort and pioneering spirit of it all. If the tide was too low or too high, we just waited for it to ebb or flow to a more favourable phase. As for the waves, we surfed anything – big, small, windy (waves on a windy day), glassy (no wind), closeouts (rough waves breaking suddenly) or peelers (smooth-breaking waves) – it didn't matter.

The only surf forecasting available to us was from the inside of the back page of the *Irish Independent*. In the bottom left corner, it displayed a pressure chart showing where the low and high-pressure systems affecting Ireland were sitting, as part of the daily weather forecast. This single black-and-white image was our solitary source of information to try to predict what the surf would be like the following day and coming week. We initially greeted the image every day with all sorts of conjecture, but eventually it became astounding how accurate we could be with the weather and surf forecasting. To this day, I'm still able to deduce as much surf forecast information from those static isobar images as I am from the ultra-high-tech surf report apps. Unlike most people, we didn't care about sun or rain; we cared about wind direction and where the Atlantic low-pressure systems were. Most importantly to us was how these lows were tracking across the North Atlantic and over the country. The ideal scenario for surfing Ireland's west coast was a dominant high-pressure system over the UK and Western Europe, stabilising weather with light or almost no wind, and blocking a big low-pressure system sitting out to the west. The only other piece of the puzzle we had was if you were lucky enough to be beside a radio to hear RTÉ Radio 1's shipping forecasts, but timing wise that never worked for us. In any case, wind in knots was hard to decipher before Google.

On the day of my inaugural surf, between myself, Frances and Joe we had two wetsuits to accompany the one surfboard we owned and the use of another surfboard from Bundoran's first generation of itinerant communal surfboards. Back then, wetsuits didn't come anywhere even close to the multitude of sizes, styles and futuristic material that are available now. All the wetsuits I had ever laid my eyes on were second hand and of a boxy two-piece unisex shape, limited to the four sizes of small, medium, large and extra large. Both of our wetsuits were two-piece contraptions with dungarees underneath and a neoprene anorak on top. Two into three doesn't go, so that November day my brother wore the dungarees of his wetsuit with a jumper underneath and a normal everyday cheap zip jacket covering his top half. I wore the other half that was the jacket part of the wetsuit, which was way too big for my nine-year-old frame by about two sizes. I would have worn an extra small if such a size existed then. The upper part of the wetsuit that was rolled around me was an adult medium. The jacket had a full-length opening metal zip straight up the chest to the base of your neck. With a texture of thick, dry shipping carboard, its lack of flexibility was compounded by skin-nipping mini-zips on the cuffs to help with application and removal. One of the peculiarities of the day for me was even though the wetsuit could have fitted two of me in it, such was its size, the harsh material still made it a tight struggle to get into.

The top was made of restrictive neoprene that offered little warmth in its construction, which was exacerbated by its ill-fitting. Both pieces of wetsuit were made with fabrics vaguely more malleable than Houdini's buckled straitjacket. The wetsuit's material triggered an instant and agonising skin rash as soon as you moved in it, as if it were lined with 60-grit sandpaper. Hauling that wetsuit on, I blurted out a few curse words. It was the first time that I got away with bold language that wasn't immediately extinguished by my sister with a well-executed dressing down.

The wetsuit jacket had a raised grandfather shirt collar that nestled its grating overlap against the skin underneath my jaw and just below my earlobes, giving me a sticky pink rash on the back of my hairline within minutes. The whole episode was exacerbated by raw skin irritation when you encountered salt and sand. The jacket's styling was a hodgepodge patchwork of black and dark blue neoprene held together with broad mustard-yellow stitching, a design that resembled a drunken Scotsman's tartan weave more than a piece of sporting attire capable of resisting at least a smidgen of the cold November North Atlantic water. Once on, the wetsuit arranged itself on me like a New Romantic Kajagoogoo blouse, all puffed out, full of collar crinkles that stripped soft, callus-free skin like a riotous pumice stone. If you surfed with any sort of regularity, wetsuit hickeys were a permanent fixture around your neck, under your arms, behind your knees and in the crease of your elbows. The abrasions would scab up but become instantly raw when you put a wetsuit on again. If you were lucky, after a few months your skin hardened up a bit. All it took to set off the flaying again was to grow a few millimetres, change to another wetsuit or not surf for a few weeks. Left unchecked, the chafing became ulcerated, which no box of Band-Aids or tube of Germolene could cure.

With only half a wetsuit at my disposal, I was destined for failure. To cover the rest of my body, I used a pair of jeans with tightly tied tracksuit bottoms pulled over the top of them. On my feet were two sets of fluffy white sports socks and a pair of old Dunnes Stores 'Sizzler' blue-and-white runners as a home-made substitute for wetsuit booties. For our hands, we all used thin, woollen, navy school gloves under a pair of yellow Marigold kitchen gloves. We would secure the Marigold gloves just behind the wrist bone to make them as watertight as we could, using a few layers of grey carpet tape, while always being very careful not to get any of the tape on our arms, as it took pelt and skin off with it when you had to remove it from exposed parts of the body. The taping made the Marigold gloves a single-use item, so we bought them by the pack. If we were caught short, Mum always had a stash underneath the kitchen sink beside the thick Jif scouring cream. The rubbery, chalky smell of those gloves reminds me of early surfs much more than any washing of dishes or peeling vegetables I may have ducked out of doing.

You lose most of your heat through your head, making it crucial to have some headgear. The only thing available to us was cheap latex swimming pool caps. We would triple stretch one on top of the other as the only concession against the bitingly cold wind, hail and water. The result squeezed the life out of our puce-coloured heads. With the throbbing tightness of the caps you could feel your heartbeat reverberating under your hair around your skull and in your face. It gave me an instant head-out-the-window-of-a-speeding-car look. We would have used the more expensive and comfortable silicon caps if they were available. While putting on these caps, the dry, tacky latex had an unrivalled ability to stick to itself, creating a pinch point that pulled the hair on your head clean off your scalp, roots and all. All this made you feel like the school bully had just given you a hair-pulling workout in the big playground.

The three of us really were quite the apparition as we walked down the beach in a sorry procession of wretched bits of wetsuit and poxy hulks of surfboard. Everything about our early surfing days, from the waves we surfed to equipment we did or didn't possess, was shaped by circumstance rather than design. We continued marching forward, blissfully light on the practical but heavy on enthusiasm for the surf that day and many more thereafter. We didn't care for aesthetics. Anyway, no one was watching because almost nobody surfed Tullan Strand in the 1980s except for the occasional sinking-sand-evading oppor-tunist. The craft for my maiden voyage was the notorious by reputation but euphemistically named surfboard known locally as the blue canoe. It was one of a hat-trick of surfboards in town that never had an outright owner; instead, the boards were passed around from perspective surfer to another as neces-sity demanded. It was a horrible lump of a surfboard the size of a canoe, hence the name. These boards would be later classed universally in the surfing world as pop-outs, with a primitive construction of two moulded, heavy pieces of fibreglass or plastic husks that were stuck together and injected with a poly-cement to fill the interior, making them implausibly heavy.

Their manufacture was cheap and somehow this beast of a board found its way to Bundoran. It was that battered and battle damaged as to have lost much of its distinguishable shape or clue to its maker and origins. In its illustrious history, the blue canoe would take a fair few teeth from and give a fair few black eyes to young and old, boys and girls, it didn't discriminate.

The board had a home-made bungee cord leg-rope that you knotted to your ankle, extending all the way to the ever-useful hardware twine moonlighting as a leash mooring. With some home DIY, the whole apparatus was jerry-rigged with rough brown squares of cobbled-together jagged fibreglass matted down onto the deck. This unwanted extra weight compounded what was already a hefty, buoyancy-challenged piece of equipment. The whole integrity of the surfboard's construction was an open-ended question of risk assessment to anyone who surfed it. Although heavy on land, the blue canoe certainly doubled its weight and sat much lower in the water the longer you stayed in the surf. As it absorbed more of the seawater like a sponge, it slowly began to sink. Taking on water through all the cracks and holes in its hull at an alarming rate is not the modus operandi for any seaborne craft. After a surf, leaving the blue canoe upright against a sea wall as you got changed, the board would immediately gush out its ballast, creating a substantial pool of saltwater around its tail within seconds. As gravity took effect, like an hourglass running the water back out again, the board would become lighter to carry once more.

The bungee cord attaching your leg to the surfboard behaved as a calamitous lasso that tripped, choked and strangled depending on what flailing body part it wrapped itself around. Its assembly gave it an ACME catapult effect as the bungee returned your board at maximum velocity with malevolent bone-breaking and flesh-taking intentions. It presented much more of a hazard and threat than any wave you may have encountered.

Already quivering with the cold and feeling more than a bit incongruous wearing my neoprene shackles, I lumbered towards the sea. With the not so seaworthy blue canoe not entirely under my arm or under my control, it was a slow procession. My brother held my hand in a sticky Marigold-on-Marigold embrace. His grip helped me get out past the first line of white water with the listing *Bismarck* attached to my left ankle. He swapped over with my sister to try to get me to a favourable depth and position for a wave. The cold shock to my body was immediate and all-consuming, the 10-degree water surging into my runners, tracksuit, jeans and baggy top before I got to waist depth, forcing me to take rapid, shallow, panicked breaths through my mouth. The jeans, Sizzler runners and tracksuit were futile against the bitter wintry elements; once my layers of cotton and denim started to absorb all the seawater, they became a sopping weighted anchor that I couldn't cast away.

I had never worn a wetsuit before, even though this one was only 50 per cent of the real deal. Being so confined and wrapped up in neoprene, latex and waterlogged clothing contrived to make me feel the absurdity of claustrophobia in the expansive openness of my surroundings. I was good in the water, but this was a much too restrictive activity for me. I hated the burden of the surfboard attached to my ankle and the tonnage of my make-do baggy wetsuit with its bulges full of water. Before the first five minutes had expired, my surfing inclinations dwindled rapidly in my rotten before it's ripe reasoning. The drudgery of it was entirely different to the freedom of swimming through waves in the summer or controlling my shark biscuit aero bodyboard in the shallow surf.

My brother heaved me into my first wave, where I instantly lurched uncontrollably forward and down, as if the front of the surfboard had just suffered a catastrophic double flat tyre at speed. The next wave offered little more, as I was blown off the board on impact, landmine style.

I did manage to catch a few successful waves that first day, so all was not lost. When I say 'catch', I use that term liberally. It was more my brother or sister who had manoeuvred me onto five or six waves. I stood up eventually on my last one in that briefest of first surf encounters. Just for a moment, I felt the sensation of gliding over the surface of a wave. But then my fleeting excitement ended abruptly as I was projected head over arse again off the front of the board in a combination of loss of balance and front-overloaded weight distribution. The board's momentum and oncoming wave allowed the Goliath of the blue canoe to tackle me from behind, smacking me hard on the back of the head. If you are wondering by any chance whether three latex caps offer any unknown property of padding and protection . . . well, I can categorically assure you they don't. That was it, my 20 minutes in the water were up. So that was my surf initi-ation: trying to get a handle on a porous board that was hell-bent on sinking itself with my ankle umbilically attached. This combination of shock, cold, tears, snots and a small stream of blood from the surfboard's impact brought the curtain down on my ignominious first surf. I told my brother I hated it, and swore at him and to God that I was never doing it again. My brother carried me most of the way back up the beach like a mini shipwrecked sailor in soaked-through Dunnes Stores finery.

A few hours later, I had warmed up enough at home to think straight. There was something about the feeling of sailing on a moving wedge of water that's other-worldly. I just couldn't shake it. The residue of that feeling outshone all the adversity of the lack of a decent wetsuit, the bitter cold and the blue canoe with a mind of its own. I found my sister upstairs and said, 'Hey

Frankie, is it OK if I come surfing with you again next weekend?' to which she replied, 'I knew you'd enjoy it.'

Within a month, by the end of December, after three or four more surfs I was completely hooked. All I wanted to do and all I could think about from that point on was catching waves. There is something in the addiction to surfing that's hard to quantify or explain to those who haven't experienced it. For many that first taste of walking on water changes your DNA. Trying to capture that essence has even crossed over as a selling point into corporate surfing with corny but accurate slogans like 'Only a surfer knows the feeling.' I've tried most sports – especially board sports like snowboarding and water-skiing, both from the same stable as surfing – but surfing has a uniqueness that sets it apart. If I allow myself to become all free-spirited about it, then the answer is simple. Every wave is different. You will never see or surf that same wave twice. Like Forrest Gump's proverb that goes, 'Life is like a box of chocolate, you never know what you're going to get.' This adage can be applied to surfing as a fundamental of its attraction. The playing field changes moment by moment where you have to decode and learn on the fly. It's a quality in surfing that can't be offered in a stadium, racetrack or something more similar, like a ski slope or skate bowl. Surfing is just wildly different to anything else, and that's the hook: the fact that the wave you are surfing has travelled thousands of miles across the ocean from some distant storm system while breaking only once. That wave gives you an exclusive experience, be it 5 feet or 50 feet. The wave you have just surfed will never be replicated in the same configuration again. If you watch advanced surfing it seems to defy physics, with steep, curving walls of horseshoeing water, deep tube rides and critical turns that seem like a lightning-fast, sleight of hand illusion in the ocean. It's as if the surfer had an engine in his board, or that her feet are somehow glued to the deck of the surfboard. Of course, neither is true, and that's the hypnotic magic spell that surfing casts over its flock.

The controversial American writer and psychologist Timothy Leary knew a thing or two about addiction. He said of the much-lauded 'instantly hooked' attraction to surfing: 'Surfers are the futurists and they are leading the way . . .' He also stated: 'The act of the ride is the epitome of "be here now", and the tube ride is the most astute form of that.' He continued: 'Which is: your future is right ahead of you, the past is exploding behind you, your wake is disappearing . . . [It's an act] done purely for the dance itself.'

## 3

# The Sea: My Sanctuary

We lived so close to the sea in Bundoran that signs of its all-pervading presence were all around me. I could automatically tell when the wind had turned to an onshore westerly, from the briny aroma of the sea blowing through our porous, single-glazed, wooden-framed bay windows. Westerly facing front doors slammed shut when onshore winds blew, with back doors swinging open. The reverse happened on south-easterly offshores breezes: out on the water in the middle of winter, with light offshore winds and thin, frost-kissed winter air, you could tell the direction of the wind as soon as fires were lit at houses on the main street, the diluted tobacco fragrance of coal, wood and peat chimney smoke filling the air. It is a smell that even now still conjures up those winter days out on the water for me.

The Catholic church behind our house was located on the aptly named Church Road. Its spire acted as a great take-off marker in the water for the prime-time, low-tide set waves at Bundoran's jewel in the crown surf break known as 'the Peak'. From a surfer's perspective, while in the water looking towards shore, if you could master the act of triangulating the church belfry in the background with the incoming lateral waves to work out your positioning, you were going somewhere, in local surfing terms anyway. Add the phases of the tide and wind direction, so that when deployed correctly with millisecond instinctiveness, this sixth-sense inbuilt protractor and set square gave you a massive advantage, enabling you to catch more waves than the out-of-town surfers, city slickers and weekend warriors. Once these skills were mastered, you could consider yourself a graduate of the Bundoran College of Knowledge.

After a long day out on the water, hearing the 6 o'clock Angelus church bell ring out meant that you would be late for dinner yet again. With only a few minutes' grace, you had to make your last wave count and ride it all the way to shore; with five children to feed and always a few extra seats filled at the dinner table, you didn't want your meal to be a second helping for someone else. The scramble was then on to scamper across the reef around 'No Man's Land' island, skirting the slippery kelp and spiky sand coral, and go for broke to make it home in time.

My mother held a few strong family values highly, especially the virtues of manners and punctuality, but none more so than our family dinner-time tradition. No matter what the day was like for any of us, we had to be home for dinner. Skipping Mass or missing a day at school was more digestible to her than missing an evening meal together. Around the table everyone got their 'through the chair' time to tell everyone else how their day had gone, with plenty of unwanted piss-taking interjection. Pleading the Fifth was not acceptable.

Dinner-time conversations would swing from the trivial of why the dogs weren't eating their new dog food to, almost in the same breath, the serious headline news topics of the day.

My brother was (and still is) whip smart when it came to current affairs, politics and history. He was unbelievably well read for a young teenager, being older than me by six years. Even back then his bedroom resembled a mini-library. Everyone had and was allowed an opinion at the table, but for me I mostly agreed with my brother even though I hadn't a clue what was being talked about most of the time. Like most younger boys, I hero worshipped my older brother; he could do no wrong in my eyes. I had the misfortune to say at one dinner time that it didn't matter if there was a World War III, Ireland was safe and wouldn't be affected because we were neutral. You will recall that nuclear weapons were a hot topic of debate for anyone in Western Europe in the 1980s. I was shot down in flames before I could eject from my neutrality, being told bluntly that it didn't matter that we were neutral; if there was a nuclear war, the front line was Europe, and we would be in the crosshairs whether we liked it or not.

Nuclear war, I thought, was only marginally more dangerous to my survival than the second-biggest threat of the 1980s. For me, that was quicksand. A whole posse of baddies and henchmen met their deserved end in quicksand faster than falling into the Sarlacc pit on shows like *MacGyver*, *The A-Team* and *Knight Rider*. By contrast, quicksand offered a heroic climax of escapes to the goodies. I liked to think of myself as a goodie back then, but I loved most baddies like Darth Vader in *Star Wars*, so I'm not sure what fate awaited me in movie quicksand.

In Bundoran we had our own urban legend about quicksand. A fable that the whole town believed in, me included. The only difference was that in Bundoran we called it sinking sand. The Bundoran sinking sand tale went something like this: 'Don't go down to the end of Tullan Strand, there is sinking sand down there and you'll get sucked in and probably die.' Now this posed a particular problem for me, as Tullan Strand is the level 2 surfing beach in Bundoran with good waves all the way along its 2-kilometre stretch, even down the far end with the dastardly sinking sand. It turns out that the sinking sand myth was to keep children away from the north end of the beach. The beach at Tullan Strand is crescent shaped, obscuring the view from one side to the other. There is also no direct access to the far end, as it backs onto an Irish army camp with a rifle range in the distance. The sinking sand story kept children from messing about down there out of sight. It wasn't until the early 1990s that surfing became popular at that end of the beach and the myth was sunk for good.

My surfing day didn't finish at dinner time. The minute clearing the dishes and cleaning up was done, I'd be out the door again and back in the water just after 7 p.m., refuelled and raring to go for another three or four hours of surfing before the midsummer light disappeared. If the surf was good, or I could get away with it, I would surf for 10 hours plus each day. If you have never surfed, it's one of the most physically exhausting and energy-sapping sports there is. When I was 12, I did one nine-hour surf without getting out of the water, with no drink, no food, no rest. My mother eventually sent my brother down to drag me out. I paid for it the next day, feeling hung-over before I even knew what a dire hangover was. Dangerously dehydrated and suffering from sunstroke, I was a puking wreck. For a few hours the following morning I was a sorry sight, but I soon got my groove back and off I went surfing again, only this time with a face covered in Sudocrem that was fit for Halloween night. By day's end, I'd be utterly exhausted as I dragged myself home after 11 p.m., a time that coincided with the main street nightclubs and late venues opening their doors to catch the overflow from the daytime public houses serving their final official rounds of drink.

If the surf forecast was good for the following day, I'd be up again just four hours later as it started to get bright again. Once again wriggling myself into my wet, sandy wetsuit, shoulder muscles aching, face still tingling from sunburn and neck stinging from red raw wetsuit rash, I'd duck and weave through hundreds of those same nightclubbers I saw queuing just a few hours earlier. As they got ejected onto the street after the 3 a.m. closing time, the pantomime of fist fights, screaming and smashing glasses would start. Running across the street through hordes of blind drunks, I felt like Luke Skywalker dodging enemy fire. Even though I was a local boy, it was as if I was some alien species in my hometown, legging it to the early-bird waves. I never failed to get a hail of drunken abuse, some of it very funny but mostly just hyper aggressive. Always a few thrown bottles and sozzled attempts at a kick followed by a stumbled lunge and 'Fuck off, ya wee wanker, I'll fucking kill yee, ya prick!' The biggest danger and most painful side effect of these early surf sessions was the never-ending splinters of glass I got in my feet from the carpet of broken glass and litter that covered the main street from the bars, nightclubs and takeaways. Running the pisshead gauntlet kept me sharp and on my toes, as I ran for the sanctuary of the sea and the rising sun.

# 4

# Land of Endless Winter

By 1983 I was almost halfway through primary school. Our school was the new Catholic one in town. It had only opened four years before in 1979, the same year I started. The school was an amalgamation of the old all-boys school and the convent for girls, so was mixed modern and practically state of the art for its time.

Like the claustrophobia I felt wearing a wetsuit for the first time, I also felt that same constriction from my first day in school until my last. I remember my mother said to me as I walked out the front door that first morning: 'You have to be there anyway, so just make the most of it.' I wasn't much trouble in school; if anything I was quiet, well-mannered and more than a wee bit shy. I avoided confrontation wherever possible in order to make the school day pass without incident, all the while hoping that the time went as fast as possible. I never wanted to draw any attention to myself in school, especially from any teachers. Being singled out or the centre of attention was my cold sweats nightmare. If I could have been invisible in school that would have suited me just fine. Regardless of what anyone told me, my overriding feeling towards school was that I never wanted to be there in the first place.

I had plenty of friends in class and can hand on my heart say that I had no enemies in school nor any group of kids that I didn't like. It was yet another contradiction, as I was sociable when I wanted to be and moved easily between all the individuals and cliques that form early social grouping in primary school. You see these groups initially in school but later replicated in adult society. I was at ease with my fellow townie kids, as well as the country children who arrived on school buses every morning from the vastly more rural areas surrounding the town. Even though they were only 5 or 10 miles away, the out of towners might as well have been from a different planet, such was the chasm between them and the local kids. From accent to attitude, they were different. Especially their accents, which were completely different to those of the town kids. I traversed between the cheeky kids, the bold boys and girls, the footballers, the loner kids who knocked about by themselves and of course my tiny but developing group of fellow wave and beach enthusiasts. I managed to establish friends in all these groups

In school, I missed the freedom of being outdoors, and the raucousness and security of our house and family life. I wished most days away in school, counting the clock down. Of course, children need the structure of school. It brought me out of my shell, it was critical in my social development, but I didn't realise it at the time. All I wanted to do any day was to be on the beach in sunshine or hail and catch waves.

On the academic side, I was good. In practice, I was open and interested in the subjects I liked and cruised through them with little fretting. My favourites were History, English and Geography. I never needed to work hard at them, as they were of great interest to me outside of school. An interest that put me well above what was required even in later years at honours level. For the subjects that didn't tickle my fancy, like German and French, I applied only moderate effort at best. Always just doing enough to get by. Ever conscious to keep the 'you failed' wolf from the door. If I had to get 50 per cent to pass a French exam, well then, I'd do just enough to get 50 per cent, no more and no less than that. To get through school successfully then was as much a test of application as it was intelligence, but I didn't see it that way, especially the application part.

My Achilles heel in school was always maths. I detested it with a passion. Maths, or doing your sums, as it was called in our house, took up all my half-hearted homework time. Trying to think my way into maths had no effect. I didn't even know where the jumping-off point was for any of the mental gymnastics. I'd be mentally kicking stones instead. The only maths that mattered to me were the parts of the subject that helped me decipher weather pressure charts and angles and speeds of waves while surfing. Real-life maths on the fly, you could say.

All my life I've had a horribly high level of anxiety to contend with. I can't remember a time when I wasn't riddled with anxiety over big or small things, especially in school. My anxiety is always there and can raise its afflicting head at any time or be prompted by a simple mundane interaction. How much it takes control of me depends on the situation I'm in and how well I've learned to deal with it. The threat of getting the cane in the principal's office hung in the air as the ultimate deterrent. That sent my anxiety into overdrive. I remember only getting a rap across the knuckles a few times with the cane. Always for maths and those wretched rectangle times tables books; I hated them more than the cane. The only time I was truly free of all my anxiety was when I was in the sea, making it an even more attractive place to be.

~

Although surfing had sprouted a few roots in coastal towns in Ireland, its growth was limited in the extreme for two decades. Ian Hill was a contemporary of Kevin Cavey when it comes to earliest Irish pioneers of surfing. Ian hailed from Portrush on the north coast of Antrim. He may not have gone into the structural side of Irish surfing, but his contribution is often underappreciated in the national surfing story. In 1963, Ian travelled to Cornwall from Northern Ireland, bringing back what is considered Ireland's first modern surfboard. Most of the boards in the country were chunky balsa-wood constructions. Ian's import was what was referred to in the early 1960s as a 'hot dog' fibreglass surfboard. It promoted more performance-driven surfing. Ian developed himself into the best surfer in the country, leading the way as to what was being done on the waves and setting off with his surfboard down the coast the following year in 1964 on his now fabled surf trip. He started in Castlerock before heading west to surfing spots all the way to Donegal, where he surfed Rossnowlagh, Tullan Strand and Bundoran's Main Beach and put his new surfboard to good use. The first known photo of anyone surfing in Bundoran is of Ian on this trip in September 1964. There was a structure in Irish surfing first established by the granddad of Irish surfing, Kevin Cavey, when he loosely formed the Bray Ireland Surf Club on the Wicklow coast with a couple of enthusiastic friends in 1963. From the innovation of pioneering watermen like Kevin and Ian came a small band of trailblazing Irish surfers.

The first Irish surfing championships were held in Tramore in September 1967. Most of Ireland's surfers at the time plied their wave-riding skills at home, only venturing to international events once every few years. Irish surfers were the perpetual underdogs at these international events; however, they made considerable inroads in establishing themselves and Irish surfing outside the country. In some cases, Irish surfing became more recognised overseas than at home. Even as late as the 1980s, surfing remained almost invisible to the general public in Ireland. For starters, Irish surfing and its dedicated bunch of protagonists mostly lived and surfed on the rural west coast. These more remote regions of Ireland were far from the big population glare and at odds with the centralised sports and lifestyles of the bigger towns and cities. By the 1980s surfing had exploded internationally as a lifestyle and a professional sport in countries like Australia and the west coast of the States. Neither the rivers of gold of 1980s excesses nor the big-time surfing seemed to hit Irish shores. In the wake of the counterculture surf scene of the 1960s and 1970s came the audacious 1980s brand of surfing. It was big, bold, tacky, showy and dollar rich with dream corporate sponsors like Coca-Cola coming on board to be associated with the professional surfing world tour. Gone were the flower power surfing generation and in came a new cocksure breed of professional surfer where ego and toxic masculinity were favourable characteristics. An example of this new 1980s driven frenzy for surfing was the annual Ocean Pacific Pro event in Huntington Beach, California. The contest attracted up to 150,000 spectators. A packed mega stadium's worth of heaving surf fans on the beach for a contest was utterly unprecedented until the 1980s.

In Bundoran, as remote as we were in global surfing terms, we were lucky to be stuck between Rossnowlagh and Strandhill. At least there were a few surfers in each of those towns who came our way when the wind swung offshore. The only other towns in the country that had a surfing community were Portrush, Lahinch and Tramore. At the time, I didn't realise that my location was central in Irish surfing terms. It certainly didn't feel like it. Bundoran had yet to catch surfing fire, but at least we had a board or two by the mid-1980s.

In the water for the next two years from my first surf up until September 1985, my interest in the sea, surf and everything about it grew at a steady rate. My development as a competent young surfer wasn't exponential but constant. I had very little to compare myself with. Our progression in Bundoran was limited by what equipment was available to us and the lack of older, better in-town local surfers to learn from. The board and wetsuit situation got slowly better over those years. If I have one burned-on impression of early 1980s surfing, it was the savage cold of winter and being in the water wearing useless bits of wetsuit. The Irish water temperature swing from winter to summer can be as much as 10 degrees in some years. Summer was no problem; it was the winter that tested your mettle. The effects of being wet with wind chill was a much bigger daily adversary than the water temperature ever was. The exposed parts of your limbs had the lifeless blue hue resembling something sticking out of a butcher's bucket. Extremities would go marble-slab cold and numb within a few minutes. Unfortunately, never numb enough to dull the excruciating pain associated with body shutdown. Riding out that pain factor to catch a few more waves: that could have been our motto. Then out of the water, when trying to walk with no feeling in your ballooned feet, your limbs got the worst dose of swollen pins and needles, with your bones feeling sickeningly brittle. If you got a nasty cut on your feet or a bruise, you wouldn't realise it until your circulation and feeling returned. After surfing for an hour, your hands and feet were in bad shape. Once home they would swell up as you thawed out in front of the fire, nursing your early-onset frostbitten limbs. It took most of the rest of the day to get the feeling back in your blotchy red hands and purple-blue feet. As the life started to come back into your extremities, a new pain sensation kicked in from the swelling as the blood flow came back.

My sister's boyfriend at the time, who had started to surf a little, went to extremes to try to trap some heat in his body to stay warm. He would rub Vaseline on his legs, arms and chest, then wrap cling film around himself for an extra insulation layer before putting his two-piece wetsuit on. Of course, surfers get in the ocean in much colder places around the world than wintertime Ireland. For example, there is a huge surfing population all along the northeast coast of America in states like New York and New Jersey, and all the way across the border to Nova Scotia. During the wintertime, this coast gets ice-bound blizzards for weeks and months on end – a feature we never see on Ireland's west coast – with much colder water temperatures than we ever experience in Ireland. Unlike these places, where they had a well-developed surf scene and industry with decent winter wetsuits available, in Ireland we had none. Years later, I would meet legions of stateside surfers from New England. In another one of Irish surfing's bizarre abnormalities, many of these east coasters would come to Ireland in winter. Most of them came from some form of Irish ancestry, viewing the west coast of Ireland in a different Irish-American light than the tropes of old Paddy sipping a pint. These statesiders saw our northwest coast as their alternative surf destination, offering them a milder winter's surfing alternative to Long Island, with a coastline that could handle big winter swells.

One thing that did change in these years was the widening of my surfing circle. Or at least knowledge of a wider world of wave riding outside of our family unit. Although our house would be the most well-known surf house in town, it was by no means the only one. The town had a handful of surfing houses. The Wards', the Meehans' and the McGloins' houses in the west end of town had some equipment as the older boys surfed. Up on Church Road, beyond the all-important church

spire-cum-surf marker was the Bowe family's home. The Bowe
brothers surfed a bit too. In the shed at the back of their house
lived another one of Bundoran's peculiar surfboards of equally
cumbersome proportions: the black-and-gold 'John Player
Cigarette'-logoed single-fin surfboard. It was another surfboard
that got passed around the surfing families in town. Having a
cigarette company on a surfboard or other sporting equipment
as a way of sponsorship or promotion was common in those
days. The John Player Special surfboard was brought back to
Ireland from the 1969 European championships that were held
in Jersey and sponsored by Player Cigarettes. The seven-man Irish
team led by Kevin Cavey made Ireland's debut in international
surfing at that event. Somehow, by the 1980s that board had
meandered its way to a shed on Bundoran's Church Road.

The dearth of surfing equipment in Bundoran for the handful
of local surfers was the mother of invention, as every board,
wetsuit and accessory that trickled into town got passed down
umpteen times, reused, repaired, glued back together and recy-
cled until they were threadbare.

Bundoran, like any coastal town, has always had 'sea families',
by which I mean there are family names in town that you automatically associate with the sea in a generational sense, as they
are made up of local swimmers and fishermen who grew up
with one eye on the sea and one foot in the water. It's no fluke
then that some of Bundoran's first surfers came from these
families. It was from this small pool of local families that I met
my lifelong best mate. He was a local Bundoran boy called
Patrick 'Po' O'Donnell. His father was the local GP in town.
When away from the surgery his dad could be found with Po
and the rest of his young family gutting pollock on the slipway
wall or launching and landing his fishing boat from the boat
quay. Po was a few years younger than me, which is a big deal

when you are young, but becomes much less so as you reach your late teens. He is the only other person I know that has such an intimate knowledge of Bundoran bay from above and below the water. We both have a mental map of the coast under the surface, especially the parts that never become exposed by the low tides. It's a knowledge of tides, seafloor, rips, currents, wind and swell, and of what lives below the water line. It's an ability to read the sea in all its moods that you only gain from decades of observation, long sea swims, board paddles, surfing and spear fishing. Po developed himself into a consummate no-frills, all-round outdoors man. He is about as close to a real-world Bear Grylls as I know. I've had more enjoyable and risky adventures up mountains and in the sea at home and overseas with Po than with anyone else. As youngsters we pushed each other in the sea; hearing someone say it's too dangerous or the waves are too big was a red rag to us, and we would make it our business to go in. I carried this with me in my surfing. Where I could be reserved and timid as a youngster on land, I was the opposite in the sea. Constantly egging each other on, the two of us savoured the stormy days when there were no other takers for a swim or paddle. My favourite days were when promenade walkers would 'tut tut' at us being too close or going into the stormy sea. We would seek out isolated, hard-to-get-to parts of the coast and areas that were deemed too dangerous. Bundoran, with sea features like No Man's Land, the Fairy Bridges and the Lion's Paw Cave, had no shortage of sea adventures for us. My friendship with Po and our joint apprenticeship in the sea was an indispensable foundation for my confidence in what would come later for me in waves of consequence.

~

Ireland may have been obscure in global surfing, but Bundoran was a small blip on the radar for the most adventurous travelling surfers in the 1960s and 70s. Outsiders arrived in town to surf a good swell and left just as quickly. One of the reasons for their speedy departures was that it was so close to the border. With Donegal being in Ulster, it was almost a dirty word to many international travellers to Ireland, surfing or otherwise. Stay away from the whole north part of Ireland was the rule of thumb. Until the 1980s, there was little engagement in surfing from the local population in town, so these fleeting visits from international surfers went mostly unnoticed.

There are plenty of anecdotes about travelling surfers, both international and Irish, discovering just how good our surf was in the 1960s and 70s. As a lifestyle, surfing promotes travel, discovery and adventure. This ethos is one of the sport's cornerstones. At the top of the pile of the world's most respected surf travel journalists sits a Californian man named Kevin Naughton. Kevin, along with his best mate Craig Peterson, travelled and discovered vast chunks of undiscovered surfing coastlines in the most far-flung corners of the world during the 1970s. They catalogued their travels and discoveries for the monthly issues of *Surfer* magazine, a progressive US publication that was considered the Surfers' Bible the world over. Their accounts of wild Africa, steaming South America and untouched Europe proved wildly popular in the imaginations of the Californian counterculture youth of that era. More than 40 years later, their articles and images have passed into legendary status throughout the international surfing community. Their contributions are still the gold standard in respected surf journalism.

Although born in the USA, Kevin is of Irish stock. Over the years, he has regaled me with plenty of fascinating stories about seeing and surfing some of the best waves of his life on Ireland's west coast as a young man. As a teenager, he would be brought against his will from the summer shores of California back to Ireland for a few weeks to visit his relatives in the northwest. He told me he hated it, until one day his parents drove through Bundoran. As luck would have it the surf was fantastic as he ogled out the car window at Bundoran's reef breaks in full flow and perfectly devoid of surfers. His opinion of what was on offer in Ireland for a restless Californian teenager changed that day. He swore to himself that he would bring a surfboard with him on the next Irish trip. He was true to his word, and has been coming back surfing to Ireland for the last 50 years. He struck up an early friendship with the Britton brothers in Rossnowlagh and Alan Duke in the north, friendships that have lasted ever since. He was so enamoured with Ireland's west coast waves that he studied for a year in the university in Galway during his college years.

By 1985, the Main Beach had become the beating heart of Bundoran's embryonic local surf scene. Weekend meet-ups took place in front of the old lifeguard tower complex before it was destroyed during a devastating storm in the winter of 1988. Everyone brought along what equipment they had in a cooperative effort to get everyone in the water on some craft or in some version of a wetsuit. If we didn't have enough equipment for everyone – there was usually about five or six of us – you had to wait for someone to catch their fill of waves before swapping out gear with you. Passing the surfboard baton was easy, but putting on a wet, cold and sandy wetsuit in the blustery midwinter weather was a real test of eagerness and stamina. The vital accessories of neoprene boots, hoods and gloves were always at a premium during winter months, so we mostly did without, or as I did just used old runners, Marigolds and latex swim hats.

Nowadays, most people in Ireland get their introduction to surfing in summertime, through the sprawling network of surf schools and adventure centres wrapped around Ireland's four coasts. If you venture deeper into surfing beyond those initial summer lessons, you quickly find out that the soul of the sport in Ireland, like almost everywhere else, revolves around wintertime. Wave-producing storm systems are abundantly more active in almost every surfing coast in the world during winter months. As a result, waves in winter are a great deal better than in summer, and in ample supply. Any dedicated surfer knows this. The much-used maxim of 'the Endless Summer' to describe the surfing lifestyle is more accurate if you flip it to 'the Endless Winter'. Wanting endless wintertime is where it's at for a committed surfer. If American film-maker Bruce Brown immortalised the phrase 'the Endless Summer', then perhaps the Roman historian Tacitus was a surfer who, when seeing the quality of Ireland's year-round surf, decided to give us our Latin name 'Hibernia' – the land of winter.

Land of endless winter or not, enthusiasm was always high in our group dynamic during our early surfing sessions. As usual, equipment continued to be our major stumbling block, especially the smaller important surf, essentials like wax, which should be applied to the deck of the surfboard before every surf. Wax gives the surfer's feet grip on the wet fibreglass surface of the surfboard. It was the most precious commodity for us, because you couldn't get it in Ireland.

My mum sold a selection of religious candles in her gift shop that now occupied the back half of the dying record shop. We discovered that the white wax of the christening and Virgin Mary candles worked best as a low-grade alternative to the real thing. We would swipe a handful of candles from the shop, scrape off the flimsy paper religious images before melting the candle down in a saucepan on the kitchen stove, fishing out the wick then pouring the hot wax directly onto our boards. My mother knew very well where the missing religious candles were going but she never mentioned it. Maybe she hoped that the candles' divine origin, 'Made in China', would keep us safe in the water (back in the day when a sticker staying Made in China was a bad thing, meaning shitty quality – the opposite is true now). It didn't matter where the candles were from, the wax hardened on the board and sharded off in cloudy milky flakes after the first few waves. We didn't know any better, nor did we have any other substitute for surf wax. So, we just made do. In this day and age, you can find surf wax being sold in many petrol stations, cafes and sweet shops around coastal Ireland, which always gives me a chuckle when I see it by the confectionary at the cash register as I tap and go for my petrol.

# 5

# Euro Surf '85

In 1985, the European Surf Championships were scheduled to take place in Rossnowlagh-Bundoran in September. Up to this point, Ireland always had a small surfing community with a dedicated Irish surf team competing at World and European events for the previous 15 years. As is the nature of international tournaments, if you compete in them, you eventually get an opportunity to hold one on your home soil. In 1985, the pool of potential venues for a Euro Surf event was limited to Portugal, France, Spain, Ireland and the UK. So, more or less every 10 years, it was your own country's turn to host the biennial event and the price tag that came with it.

Ireland had held two international events previously. The 1972 Euro Surf was pencilled in for Lahinch, Co. Clare for a two-day event in September that year. As is the curse of many surf events around the world, you are subject to conditions of either too much surf or too little, as was the case in Lahinch that year. The event was run off in beautiful weather but tiny 1-foot knee-high surf. On Sunday England claimed the 1972 European crown to an enthusiastic local crowd on Lahinch beach. What the surf lacked that weekend was made up for by teams enjoying the sights and sounds of the majestic Clare coast of the early 1970s. It may have been a disappointment for the surf on offer, but it was a statement of intent by Irish surfing of what we were capable of hosting. We were a tiny nation in surfing terms, but we were already punching above our weight in and out of the waves. A few years later, in 1976, an international invitation contest was held in Easkey, Co. Sligo. The tournament was sponsored by Smirnoff Vodka. This time the event got plenty of surf but was marred by protests against the perceived commercialisation of surfing by the mostly ex-pat community of alternative surf lifestylers who lived in the area.

The 1985 Euro Surf was the third crack at the whip at Ireland's ability to hold a successful international event. One thing that was for sure, there would be no protesting or any chanting or drum banging from surf hippies in Bundoran in 1985. I can't think of anything on the planet more unlikely to be seen and tolerated in 1980s hard-tack Bundoran than anti-commercial, new age surfing hippies. It was a time when you'd get a kicking if you went down the town on a summer's day with the wrong football jersey on.

I've experienced most surfing cultures around the world over the decades and feel well placed to draw the conclusion that our own Irish surf culture has developed in a more individualistic direction than anywhere else in the world that I have been. What sets our surfing culture apart? Ireland as a nation has a healthy cynicism for globe-sweeping trends and idealism. We constantly take a self-deprecating, introspective look at ourselves, which has always made us wary of jumping on the bandwagon or making a fuss. In Irish surfing terms, the same is true. Flower power, transcendental meditation or any other buzzwords associated with the 1960s and 70s in places like Australia's east coast and California didn't take hold on the west coast of Ireland, that's for sure. Along our coast, what would have looked on paper as the perfect fertile candidate for a bit of social revolution was Ireland's small but self-aware surfing population of the 1960s and 70s. The counterculture movement is something that never took any meaningful root in Irish surfing. Ireland's prime movers in surfing were not easily impressed upon. As a country, we have such an ancient and longstanding sense of national identity of who we are that global idealism and sweeping fads don't catch on here as they do in other countries. Mercifully, the 'Yo Dude!' surfing mentality has never crept into Irish surfing. I can't even imagine someone in a thick Donegal, Sligo or Waterford accent acting or speaking in the southern Californian lingo. Irish people from birth are installed with a brilliant bullshit detector; it's part of our national psyche. As a people we are not the easiest to influence. This stands true for Irish surfing. Even in its infancy, structured and non-structured surfing went in its own direction, acknowledging and learning from outside influence when necessary but never embracing it wholeheartedly. It can be counterproductive of course, but this is how we Irish are in a cultural sense.

From the end of the 1960s and through the following decade, surfing had grown hugely in the UK, especially in the southwest, where south Wales and the counties of Devon and Cornwall became the powerhouses of European surfing. No such expansive growth in numbers, culture or industry took place in Ireland during this time. By 1985, the addition of a few newer European countries competing at the championships meant the event presented a bigger proposition from the two-day event that was scheduled for Lahinch 13 years previously. The championships were now a week-long event for south Donegal. The very fact that a big international surfing contest was being held in our town was mind-blowing for an 11-year-old local lad. I really couldn't comprehend it. Witnessing my first surfing contest – and it being a big international one – didn't seem real at the time. The whole week is seared into my mind. What was possible in my hometown made surfing become even more of an obsession to me, if that was even possible.

Years before Irish Surfing Association (ISA) president Brian Britton passed away, I sat down and spoke to him at length about Donegal hosting the 1985 European Surf Championships. I feel most fortunate to have met and become friends with many from this small but massively influential first generation of Irish surfers. Hearing their first-hand accounts of the earliest Irish surfing days is something I treasure. It's even more poignant to me now as many of these legends of Irish surfing are no longer with us. It is and was a privilege for me to have been in touching distance of them. Brian was the main driving force responsible for attracting the championships to our northwest coast. While talking to Brian I was more interested in finding out how exactly the event was brought here as much as my own memories of the contest itself. My reason for taking this line of inquiry with Brian needs a bit of perspective. In 1985, there was no commercial Irish surf industry in the area. Surfing had roots in Rossnowlagh and Strandhill but was still almost unnoticed outside of these towns. It was still virtually undetectable in Bundoran.

Ireland was still three years away from the start of Jack Charlton's Boys In Green Euro '88 footballing success that energised the nation, giving us all a new sense of national optimism, self-esteem and pride that set Ireland on an upward trajectory to the long-overdue good times. With surfing being such a minority sport locally back then, the notion of holding a big international event in the northwest seemed like an unattainable and unnecessary pipe dream. I asked Brian when he stripped it all back what was his single motivating factor more than any that got the contest here? He said unequivocally to me it was the perception that persisted at the time about surfing in Ireland, which was something like this: 'What? Surfing in Ireland? There is no surf in Ireland, what are you talking about?' Brian also told me that all he ever heard was that you could never hold a big surfing event in our area. There was no precedent for it. Dublin had always been the home for big sporting events.

Brian realised then what much of the surfing world knows now, and that is that we had the waves to rival anywhere on the planet. Ireland has a beautifully unique, boutique countryside. We don't have Alpine mountains or the Colorado River, but we do have an abundance of truly world-class surf on our west coast. A coastline with a surf quality and vintage to rival and often surpass the world's very best, even the coastlines of big superpower surfing nations. This realisation of that fact and being told it wasn't a realistic ambition drove Brian on more than anything. He had his vision for the future of surfing in Ireland and where he thought surfing could and should be, and at the very least bringing surfing into that national sporting conversation. It wasn't everyone's view of course; some wanted to keep the brakes on. The ISA, however, as the driving force of Irish surfing at the time, had much more influence than it has today in our modern and much larger coastwide surf industry. In 1985, Ireland's surfers were tiny in number but high in standard. The group of surfers including Andy Hill, the Tobin brothers and Grant Robinson, all from the northwest, who had the ability to stick it to the best in Europe. The 1985 Euro Surf was to be the flagpole event in a new, evolving, vibrant and coming-of-age Irish surfing scene.

In a very Irish solution to sponsorship of the event, Guinness came on board for Euro Surf '85. A behemoth like Guinness becoming involved with Irish surfing was a serious vote of confidence, if one was needed with Brian at the helm. From that moment, Guinness and Irish surfing went hand in hand for many years, right up until the end of the 1990s. Even though Guinness is a commercial entity it is as much a symbol of Ireland as any. Especially overseas Guinness screams IRELAND just as much as the shamrock or the harp do. Back in the 1970s the marketing and advertising department at Guinness had commissioned a surfing-themed TV advert to be shot on the north shore of Hawaii with its world-famous surf breaks. The advert was made, but for reasons that have never been revealed it wasn't released, and was mothballed to the Guinness archives. When Guinness jumped on board with Irish surfing and Euro Surf '85, some young executive at the company dug the advert out of the archives and dusted it off. Shortly thereafter it was rolled out as part of a new marketing campaign for Guinness, making its first appearance on Irish terrestrial TV. It's now looked on as the most classic and iconic Guinness advert in the pantheon of memorable advertisements the company has produced over the years.

The advert became an instant favourite in our house. As a young boy, I would come sprinting into the sitting room to watch it when we heard the music. It was the only way at the time that you could see surfing screened on TV in Ireland. The internet, iPads, mobile phones, YouTube, Netflix, Sky TV and even surfing DVDs were still way off in the future.

When the Euros rolled into town, it had its HQ in Rossnowlagh, where teams were based. The contest had three different surfing venues that could be utilised depending on the surf conditions. First up was Rossnowlagh Beach, the second venue was Bundoran with Tullan Strand and the Peak, and the third was spot-on: Leitrim's small but oh so good 2.5 miles of coastline. In the end, the whole contest was run off in Bundoran, with early rounds taking place on small waves at Tullan Strand. The finals were moved around the corner, where they were held in ideal six-foot waves on the Peak. This combo of Tullan Strand on small days and the Peak on the bigger days has served as a winning blueprint for almost every International and domestic surfing contest in town since then. Englishman Paul Russell was the 1983 European Surf Champion, and he was still part of the English team in 1985 for the event in Bundoran. He famously said of the area to the media after the contest: 'Ireland has the best surf I have seen outside of Hawaii.' It was high praise indeed for our patch of coastline, as Paul was one of Europe's best and most respected surfers at the time.

The junior event that held the most interest for me was won by a 17-year-old Tahitian surfer named Vetea 'Poto' David. A young lad from the south Pacific winning a surf contest in Bundoran in 1985 made for what sounded like a fabled headline in the local newspaper.

The 1985 Irish team were mostly from the northwest Donegal-Sligo area and the Causeway coast in Northern Ireland, with a few from Tramore in Waterford. Most of their names and faces were unfamiliar to me at that time. The northwest and southeast home counties of these surfers is a good reflection on where surfing was in Ireland at the time. Irish power surfer Brian Tobin was the hot favourite to take the title, surfing Bundoran's reefs with a modern, aggressive surfing approach that was a positive shock to the established Irish surfers. For Ireland to have a top seed in the event broke new ground. Brian had learned to surf in his dual upbringing along the Gweebarra coastline of Donegal and the waves of Jupiter Inlet along Central Florida's Space Coast. After blazing all his heats, Brian became unstuck in the semi-final. He looked a dead cert for lifting the European title before committing an unforced error of riding a wave after the hooter had sounded. It was a mistake that cost him the points of his highest-scoring wave and eliminated him from the final. The Irish camp on Bundoran's Atlantic Way was always a hive of activity and well supported, especially on finals day. To the unaware onlooker, surfing contests can be confusing, as they can be as much about interpretation by both competitive surfers and the judges' subjectivity. Without rolling out some trite sporting cliché, I will say that surfing requires you to apply quick thinking, on-the-spot innovation and adaption, skill, experience and repetitive techniques to elements outside of your control, almost more than any other sport I know. Bundoran's platter of waves offers up all those elements to test the most skilful international surfers, as it did in 1985.

I have such a strong memory of the Euro Surf '85 in town. I spent most of the time running around the contest site foraging for and collecting bits of discarded surf wax. I'd press these offcuts together into a mutant vomit-coloured wax ball that was one part wax and two parts dirt and grass. It was a revelation to me to not have to melt down our 'Holy wax' from religious candles for the next few months, as I made my scavenged wax ball last an absurd length of time.

After the contest ended and all the teams and fanfare pulled out of town, all fell suddenly very quiet in Bundoran, leaving its hardy band of school-aged surfers to settle back into Bundoran waves and ways once again. For me, the whole thing created a renewed, energetic enthusiasm for surfing. The contest also left behind a legacy of sorts in town. As I've said, in reality there were only a few dozen surfers in total between Bundoran, Rossnowlagh and Strandhill at the time, with fewer than 10 surfers in Bundoran (three in our house alone). What it did do was turn the tap a notch that started a dripping chain reaction in local surfing. The contest's legacy would eventually contribute to the flood that pushed local surfing to new levels not seen before, propelling Bundoran and Ireland's northwest into the 1990s, when the area with the town as a centrepiece would become its own surfing 'buzzword' and must see for globe-trotting pro-surfers and every manner of surf media. Euro Surf '85 even solved a few equipment issues for us, as we managed to pick up a surfboard or two. The fact that there were very few surfers in town restricted a mass injection of equipment. With so few surfers, there wasn't really a local surfing population to suck up the opportunity of purchasing second-hand boards and wetsuits from departing competitors as they were being offloaded.

As eye-opening as that week was for me, I was still green behind the lugs and knew almost nothing about the complexity and sometimes the simplicity of real surfing. I still had a lot to learn, but I was on the right road. Seeing surfers like stick men dropping into double-overhead waves on our local breaks, figures disappearing in and out of long tube rides that I'd only ever watched on *Crystal Voyager* – all of this was spellbinding to me.

On a national scale, an event like Euro Surf '85 breathed oxygen into Irish surfing, but it was still just preaching to the local band of surfers on the coast. The holding of the contest didn't initially expand participation in local or Irish surfing to any great degree. It would take the following decade before Irish surfing received national exposure beyond its already converted community.

～

Just as songs from bands like the Beach Boys formed the soundtrack to surfing communities in California during the 1960s and 70s, music played an important role in my life growing up by the sea. Music was everywhere in our house and was always an integral part of our everyday lives. It defined our family long before the surf did. When at home, I would sit by the record player flipping LPs, and out on the surf I'd cycle through whole albums in my head.

I adored the music of Queen and Elton John, who both produced elaborate eye-catching album art to go along with their records. With all of us in the house, our music education as children was wide-ranging and eclectic. It gave us all a cultured knowledge way beyond our age. Guitar heroes were my thing then and still are today to a large degree. Rory Gallagher, Phil Lynott, Gary Moore, Van Morrison, Dire Straits, U2 and Eric Clapton were among my most played rockers. The connections between surfing and music run very deep from every angle you can think of, from bottom up to top down. There is a musicality to surfing, from famous musicians who surf, to surfing inspiring music. It was and still is especially true in such an abundantly musical country as ours. The Irish surfing-music connections are rich and deep. Outside of Ireland, when I started to spread my surf-travel wings the surf-music connection was something I ran into everywhere at every level.

As a family, the business of running record stores offered up more practical requirements than having the opportunity and accessibility of listening to every genre of music imaginable. As soon as you were old enough to get a provisional driving licence, you were put on deliveries, or running some messages up to Monaghan, as Mum called it. By the end of 1985, my older brother had his beginner's driving permit. We were on the road for pick-ups and drop-offs across the rally stage roads of 1980s Ireland. We would be regularly dispatched to Hector Grey's and Waltons in Dublin on days off school for stock pick-up. At the time, they were the biggest music store wholesalers in the country.

My brother and I faced a dilemma on the return journey to Donegal. If we drove to Dublin through the north, it was faster, but we had to go through the rigmarole of crossing the border twice, with the drama of sealing and opening stock on at least two stops both ways with British and Irish customs. On top of that, there was the domino line of RUC, Garda, Irish army and British army checkpoints on the border crossing roads. Depending on how busy or locked down they were, it could occasionally add an additional hour or two to your journey time. If we went via the south, it was a longer journey with worse roads, but we would avoid customs and the last part of the drive was on the northwest coast again. The added attraction to taking the southern route was we could pop into Strandhill, or a quick detour to Easkey, on the way home for a surf. You never wanted to get home too early, because you would be given another job to do. So, we stretched out the arrival time as best we could. We would always leave early to be at our pick-up or drop-off destination at the stroke of doors-opening time.

The big delivery van we drove soon began to serve its real purpose for us, and that was a chance to see more of Ireland and explore parts of the coast we had never been to before. My brother had become a regular scuba diver by this stage, so it was handy for the dive tanks too. Although bringing explosive compressed air through Northern Ireland's British army check-points was just asking for trouble, so we left them out of our surf missions. The staff at Hector Grey's would often help us to fill the van with stock. They always wondered what on earth the surfboards and bits of wetsuits we had in the back were for. These lads were real northside Dubs. Standing on Upper Liffey Street and looking at surfboards in a Donegal-registered panel van while filling it with stock was quite something for them to wrap their heads round.

We might as well have told them that they were ironing boards. Arthur C. Clarke once famously said that 'Any sufficiently advanced technology is indistinguishable from magic.' It's a phrase very suited to early Irish surfing communication with non-surfers. Not that surfing is advanced technology, it was just so alien to the Irish population. We had some time convincing the salt of the van loaders at Hector Grey's that we really did use the surfboards in Ireland. My brother and I still laugh about that time. Thinking back on all those delivery trips, it seems like an alternative universe, or at least a very unrecognisable Ireland, which I guess it really was. Now Dublin has Ireland's biggest population of surfers on the island, with brands like Quiksilver and Vans opening flagship stores in the city centre, and a plethora of surfing schools and watersports shops sprouting up from the docklands to the beaches of the greater Dublin coastline. Thanks to Euro Surf '85 and the shift in attitudes in the following years, surfing in Ireland had become much more than a cult-like pastime.

# 6

# The Rope and Christian Beach Missions

Of the many surfers who have influenced me over the years, none have more than my older brother Joe and sister Frances. I wouldn't be surfing if it wasn't for them and their passion for the sea and surf. Bundoran is blessed with world-class surf in every coastal nook and cranny. My early surfing was very singularly focused on one location. My universe was Bundoran, and my surfing solar system revolved around Bundoran's Main Beach. Within walking distance from anywhere, it was perfect for all the kids who surfed from the West End, East End or Main Street. The beach sits at the end of the Promenade, a stretch of sand between the Peak reef and the iconic Rougey cliff. We used to call it the 'mean bitch', a fitting wordplay at the time due to the heavy shore-dumping waves it had at high tide. It is one of the best beaches to learn to surf on, not because it's easy; quite the opposite, because it really is quite dangerous and unpredictable. Being a narrow beach with a funnel-shaped sandy approach between the rocks, everything from swell to water depth is concentrated and quick to change.

The Main Beach presents an all-star cast of surfing and beach hazards all squeezed into a small strip of sand. It has rips in all directions (pulling everything left, right and out to sea), swift depth changes, exposed reefs and a skin-grating reef break called 3D, which links up with the beach break waves on bigger high-tide days. On the low tide there is a fantastic almost below sea level sandbar that produces an ultra-shallow powerful wave that churns along the ever-changing spit of sand. The parallel currents have river-flowing strength pulling through the flats up into the wave face, which helps the wave peel along in the tight confines between the reef and point. The rip can also pull you well beyond and into rocks off the point and out into the bay. It was a baptism of fire on the Main Beach for anyone, swimmer or surfer alike, not used to its complex mood swings. You learned pretty hard and fast lessons of where the dangers were and how to deal with them. The biggest danger on the Main Beach was, however, man-made. It came in the shape of the barrier rope that stretched across the beach during the summer months. It was heavy, hard-wearing industrial rope about 2 inches in diameter that was permanently coated in sharp barnacles and immature black muscles that could slit your skin like a box knife. At low tide, the rope was marooned well above the low-water mark, but as the tide flowed back in the rope slowly and morbidly floated back into play.

Bundoran has very few 'wave-free' days year-round. Even on the flattest days in the summer months, you would still get a few bumps of swell riding into the bay, or afternoon choppy sea breezes creating small, irregular, disorganised surf. From mid to high tide was always the best time to surf or swim on the Main Beach, but this was also when the rope was at its most deadly. It became like a macabre, elasticised horror version of Robin Hood's bow. There was a bit of slack in it but not much, and it would be taut on either end of the ebb and flow of each mound of swell. It became more extreme in breaking waves. It would snap back and forth with ferocious speed between the crest and trough of a wave. The Bundoran Main Beach rope would have had pride of place during the French Revolution as contender for best guillotine on show for most heads taken off.

I remember my mate Jimi Meehan developed a unique bunny hop on his surfboard that enabled him to jump over the rope hands free with his surfboard. Inexplicably, the surfboard remained stuck to his feet. No matter what state of play the rope was in, this hopping manoeuvre allowed Jimi to ride a wave from the outside, clearing the rope all the way to the sand. What Jimi managed to do was quite a feat of timing and balance. I never once saw him miss or get clipped by the rope.

There was method behind the madness of the Main Beach rope, but it had its origins in Bundoran Georgian and Victorian antiquity. In the era of bathing boxes and Victorian sensitivity, the rope was a boundary beyond which signalled the end of the flat earth and certain death. In a 1996 survey for a proposed marina in Bundoran, the town's coastline scored 10 out of a possible 10 on wind and swell exposure. In 1980s surfing, much had changed since Victorian beach rope times in Bundoran, with newfound attitudes and appetites towards the sea and a confidence in swimming and surfing reaching heights previously unseen.

Before the boat quay was constructed there was a sandy beach that was the centre point separating the old single street from the rest of town. A rope with metal posts can still be seen today marking the divide between Catholic and Protestant bathing areas. Once the boat quay was constructed it stopped the sand flow and the beach disappeared, bringing all the focus onto the

Main Beach, where the Doran River meets the sea. Hence the town's name Bundoran, meaning 'The bottom of the Doran River'.

The Main Beach rope was lethal to all sea-goers and could (and often did) injure people. The head lifeguard on the Main Beach was Mickey Rooney, who was affectionately known locally as 'Mickey Geldof' due to his charity work. Mickey was old school, and in a comical twist for a head lifeguard, Mickey couldn't swim due to a skin condition and was advised not to spend any time in the sun without being covered from head to toe. Even as young kids, the hilarity of the situation wasn't lost on us. Bundoran had to be a world's first: a popular seaside town with a head lifeguard who could neither swim nor go out in the summer sun.

In my younger rope-hating days, Mickey and the rope were my public enemy number one and two, in that order. Determined to do something about this, me and my surfing mate at the time, Patrick Daly, hatched a cunning plan to get rid of the surf-spoiling rope. We would get up very early: it got bright from 4 a.m. so that was our zero hour. We would dodge all the revellers leaving the nightclubs and drinking spots at first light, scuttle down to the water, cut the rope and be back in bed before anyone noticed we were gone.

And guess what? The plan worked. We swam out to the rope with just enough light in the westerly sky. Using the mini-saw on our Swiss Army knives (everyone had one of these in the 1980s), we cut the rope at both ends. It worked, and the rope was no more . . . until the tide went out and the council men dragged it back, re-attaching it to its equally dangerous submerged metal posts by lunchtime. Those metal posts either side of the beach posed a different type of danger no less menacing to surfer and swimmer alike. The posts were concreted into the reef and stood over 2 metres clear of the water on the low-tide mark. They were heavily encased in rust, with sharp and horribly disfigured sections of rolled steel joists, of the type used in building construction. On the mid to high tide, they acted as a submerged booby trap to any unsuspecting swimmer or surfer.

The game of rope-cutting cat and mouse went on for the rest of the summer. We were never apprehended, even though my brother found early-morning suspicious sand on my runners at the front door. Mickey was backed up by four capable young lifeguards from the local area who kept the waters patrolled. In modern times, we would look on Mickey's position more as a beach marshall than head lifeguard. He was fierce on the loud-speaker, especially to summer holiday makers. He never held back. His favourite line was, 'Get the fuck out of the water, ya cheeky bastards!' You could hear his version of mallet across the head verbal diplomacy from the promenade.

After Mickey retired, I would still see him around town every now and then, and I always made a point to stop and have a chat with him. He was a great character, and I grew to be very fond of him. When I told him one day that it was me who had been cutting the rope all those years before, he burst out laughing and said, 'I knew it was you, ya cheeky bastard, but I could never catch you.' Mickey organised the annual Bundoran Bay Swim every year and raised a lot of money for Conquer Cancer, a charity that was close to his heart and mine too.

～

My primary and secondary school classmates who surfed were Patrick McGloin, Damien Granaghan and Richard Carmody. I did have a much wider circle of friends, but those three boys surfed so it made them by that virtue the inner circle. Every summer for a week or two, Bundoran, like so many seaside towns at the time, got a visit from the Christian beach missions spreading the gospel. This group set up in front of the lifeguard tower every year with a 'Kum Ba Yah' campfire enthusiasm that would have been the envy of any chirpy children's TV presenter. They were a non-denominational evangelical church without walls, made up of girls and boys in their early twenties. Some of them came from another part of Ireland and the UK, but most came from Canada and America.

Like the entirety of my surfing world, the beach mission's HQ was not surprisingly also the town's Main Beach. They would set up in their red T-shirts early in the morning through to early afternoon before the promenade got too hectic and rough. They knew afternoon abuse from summertime piss-heads was to be avoided. Patrick McGloin, Patrick Daly and I were regulars, making sure we went down to the beach most days. Mum would say after breakfast, 'OK, off you go now, and I don't want to see you until teatime.' Before and after surfs we would sit with the beach missions for their singsongs and get fed with sweets, buns, cakes and drinks – which, let's be honest, were more appealing to us than their food for the soul.

They also distributed Christian-themed stationery and pamphlets. I remember one 6-inch ruler with a lenticular 3D image on it. Moving rulers and moving statues were the new-fangled must haves for the 1980s. The beach mission's ruler differed quite considerably from the *Masters of the Universe* one I already had. When you held it down, it had an image of Jesus in his everyday carpenter's outfit of robes and sandals going about his business. When you tilted it up, in the blink of an eye he was yet again torturously nailed to the cross with a blood-flowing crown of thorns. I had that ruler for years and it wouldn't have looked out of place among the made in China souvenirs available from the gift shops at Knock.

As schoolkids we toured every year to the Knock Shrine, which was the nun's favourite and a handy one-hour bus drive south from Bundoran. By the middle of primary school, I was an old hand in the Knock gift shops. I once bought Mum a whole set of Mary, Joseph and the Child of Prague statues for 99p. They had the null-and-void life-likeness and articulation of a Russian doll, decorated with a couple of different ecclesiastical go faster stickers with the adhesive strength of a feather on them to differentiate between the figures. Each figure had a painted face taken up mostly by way oversized bursting red lips that Kim Kardashian would have been envious of. I was chuffed with my purchase, even though they immediately lost their identity due to the stick-free stickers that attached themselves to the inside of the blue-and-white-striped plastic bag. Mum said she loved them so that was good enough for me, money well spent. The figures mysteriously disappeared shortly thereafter from our mantlepiece. Maybe they were wearing too much red lipstick for Mum. I suspect they were too good for everyday use and ended up in the 'best for Christmas time only' cutlery cupboard.

The two Patricks and I were respectful to the beach missions, but I can't remember any of the preaching sinking in. We had heard it all before. One of the booklets they gave out told a cautionary tale about a very bold boy called NIS, who was devious, deceitful but also attractive, convincing and, most importantly, a liar full of empty promises. All very common traits shared with all Catholic baddies we already knew. Nevertheless, we were warned to stay clear of NIS and his ilk. His antics and temptations were seductive, we were warned. We were made aware of the tell-tale signs of his influence. NIS of course was SIN spelled backwards and represented the temptations of the devil in the beach missions' child-friendly world. As is the way of almost all teenaged boys, NIS sat squarely on all our shoulders as we joined in daily with the happy-clappy beach missions. As we sat in our wetsuits, NIS whispered lustfully in all our ears as hormones coursed through our veins, magnified by the main attraction of the beach missions, which were the born-again Christian American princesses. So those impure thoughts were down to NIS whispering in my ear then; he really was a hallion putting black marks on our souls.

When we returned to school after the summer, our NIS confessions would be heard by the half-fossilised Father McNulty. Our old priest was a much less attractive proposition than the beach missions' girls, but Father McNulty was the real deal with a direct line to God, and we knew it. He would absolve you of all your original sin, thank Christ for that. Wiping the slate clean of impure thoughts and all the evils of July and August to boot. It was a good deal, confession. It was like admitting to the crime but entering a not guilty plea.

In hindsight, Father McNulty couldn't hear us anyway, so I think my soul is still blackened by NIS and his wicked ways. As secondary school beckoned I was getting stronger and more confident in the sea and more capable in the intricacies of surfing along the face of a wave.

## 7

# The Big Storm of 1988

In the 12 months of 1988, I learned an accelerated lesson in just how good surfing could be, how ugly the sea could get and how badly I wanted it all. It was a pivotal year for me where I became aware of a few more rings in the ever-increasing circles of the surfing world. The small injection of surfing equipment snapped up after Euro Surf '85 had been put to good use by us over the three years since the event. We were surfing more than ever before. My progression was impossible to judge, as it was mostly within the Bundoran surfing community of still less than a dozen. My self-awareness about my own surfing progress didn't go beyond having fun, getting my fix of catching waves and surfing a few more intermediate waves in the bay.

I passed a milestone that year. However, it was on the second attempt after narrow shortcomings the year before. There is a limit to how much sea swimming you can do year-round in Ireland, especially in those days without proper wetsuits. Over the winter months, I had applied myself to the local pool. I found I was a natural strong competitor in the pool in most swim strokes. I loved swim galas and the nervy excitement of competition. I amassed a drawer full of gold medals at county and Ulster under-age level over that three-year period. As much as winning in the pool felt special, the monotonous repetition of swimming lengths in training for hours and days on end lost its appeal to me after a few seasons. It was only a stop gap for me until the summer months came around again and I could jump in the sea.

At the end of that summer, I was determined to complete another local rite of passage challenge: the annual 2.5 km-long Bundoran Bay Swim in aid of cancer research. As much as the event is a worthy fundraiser, it was also an open challenge to sea swimmers. It was always experienced adult swimmers who took part; no youngsters ever attempted it. Going from age 11 in 1985 to a teenaged 14 by 1988 helped me a lot physically with surfing and swimming. If you can't power yourself out beyond breaking waves, it's hard to progress at surfing. Starting secondary school was a big thing for me. It was not as penned-in as primary school, so I relished that extra bit of freedom. I was still spindly but had become considerably stronger with broad shoulders from hundreds of hours spent surfing and swimming. That extra strength helped develop me into a strong and confident paddler in the sea. As 98 per cent of surfing is paddling your surfboard, this extra strength was crucial in allowing me to get in and out of some bigger wave conditions, of which Bundoran had plenty.

The Bundoran Bay Swim seemed the next logical step in my sea trials, as my sister and brothers were already swim veterans at this stage. To be able to say that you had made the swim was a big feather in anyone's cap. I didn't know anyone my age who had attempted it. At the end of that fantastic Euro football summer of 1988 and at the second time of asking, I finished the bay swim handy enough, coming in alongside my brother and sister, which was in stark contrast to my first attempt the year before. The bay swim is always held in August, theoretically when Irish sea temperatures are at their warmest, but it's not always the case. The swim consists of a fiddler's elbow 2.5 km-shaped course across the bay from beach to boat harbour, although the length of the swim varies wildly depending on the tide and sea conditions. It's a tricky swim, even for experienced sea swimmers, the course taking in a long, deep cliff section of open water with all the unpredictable rip and wave movement in the bay. On a calm training day, it's much easier to complete, but without fail the day of the swim dawns every year with some form of less-than-ideal swell running and choppy sea conditions to contend with. The first time I attempted the Bundoran Bay Swim, I was a year younger and even more rakish at 13. The day of the swim was typical Bundoran weather, with afternoon northwest onshore chop and 3-foot seas, and only momentary bursts of bright summer sunshine breaking through the fast-moving, low wispy clouds above. It was a day where the sea was speaking to the sky, making it almost impossible to tell where the water ended and the sky began. The mirroring gave the sea an unearthly colour scheme in its reflected veneer. Added to this patchwork seascape was the very healthy but brownish-copper hue of the breaking waves, garnering their colour from the late summer iodine secretion caused by the local kelp forests just offshore. It wasn't cold but far from comfortably warm either. A typical Irish summer's day then.

In those days you did the bay swim in your togs with no swim fins or any wetsuits or accessories, full stop. Anything more than togs, a swim hat and goggles was seen as blasphemy by the old, established swimming martyrs in town. That first attempt, I managed to make it the whole way around the bay, feeling good but a little cold on the final 200-metre leg. On the home

stretch to the boat quay, I swam into a thick swarm of brown
compass jellyfish. I felt a few stings under my arm and across
my face. Foolishly, I stopped swimming to have a go at trying
to rub away the stings. After only a few moments, I felt disoriented, which had nothing to do with the stings and everything
to do with the cold gaining an even tighter and more immediate
grip on me once I stopped moving. I heard the hum of an
outboard engine and a few familiar voices. I looked up to see
the smiling faces of the lifeboat crew looking down at me. One
of the crew said to me, 'Hi, young Fitzgerald, are you OK?' I
replied, 'Oh I am, aye, I'm grand Mr Granaghan, I just got
stung by a jellyfish' with my lips quivering. I put my goggles
back on through equally frantic, shivering hands and off I swam,
completely disoriented by the cold, in the wrong direction
heading back out to sea. I was whipped into the lifeboat in a
flash as I meekly protested my unjust extraction, the crew re-
assuring me that I'd made it. They were just going to give me
a lift to the boat quay as I was almost there anyway. I can't
remember much after that until I came round again in the back
of the ambulance at the top of the slipway. As I warmed up,
the paramedic told me I was in early-stage onset hypothermia
and was pulled out just in time, wrapped in blankets and silver
foil like a purple crash-landed Roswell alien talking nonsense
in the back of the ambulance. Hypothermia, as I discovered that
afternoon, is as seductively comforting as it is lethal. You don't
feel cold at all, you just feel warm inside, lightheaded, that nicely
drunk stage of no inhibitions where everything is perfect in the
world accompanying faint hallucinations and babbling talk. All
I wanted to do was curl up, close my eyes and sleep, which is
its most lethal element. After regaining my senses and feeling
somewhat back to normal, I was given a pat on the back by
the lifeboat crew with a 'well done, young cub' cheerio, before

walking home with my brother and sister. I felt proud of myself as the youngest swimmer that day but also burning disappointment in the pit of my stomach as I knew I had failed to cross the line. For me that sickening sense of personal failure spurred me on to train hard and smash the swim the following year, which I did with plenty left in the tank.

By 1988, the shorefront of Bundoran had become as familiar to me as the inside of our house. I had an intimate knowledge of the nuances and peculiarity of Bundoran bay, both in and out of the surf. To me, it seemed as constant and immovable as Yeats' much loved Benbulben mountain standing to attention behind the coast. All that changed during early January that year when the northwest was hit by one of the most powerful and destructive storms I had witnessed up to that point, or since then for that matter. The northwest is no stranger to severe weather, and in winter it is storm battered. The town of Bundoran is mostly set quite a bit back from the immediate shoreline, a lesson learned by older generations not to build too close to the sea. The West End is however nestled above the cliffs and sea wall for good reason, as a beachfront villa wouldn't last a month on our surf-pummelled coast.

Back then, the seafront of my youth looked considerably different to how it looks today. The Main Beach had a double-storey lifeguard tower with changing rooms, showers and an upper viewing platform with a mini-elevated promenade that was perfect for BMX Beat bunny hops. The Thrupenny outdoor pool had a boat-shaped double-level complex complete with changing rooms, seats and lookout platform that offered a panoramic view of the bay.

When a ferocious storm struck the northwest of Ireland in February of 1988, it decimated the coastline. The eye of the storm passed over Rossnowlagh, wrecking the newly built surf clubhouse (Ireland's first purpose-built surf clubhouse building). Waves and hurricane winds smashed in most of the doors and windows of the adjacent Sand House Hotel. Both Bundoran and Rossnowlagh were declared disaster areas in the aftermath. My mother was always up for an adventure, life threatening or not. She decided a drive around the town was in order on the day of the storm – we were definitely not a 'batten down the hatches' family. We piled into her station wagon and off we went down the Main Street in the middle of a mid-winter hurricane with winds touching 135 mph. We barely made it into the car outside for starters, as it got mercilessly battered by a swirling mass of debris. Most dangerous of all were the flying roof tiles and slates smashing into everything like missiles. We made it about 400 metres down the road to the West End and had to turn back. It was a day that had all the hallmarks of a Hollywood disaster movie, as the bridge in the centre of town was being swallowed with every onrushing set of mountainous waves. My mum made the dash over the bridge in the car twice. She timed her game of chance perfectly, missing the frequent charges of seawater over the thick, grey cut-stone walls. Enormous high-tide waves were breaking over the roof of the old multistorey Imperial Hotel in the West End. Incredible cubic metres of seawater formed pulsing waterfalls, deluging down off the pitched roof and smashing parked cars on the street below, each wave leaving in its wake a swampy soup of flotsam and jetsam on the roads and buildings. To put that into context, the Imperial Hotel stood on top of the West End cliffs and was four storeys high, giving it well over a hundred feet of elevation. Waves were clearing the roof and causing all sorts of chaos. No storm since has come close to that level of destruction.

The next morning, when the winds had calmed down some-what, we were like ants crawling all over the wreckage and debris that was once the foreshore. All the local kids and families were out after surviving the salty apocalypse and poking around in what was left. The Main Beach, outdoor Thrupenny pool, lifeguard tower and viewing platforms were completely gone, with only shards of twisted metal remaining. The lifeboat from the West End had been lifted out of its station and dragged across the bay, where it was impaled on a piece of deformed steel where the lifeguard tower once stood. It was a disturbing and almost inconceivable scene to digest for me. I learnt that morning what a cruel mistress the sea could be. Before, it had been my playground and location for good times, but here it showed its most merciless, malevolent side. I took it personally. I felt betrayed by its rampage.

As the week wore on, the extent of the damage to the shore front and town became even more apparent. Destruction was everywhere. However, it seemed that Manannán, 'the Irish Lord of the Sea', was trying to make amends with us for his angry outburst as we witnessed the inexplicable sight of a few surfboards and wetsuits washing ashore. It later transpired that the source of these gifts from the sea wasn't a repentant, mythological sea god but Rossnowlagh Surf Club. The new clubhouse had its doors and windows blown out by the waves and its contents flushed out by the all-day storm surge and mammoth waves. Most of the boards came ashore unscathed on the rocky West End of town after a rudderless sea journey of many kilometres, which was a miracle in itself. Most were rounded up and returned to the club. A few strays never made it back around the estuary to Rossnowlagh. These boards and wetsuits were claimed by Bundoran surfers in a local version of the Law of Maritime Salvage.

In the 1980s, local surfers in Rossnowlagh were the enviable haves and Bundoran locals were decidedly the have nots in terms of equipment, experience and ability. The two surfing communities today are indecipherable in most ways, and can be seen as one grouping, the links are that tight. Rossnowlagh has a long heritage in Irish surfing built around the pioneering Britton family. In the early days that heritage made a big difference, especially for equipment. The waves in Rossnowlagh are mellow. It's a beginner's beach perfect for longboarding, kids or big battleship soft-top surfboards. Its surf offers little challenge beyond a learner's wave, so it's not much of a challenge for intermediates and above. Bundoran, on the other hand, just around the corner, has a spectrum of different waves for every level. On any given day, most of the Rossnowlagh locals who were looking for a challenge could be found then, as they are today, out surfing on one of Bundoran's main surf breaks.

What Bundoran lacked in surfing heritage in the early 1980s, it made up for in perfect surf. It's hard to imagine now as Bundoran is branded 'Ireland's surfing capital' with all the surf businesses it has and the legacy of hosting all of Ireland's big international events and high-profile pro surfers over three decades. For us growing up, it would be the early years of the 1990s before the pendulum swung and Bundoran found its surfing feet. The two towns are still vital to each other and exist in a symbiotic surfing microclimate of waves and surfers, with one town offering surfing simplicity and the other offering every technical wave challenge you can imagine. It's a tiny coastal area but combined it has produced way more than its fair share of the surfers, personnel, events and industry that has pushed Irish surfing forward in the last 30 years.

As small as the Bundoran surfing community was, it was dedicated and began propelling forward at a faster rate by the end of the 1980s. The number of local surfers was just into double figures. We still all knew each other in Bundoran and we could easily pick out individual local surfers from land by their style in the water. If that visual ID failed, you could tell who it was in the water by their surfboard, its colour and the wetsuits they wore. It was their surfing family crest and instantly identifiable. I could pick out the bunny-hopping virtuoso Jim Meehan surfing the Peak way off in the distance from the top of Rougey cliff by his neoprene uniform alone.

The year 1988 was also when I invested in my first proper winter wetsuit, one that would actually fit without a half decade worth of growing room. Up until then, I had been using hand-me-down wetsuits and an inadequate summer weight 2 mm wetsuit brought back from holidays in Orlando, Florida. Considering what was needed in wintertime Bundoran, wetsuits available in tropical Florida had about the same effectiveness for us as someone wearing a Lycra onesie in Lapland. If my brother or sister weren't surfing that day, I often wore their two-piece summer wetsuits over my one-piece Florida import.

In those days, the must-have wetsuits were from a company in the UK called Second Skins. They were custom made in England to fit the individual's exact measurements, which was essential when neoprene at the time had the tactile flexibility of Sir Lancelot. Ordering wetsuits was all done by post. Most were mail order. If you had a telephone number to ring, that was a bonus. Second Skins advertised their service and products in the UK's main surfing magazine, *Wavelength*, and we managed to get hold of a copy. I called Second Skins to order myself a wetsuit, and about six weeks later I received a big brown parcel in the post (the magic of waiting for the postman to deliver was just as exciting as Santa Claus was years earlier). My wetsuit had a black body and purple legs. I thought I was as cool as a cucumber, but when I look at old photos of the colour combo, it looks like a Joker and Batman abomination melted into one. The quality of Second Skins wetsuits was sublime in comparison to what I'd used for the previous five years. These wetsuits were warm, and for the first time I wasn't losing all my heat after two minutes in winter water. The exterior torso of the wetsuit was made of a material called double-lined smooth skin, which was a rubbery black finish that looked slippery when wet. From the waist up, I had a 'bring out the gimp' aesthetic.

Rashing has almost disappeared nowadays, but back then it was as common to ask someone for Vaseline as it was for wax. The world's most popular surf wax is called Mr Zog's Sex Wax (I'm not joking). When it came onto the market in California in 1972, it was produced by Frederick Herzog, chemist Nate Skinner and artist Hank Pitcher. Its bold candy-pop colours and moreish smells struck a chord with everyone. The wax was an immediate cultural and economic success that went well beyond surfing. The three Californian surfing amigos used the smart marketing ploy of calling it sex wax rather than just plain old surf wax. The risqué name gave it a rude curiosity irresistible to anyone who saw it for sale, surfer or otherwise. Even in my own surf shop today, almost every non-surfer who comes into the store picks up the wax and has a giggle. Most leave with a bar or two regardless of board ownership. It doesn't hurt that every bar of sex wax now has the singularly beautiful aroma of bubble gum coconut.

For me in 1988, turning up to a surf spot dressed in my dominatrix black rubber wetsuit, holding a bar of sex wax and a tub of Vaseline was normal enough. I wouldn't have looked out of place heading for one of Berlin's famous S&M clubs. It was the 1980s after all, and if Adam Ant could get away with looking like an Edwardian pimp, then so could I.

After the initial success of my parcel smuggling of wetsuits from England (without Mum finding out) and the relative ease of their arrival, it gave me a brazen confidence to see what else I could order. My new escapades focused my efforts and all my money towards bringing in more merchandise. Mum did notice the new wetsuit and let it slide. She was disappointed though that I tried to hide it by intercepting the postman. My mum supported my quest for waves, and at that age I was very much sponsored by my mother, like everyone else. Nevertheless, she did warn me enough was enough and no more wetsuits and gear from the UK until the next year. She was aware that surfing was something I'd been doing for a few years and that I was taking it seriously, but she feared that it might be another passing gadget fad that the 1980s were so famous for. In fairness, '80s fads like the Rubik's Cube, the Space Hopper and yo-yos had sucked me in, but inevitably they all ended up on the scrap heap. The only difference between these fads and surfing was that a yo-yo was distinctly cheaper than a new surfboard and wetsuit.

I had rushed headlong into most of the '80s crazes. In general I was influenced by music, American films of the time and the growing Americana that was creeping onto our TV screens. It was hard to resist. I was part of a breakdance group called 'Freeze Frame' with my rope-cutting surf buddy, Patrick Daly. We even managed to win best dance act at Opportunity Knocks in Ballyshannon's Abbey Theatre. It was bright lights, big city stuff. Dancing to the soundtrack of *Breakdance: The Movie*, we were dressed like MC Hammer with big Adidas runner boots on looking pretty fly for a white guy, or so we thought. In another '80s fad, Steven Travers over the bridge from us on Church Road built a BMX quarter pipe and we were all BMX bandits for a few years. In my mind, I was Elliott from *E.T. the Extra-Terrestrial* and only one step away from flying over the bike ramp. In the middle of all these flash-in-the-pan fixations, there remained one constant throughout, and that was surfing. As the novelties came and went, surfing stayed permanently anchored in our house. For me, the endless adventure of riding waves was front and centre, and wasn't about to fade away anytime soon.

## 8

# 'I'm taking you to the Irish National Surfing Championships . . .'

There was one more seismic moment in store for me in 1988 before the year was out. At least the threatened confiscation of my purple-and-black apparition of a new wetsuit was given a welcome stay of execution. I was so excited at the prospect of surfing through the coming winter in a real wetsuit. Little could I have imagined it would soon be put into action in the Irish surfing contest circuit.

The success of local surfers in Euro Surf '85, in particular Brian Tobin, helped raise the profile of surfing in Ireland. The other half of the Florida/Donegal surfing Tobin brothers was the wispy blond-haired Kevin, or KT, as he became known to everyone. KT had a vivacious, livewire personality, and coupled with his expertise on the waves this made him an instant hit. Along with his older brother Brian they burst onto the Irish surf scene in the mid-'80s with much colour, skill and vibrant surfing modernism. Both brothers had competed so well for Ireland in Euro Surf '85, raising the bar of Irish surfing in the process. KT was the first and perhaps the only surfer I have ever hero-worshipped. His surfing ability and timing was incredible. His style was more relatable to me than his brother's because KT surfed with his right leg forward, the same as me. In the world of surfing, this is less common than someone surfing with their left foot forward, so I could appreciate and understand what KT was doing on the waves easier than his brother Brian, who surfed with his left foot forward. It sounds like remedial stuff but that all counts when you are learning without any real coaching or direction. After finishing high school in Florida, the two Tobin brothers decided to return to Ireland for good. With their injection of what was possible on Irish waves, surfing in the northwest would never be the same again.

At the time, I could barely manage to close my mouth in awe while talking to KT. I asked him, with a certain perplexion in my conversation-making, 'Why would you want to move back to Donegal from Florida?' To me, Florida was that magical land of Disney enchantment where we'd had a few big family holidays. I would always cry when leaving Florida for the airport and the flight home. KT replied immediately: 'It's for the waves, little Richard,' as he always called me, spoken with a purposeful Rick James twang. 'The waves around Bundoran are one in a million,' he said, 'especially the Bundoran Peak.' During the summer, KT had a fleeting romance with one of my older sisters. Although it was just a brief summertime thing, Kevin was such an endearing character that he became a fixture in our house thereafter.

Neither of my parents were the type who stand on the sidelines cheering for their children at sports events. In fact, they never did any pick-ups or drop-offs either. I remember being left behind one cold winter's evening by a swamped-with-kids mother after a swimming session at the pool in Ballyshannon.

I was still in primary school and came running out of the changing rooms dripping wet as she drove off, her red tail lights disappearing up the hill in the sideways wind and rain. With no money or payphone, I had that feeling of dread. Too shy to say anything to an adult, I got dressed and thought to myself, harden up, you know the way home. I set off walking the 7 kilometres back to Bundoran in the dark along the busy main road. Mum wasn't overly fazed when I got home late, there was no search party summoned. I never felt I missed that parent-sport involvement, it was just the way it was for us. I could never imagine either of my parents standing around a junior surfing contest arguing over judges' scores. They had raised us well to be independent and free from what you'd call 'helicopter parenting' nowadays.

One evening in our kitchen (and he had this uncanny knack of arriving at our house just in time for tea after a day's surfing) KT said to me, 'I'm taking you to the Irish National Surfing Championships in Rossnowlagh next weekend, little Richard.' I didn't even know the championships were on, and knew even less about the reality of surfing in a contest. Kevin informed me that I was well able for it. He was true to his word and picked me up in his wee, faded powder-blue, two-seater van on the Saturday morning. With the B52s blasting from the speakers, off I went, sardined between surfboards in the back for the 17-kilometre journey up the coast to Rossnowlagh. Kevin gave me a crash course in surfing a heat on the drive out. I listened as best I could, huffing and puffing as I changed into my wetsuit while lying down crammed in the back of the van, a wriggling mass of arms and legs. Surfing a heat has changed a lot from the 1980s to today's modern surfing contest. In 1988, it was all about squeezing as many manoeuvres as possible in on every wave. Length of ride was a close second in the scoring criteria.

Two things that don't count for much in the modern format. Catch three good waves in 30 minutes and ride them to shore, were my instructions. Critically, surf no more than 10 waves was the basic don't-screw-it-up blueprint I was to follow. KT warned me to never stand up on a wave after the end of the heat, once the buzzer sounded. 'It cost my brother Brian a European title [in '85],' he warned me. Serious stuff then. I didn't know what to expect, but I was putting my wetsuit on in the back, so I'd be ready for anything once we hit the sand in Rossnowlagh. My main concern was how would I hear the heat start and finish buzzer way out to sea, or see the colour changes on the board that indicate the time remaining? I wasn't overly concerned about the surfing side of things: I knew I could paddle and surf waves till the cows came home.

Rossnowlagh Surf Club (RSC) was established way back in 1966 at the very birth of organised surfing in Ireland. It took another 22 years before the building of RSC clubhouse right there on the beach when it was completed in May 1988. We all took a drive out for the opening of RSC. There was a good crowd of about 60 people gathered from the local community, surfers from Bundoran, Ballyshannon and a few who had come up from Strandhill and Tramore. RTÉ News sent a reporter and cameraman to cover the big day as the clubhouse was opened by the then Minister of State, Frank Fahey. At the time, the report suggests that there were 600 surfers in Ireland. Small though that number seems, it was most certainly generously stretched for the minister and TV cameras. The real number of surfers in Ireland in 1988 was much lower than 600, coming in at half that number of around 300 at the most optimistic. Even so, by modern estimates, if we take that figure against the impossible to accurately calculate number of surfers in Ireland today, we can see the dramatic upward trajectory. Surfing's increase in popularity is impressive, with participation figures sitting somewhere well north of 150,000, even 200,000 by some estimates. Whatever the uptake figures, it's only moving one way, and that's upwards.

I spent the duration of the TV news report the following evening trying to spot my 14-year-old self in the crowd, but to no avail. RSC's construction was also the first permanent surf club building in the country. Although the new surf club didn't affect the day-to-day surfing for us in Bundoran, it proved to be a major kudos for the area and a statement for Irish surfing. Surfing as a pursuit can be so flighty and unspecific, especially for outsiders trying to understand the sport. What I mean by that is you can turn up to the beach one sunny day with hundreds out surfing. Turn up the next day, the sun is still out, the waves are still breaking on the beach, but with a change in wind or swell direction it has put the beach out of favour. Where there were hundreds the day before, you may only have four or five beginner surfers in the water, even though conditions look 95 per cent the same as the previous day. It makes no sense to those looking in on the sport. It comes across as mad. You could compare it to only playing football on a pitch if the wind is blowing in a certain direction: any change and the match is off.

Surfing is also a hard activity to attach any bricks and mortar to. Most sports will have club changing rooms at their local venue, such as tennis, football and so on. Surfing doesn't lend itself to that model. Nevertheless, here at the end of the 1980s in Rossnowlagh, there was a new surf club building. I didn't use it for the simple fact I didn't live within walking distance of Rossnowlagh. However, if I took a Sunday drive with an older family member to surf there, it took me a few years to stop getting a kick out of seeing 'Surf Club' written on the roof as you drove down from the cliff top. A surf club building in

Donegal like the ones you saw in Australia – it was cool for my teenage years every time I laid eyes on it. The club provided a hub for the legions of summer holiday makers from the north as well as the core locals. Rossnowlagh had only a resident population totalling less than 50 people, including the local surfers. So, it was a real credit to that handful of local surfers pushing to get it built; having a physical presence of the RSC on the beach sent out a massive signal. The new RSC encouraged so many kids into the sport, especially from Northern Ireland. From that small clubhouse emerged many mainstays in the checklist of Irish surfing families.

We arrived for the contest in Rossnowlagh at 8 a.m. I had managed to get fully shuffled into my wetsuit like a jack in the box in the back of the van. Now I was stinging to get into the water as soon as KT opened the back doors. I had surfed Rossnowlagh before, but only occasionally. I wasn't overly familiar with its waves. KT told me the surf forecast was good for the weekend. I knew the surf in Rossnowlagh was an easier proposition than the waves in Bundoran. That morning, the Rossnowlagh car park was a buzzing hive of activity in front of the RSC. I couldn't contain my excitement at what was to be my first ever surfing contest. The weather was mild, with no wind. KT was right about the surf, it was glassy with peeling 3-foot waves on offer. I registered at the surf club and was told to be back at 8.30 a.m. to check the heat sheets as the contest started at 9 a.m. sharp. That gave me 20 minutes to jump in and have a warm-up surf, so I ran for the water like a scalded cat. I never did get changed out of my wetsuit again that day, staying suited up until just before dark. Between heats, I'd go free surfing with all the other juniors in the contest. I had that boundless energy and enthusiasm to keep going for eight hours straight in the water. Adjacent to the RSC was Surfers' Bar owned by the Britton family. The bar was an Aladdin's cave of Irish surfing memorabilia. Photos, boards and posters adorned every square inch of wall space. The images were a feast for the eyes, highlighting Irish surfing greats and events past and present at home and abroad. The only refuel I had that day was standing awestruck in the bar staring up at the photos while gulping a bottle of club orange, a fistful of Tayto crisps and chomping down a Marathon bar in two bites.

KT had already garnered a huge persona within Irish surfing. He was full of wacky wit that benefited from the distinct contrast of Donegal and Central Florida living. My guts would hurt from laughing after spending a few hours with KT. His years in Florida had given him a pitch-perfect rendition of the redneck, brain-dead surfer dude. Complete with a Jim Carey ability to rubberise his facial expressions in tandem with his pantomime southern hillbilly surfing pomposity. He really should have been on stage. KT would keep the whole car park in hinged-over stitches with his demented role play impressions of a half dozen characters all at once. Kevin and Brian don't get the credit or the recognition they deserve in modernising Irish surfing attitudes and abilities in the water. To me, in some ways they are the forgotten men of that time. They both played such a crucial role in breaking down the doors of what was possible on Irish waves and by Irish surfers. They didn't miss a beat surfing heats against Aussies, Americans or any other big surfing nations. They certainly never saw themselves or any other Irish surfers as the underdogs in or out of the contest surfing arena. The brothers were a blast of Florida heat on the Donegal coast just when it was needed. For me personally, the Tobin brothers were a window into what was going on in the surfing world outside of Ireland. Both brothers represented Ireland for years and won many national titles between them. Brian, as part of the Irish surf team, made it all the way to the semi-finals of the World Surfing Championships before the decade was out, an achievement that hasn't been matched by any Irish surfer at that event since.

At the contest, I was to meet three surfers my age who have remained friends ever since. John McCarthy and David Blount from Tramore and Adam Wilson from Portrush were competing in my age group for the event. For the decades that followed, we would be sparring partners in heats, surf travel companions and Irish surf teammates through the year and age categories. The boys have endured as three of the most respected surfers in the country, becoming part of the tapestry of Irish surfing. Attending that contest in Rossnowlagh was a big eye-opener for me. It was a national event where meeting like-minded teenagers cut from the same cloth as me was a momentous discovery to make. I had found my tribe right there: this small gathering of Ireland's best from the compact selection of surfing towns. Being among Ireland's top surfers gathered underneath the overhang roof of the RSC felt like I'd stepped up a few notches. Getting into surfing didn't come easy to any of us. We all had similar backgrounds and neither me nor any of the other juniors had all the right equipment. Nor did any of us have a by the numbers introduction to surfing. My board was crappy, but my purple wetsuit was impressive and that was enough. To surf, especially as a youngster back then, you had to really want it. Nothing was handed to you, there was no easy way in. You had to chase it, grabbing onto it as hard as you could. That scrap-like-hell desire to surf was etched all over this new tribe I had just discovered.

By Sunday afternoon, I made it all the way to the junior final, which was surprising, especially to myself. I couldn't believe it. I finished third and loved every minute of competitive surfing. I had gained enough points to be in contention for the Irish junior team for the upcoming Euro Surf. If I managed to get a decent result in the following event, I was in. On the drive back to Bundoran that Sunday evening, I was in a daze of delight and surfing possibility. It was a whirlwind from being clueless on Friday to being in contention for a spot on the Irish junior surf team by Sunday evening that was way beyond my expectations. I had gained three new, like-minded surfing friends from different coasts, including the new Irish junior champion, Dave Blount. We all swapped home phone numbers and addresses. Before leaving, we invited each other to come and stay and surf in our respective towns and houses to sample the waves we surf. It was quite the weekend for me.

That one simple act of kindness and encouragement by Kevin Tobin in picking me up and bringing me to that first contest had a huge effect on me. Over the next 10 years, I'd surf for Ireland at three European and three World Championships. Along with Jimi Meehan we were the first Bundoran surfers to make the Irish surf team and compete abroad. Of the many accolades I have achieved in surfing since, those events will remain some of my proudest moments. Standing under the Irish flag with my teammates at opening ceremonies, or at the contest sites from Rio de Janeiro to Huntington Beach, California, are memories I cherish. All the friends you make and camaraderie you feel while surfing on Irish teams is like no other. To represent your country on the international stage is a bursting-with-pride fulfilment that's hard to explain if you haven't done so.

After that contest, I had an added spring in my step and a new purpose when looking at the surf and what was contained out there in the waves. Surfing now represented something even more to me. The horizon felt bigger. Surfing internationally was a real possibility, and competing at all the Irish events the following year was purring away in my head. I was bristling with possibilities and the targets I wanted to set. My new wetsuit was as good as the hype said it would be. It held together and kept me warm in the water that autumn and winter until I grew out of it. One October Saturday, a few weeks after the contest, Bundoran was hit with a big triple-overhead swell of perfect shape and proportions. I could hear it rumbling from my bedroom before first light. I checked the surf before first light. The bay was lined up with flawless, double-ceiling-high, powerful tubing waves all across the reefs. I could see that no one was out, with nobody parked up waiting either. This reality snapped me into a kind of trance of denial. At age 14, I discounted my relative inexperience in waves of this size and the fact that no one else was in the water. All I knew was that I wanted to surf that day. I couldn't resist it. I'd never forgive myself if I didn't paddle out and give it a go. I'd never tackled anything quite so big or powerful before, but the prospect of being out alone was pushed to the back of my mind almost immediately. I was hoping someone would paddle out by the time I got suited up. Within 10 minutes, I was back down on the edge of the reef ready to paddle out. I couldn't see anyone else in the water over the emerald walls. I made it halfway out to the take-off spot, weaving and dodging the green and white hammer blows. As I neared the point of no return, when you are too far from the safety of the shore, I saw what looked like a little black creature paddling up a jade wall several times its size. I could see him look back and register that there was another surfer in the water. Maybe he felt relief at having company. I know I certainly did. I paddled like a maniac to his position with a safety in numbers rationale.

Before I reached him, I recognised who he was. It was Brian Tobin. I remember his exact words as he called out to me in earshot. 'Hey man, I can't believe you paddled out, you're a fucking animal to be out here. It's just the two of us.' As I got closer, he had a massive smile on his face. I told him that I hadn't seen him from shore but couldn't resist the lure of surfing a swell like this even if it meant a solo mission. I sat on his wing for the surf where he called me into the biggest set waves I had ever ridden to that point. Dropping down those big emerald walls and seeing it pitch up the whole way across the bay in front of me felt like no surfing I had ever experienced before. It was dream two-hour surf, just the two of us with me on the steepest of waves and an even steeper surfing graduation. I savoured every moment of it. Walking up the reef with Brian afterwards with my tyres pumped up, I felt 10 feet tall. Brian said, 'You're a ballsy wee prick, aren't ya? No other kid your age is surfing waves like this.' Both the Tobin brothers affected me that autumn, first Kevin and then Brian. With his direction of me in the big surf that morning, his vote of confidence went a lot further than I'm sure he ever realised. That day and that one surf gave me self-belief in something that I had already realised I was heading for. That recognition was that I was drawn to big surf and felt remarkably comfortable out there in it.

# 9

# One-Eyed Willie

For as long as I can remember, I have always set targets for myself. Whether I reached them all is another story. There were goals I really wanted to achieve that I wrote down and worked towards, sometimes for years, without ever getting close, while others I eventually reeled in. I didn't set the standard short-, medium- and long-term aims. I looked on them rather more like this. Firstly, the achievable ones, even if they took a long time. Secondly, targets I knew I could get to but required alot of effort, hard work and a bit of luck here and there. Lastly, there was the Hail Mary, hit and hope ones that mostly turned out to be pipe dreams. My list wasn't all based around surfing of course, but surfing objectives were a major part of the inventory.

From 1988 onwards, after I got a whiff of competitive surfing I couldn't shake the desire that one day, somehow, I would be good enough to get paid to surf, in big waves or small. It sounded mad at the time when I said it out loud to myself. Nevertheless, every time I redid my list, I rebooted that goal to the top of the page. Ireland had no paid professional surfers at that time, or any history of them for that matter. We had never produced a professional surfer. There was no shame in that. Professional surfing as a global sport had only emerged in organised form in 1976, although surfing's first official professional surfer was George Freeth (1883–1919). By the 1980s Europe had only a fistful of semi-pro surfers, with most of the early pro murmurings coming out of the UK.

As the 1980s ended and the new decade began, my addiction to surfing was complete. I'd surfed for Ireland at European Junior level and had become a regular on the growing Irish surfing contest scene. Surfing really started to dominate every aspect of my life: my physical shape, my desire, my mental attitude and financial thinking. It's a sport that makes you single-minded verging on the obsessive, which leads you down a road of insatiable greed with your free time. I also came to realise early on that much of the sport is taken up with chasing waves and swell up and down the coast, or in later years for me across the planet. It's a lifestyle that becomes all-consuming. Whispered cat and mouse rumours of phantom surf breaks over yonder; mile-long waves in Kerry; mystic island waves in Mayo; cavernous tubes in Clare; seamount monster waves in Sligo; and Tahitian reef pass perfection in Donegal. I'd heard it all. There was little hard evidence bar the odd grainy photo, but it was mostly a time of stories exchanged between local surfers of something better beyond the next hill, round the bend or across the bay. It's a way of thinking that propagates wanderlust, fostering an adventurous spirit whether you fully register it or not. The possibility of new discoveries, even if they were only new to me at the time, filled my thoughts. The dreams of far-flung exotic travel destinations halfway around the world triggered my imagination as much as anyone. From my first tentative steps into the surfing world as a child, I was always a dreamer. Forever searching for something different at home, at school and in my hometown.

I loved getting lost in make-believe, first with my toys then later in films, books and music. I loved anything sci-fi. I must have watched Mike Hodges' campy *Flash Gordon* film 50 times, loving every second of it. Above all, I adored *Star Wars*. George Lucas's game-changing space opera hit me and almost every other child growing up in the 1970s like a thunderbolt. I couldn't get enough of it; even now as a middle-aged man-child I still can't. I was totally taken in and absorbed in its classic fantasy themes. When it came to the real world, I would still let my imagination run wild. Yes, the countryside and coast around me kept me fascinated. But the dreams of travelling to exotic places on this planet, or to a galaxy far, far away, were never out of my mind either.

In the sea with surfing, I found that same contradicting feeling of a deep connection and unbridled escapism all at once. I had found my groove in surfing, and it felt specifically mine. Surfing was something I could take ownership of. I felt immediately at ease but holding on tight to this sea world where everything made sense to me. Surfing had become my thing. It was something I identified with. Most importantly for me, it couldn't be controlled by anyone or readily understood by many at the time.

I could self-determine who I was and what I wanted to do, giving myself an identity with surfing and within that initial sphere of Bundoran's sea and waves. On a day-to-day basis, I didn't need a team to play for, and there were no green fees either. The waves were there on my doorstep for free and I was all over them with that unquenchable thirst for more. I knew even then that surfing was uncommon and individual for the time, so I had a guarded passion for it. For much of my school years, if I met someone new like an adult or a friend or work colleague of my parents, they would invariably say, 'Oh, you're Ritchie Fitzgerald's son. What instrument do you play then?' to which I would reply, 'Well, I don't play anything.' This response always received an incredulous face and quizzical frown, implying that I must be in some way the trouble-making black sheep of the clan.

It wasn't that I somehow rebelled against that automatic musical assumption, my dad or the famous name I shared. My non-engagement with becoming a musician was more a strive for my own identity rather than any planned velvet revolution against the family tradition. In fairness to my father, he was the least pushy parent imaginable. There was zero pressure from him to following in his footsteps. He was gentle as a dad: he never raised his hand or voice to any of us. He never understood surfing, but by the same token he never tried to hold me back from its calling either.

Finding my own personality was a yearning I felt from a very young age. In surfing, I found the vehicle to shape my identity. In many ways, I knew almost immediately in an instinctive way that the sea was what I was looking for. The waves became second nature. It was where I felt oddly safe and totally at home. The water never scared me underneath the surface either in that subterranean alien world I'd see when diving or snorkelling. Nor was I ever overly cautious of the fearsome dredging waves on the surface. The sea and everything about it just fit perfectly with me.

Surfing has always been a difficult activity/sport/lifestyle to classify, quantify or to even bookend in any satisfactory fashion. It can be seen as regular sport with a world governing body, a polished globetrotting contest circuit competed for by highly motivated professional athletes, and now even an Olympic sport. On the other hand, it can just as easily be identified as an alternative lifestyle, pigeonholed by stereotypes and populated by a fusion of eco dreamers, drifters, counterculture dropouts and anti-establishment free thinkers. It can even be viewed as an all-consuming addiction for the faithful, with an almost cult-like compulsion that converts to a passionate way of life. The very nature of surfing means you must have had one toe in that off-kilter lifestyle choice to pursue it 100 per cent. Waves don't just switch on or show up at 5 p.m. after work, or at the weekend when you clock off. You can't just go and catch 18 waves like you can play 18 holes of golf. To chase a surfing dream, you must be flexible to the extreme, having the ability to drop everything at a minute's notice and walk out the door when the swell hits or the winds turn offshore. This lifestyle is not very conducive to having a conventional 9 to 5 existence.

Good surf can appear anytime and almost anywhere along a decent body of water or stretch of coast. This unpredictability lends itself to the surf travel bug. Exploration and travel are evocative to any surfer past or present. Travel is and always has been a major part of the lifestyle that surfing offers. In a modern context, a significant chunk of that free spirit of adventure into the unknown has been lost by the shrinking world of information-heavy personal technology we all live in. Now in 2022, you have at your fingertips endless online surf information, with up-to-the-minute surf reports and webcams that make it easy the world over. In many ways, it has diminished what was once the accumulation of a lifetime of ocean knowledge gained by a few but valued by all. Understanding or being able to read weather patterns was such an important part of becoming an all-round surfer/waterman. To acquire that understanding of weather, pressure systems, swells, winds, tides and an intimacy with the coast, you had to spend an apprenticeship of many years around the seashore and in the water. Total immersion in surfing and the coastal environment was the only way to learn the subtle mood swings and violent unpredictability of the sea.

It's lucky that nature doesn't do straight lines or acquiesce to technology. Neither does it follow a uniform, predicted design. So even today, there is plenty of scope for local knowledge and that strangely hard to find elusive spirit of real adventure in the modern world. As much as the forecasting and surf travel companies try to box it all up and present surfing in a neat package, it's really impossible to tame or gift wrap surfing and ocean swells on a screen. Accurately predicting surf from a global online surf website based in London only works a certain percentage of the time. Nothing yet has replaced local knowledge and boots on the ground. The global leaders in online surf companies get it wrong as much as they get it right, which can really hinder your plans if you are landlocked or an urban-based weekend warrior. On the flip side, it can give you unexpected reward if you are still willing to take a leap of faith.

Where I grew up, I was extremely lucky. By some freak of nature, Bundoran has a playground of world-class waves on offer all year round. Year on year as my ability in surfing increased, so did my horizons expand in the hunt for new breaks and unsurfed potential. At the time, undiscovered surf breaks were still all over the west coast of Ireland; sometimes we barely had to leave the town boundaries to experience them. Jimi Meehan and I made hikes out to waves on the fringes of town at weekends and after school to expand our surfing universe. These very surf breaks are now known by surfers the world over, and you'll see them included in every online surf guide, print publication and surf report. After we surfed them, we adopted the method used in Roy Walker's TV game show *Catchphrase* ('say what you see') in naming the spots. We really didn't put much thought into it, the waves christened themselves in many respects. The famous PMPA point we named after the PMPA insurance (later AXA insurance) office that sat on the main road in front of the waves. You would cross the field directly in front of the PMPA garage so that was our marker and so the wave was named. Black Spot, now one of the most popular and photographed waves in Ireland, was just before the Leitrim border. It's one of those waves where you take off in Donegal, and if the conditions are right on a long wave, you end your wave in Leitrim. Jimi had the place to himself when we were growing up, except when I made the trek with him. He was the first local Bundoran surfer I remember going out there; he ruled the place. He named the wave after the old traffic sign on the road above that warned 'Beware: Accident Black Spot Ahead' in bold black letters in reference to the twisty road and tiny bridge. My dad, who was the embodiment of a cautious driver and a man who never touched a drink, once rolled his van on that spot. It was a treacherous piece of road that just happened to have a class wave beyond. The hollow slab wave that breaks just off the Main Beach in Bundoran is called 3D, which sounds very cosmic and suitable for a wave that turns itself inside out. We called it 3D for much less of a trendy reason than is often assumed. On the beachside of the wave, there's the outdoor Thrupenny pool which we used to paddle out from to get to the wave. When I was young, there was still an old metal sign at the entrance that said 3d (shillings), the old entry price to the pool long before my time. Nonetheless, the sign was still there, so we named the wave 3D.

Growing up across the street from the beach and the majestic waves of the Bundoran Peak didn't hurt in incubating my general love affair with the sea. I think my fascination for the ocean is more deep-rooted in me than just location. I feel it's in my make-up somehow. My friend Chris Malloy always professes that you get 'sea people', which sounds oversimplified but there is a truth in what he says. What he is really getting at is people who have grown up in a particular environment become most intimate with their surroundings. They instinctively understand its rhythm, nature, moods and the heartbeat of that local environment. It's something you can't teach, it just organically happens from childhood onwards. In the case of where I grew up, the sea was ever present. Walking to school you could hear it, see it and smell it. It got into your veins like a virus, and once you lived a life by the sea it's painful to be away from it for any length of time.

Bundoran had a community of sea people: the local families that were engaged with fishing, swimming, beach combing, and the divers, winklepickers, canoeists and eventually local surfers. The most famous and wonderfully unusual of all these sea people from my childhood was Babs, the eccentric three-piece-suited and wellingtons-wearing seaweed man. Babs would dry and sell carrageen moss seaweed on the shore side of the reef. When the seaweed was dried, Babs would make a few deliveries. He would drape the dangling limbs of dillisk (red algae) and carrageen moss over both ends of his old black 'High Nelly' bike before walking it up the town. My mum always bought a 'crisping on top and spongy in the middle' armful of it. She would make a fermented milky drink for us with the carrageen. 'It's good for you,' she would assure us. Good for you or not, I hated it. I'd screw my face up at the mere sight of it. If it didn't look visually appetising, it tasted even less so. If Babs was alive today, his knowledge, techniques, delivery system and product range would make him the authentic toast of the apothecary world.

~

On a cold but perfect winter's Saturday in 1989, I bumped into Willie Britton on the Main Street in town. He asked me if I wanted a lift out to the Sligo coast to surf an area I'll call 'Gore

Booth's' for the sake of posterity. I immediately said yes, abandoning in an instant all other plans for the day, and sprinted home to grab my gear. Willie was from Rossnowlagh and an integral part of a group of older surfers that you'd see on the coast when the surf was good. Willie took on almost superhuman status in my mind with the waves he surfed. He was the original big-wave surfer in our area. Back then, we referred to big, powerful days of surf when no one considered paddling out as 'Willie Britton Days'. Because eventually Willie would arrive in the car park, suit up and surf triple-overhead waves by himself. His surfing was conservative, measured in his execution and conciseness with his wave selection. He rarely fell off or did anything showy or spectacular. What he did do was surf big waves with amazing flow and a cultured style born of the powerful local waves we have. With little fuss, Willie would surf liquid wedges and walls of fast-moving ocean with such consummate ease. He was a connoisseur of smooth style and soulful understatement.

I was 15 years old at the time and to be asked by a senior surfer of Willie's calibre to come for a few waves was a huge thing. 'Gore Booth's' was just down the coast from Bundoran, but it might as well have been Outer Mongolia to me. It was a place I'd heard about but never seen or surfed. That day was my first experience surfing the fabled Yeats Country selection of reefs. The main break there offered a softer alternative to Bundoran's seat of your pants waves. The north Sligo coastline suffers the same swell as south Donegal, and it holds similar-sized waves. The only real difference for me was that I could really open up my surfing on the faces of the waves there for the first time. Surfing 'Gore Booth's' was a cutting-loose revelation for me, as the lip of the breaking waves crumbled more forgivingly than the pitching, unforgiving hollow waves of

Bundoran. Surfing is like a blank canvas: every surfer will approach a blank wave face differently, drawing their own individual lines across it. Some even refer to surfing as an art form. Perhaps it is, but that sentiment is too high a concept for me to wrap my mind around with any overarching authority.

The Sligo waves that day gave me a whole new experience, letting me surf top to bottom as hard as I liked, drawing out big carving turns on translucent cyan-tinted walls with relative impunity. The waves of 'Gore Booth's' sit between two of Ireland's most well-known surf towns in Bundoran and Strandhill. Back in 1989, in the unlikely event that you'd meet another surfer out there, the odds were very high that they were from one of the two surf towns. The only locals claiming the place back then were the herd of curious mousey-coloured jersey cows who hung their necks over the mangled barbed wire and broken-down stone wall in an act of both nosey curiosity and scratching their hide.

Willie and I pulled up that afternoon to eye-wateringly perfect surf. The waves were flawless winter A-frames that equated to double-overhead wave faces, with uninterrupted corrugated lines to the horizon producing ruler-perfect walls hitting the coast and the reef, causing the waves to split into breaking left and right V-shapes. With only three Strandhill surfers in the water for company, we were quick off the mark to get togged out. Even with five of us in the water that afternoon the lion's share of waves went unridden, as is always the way in uncrowded surf. I remember that session the waves were incredible.

The Strandhill crew of surfers can claim ownership of this special piece of surfing coastline more than anyone else. There is a bizarre but true story of how it was located as a surf spot. Strandhill has always had a little airstrip and aero club where you can book flying lessons or go on a sightseeing flight. The runway stretches almost out into the breaking surf, giving you the impression that you are making an emergency water landing every time. Sligo has a tradition of some brilliant fixed-wing pilots. So back in the 1970s, Strandhill surfer Stan Burns took a local flight with one of his mates. They flew low level up the coast towards Donegal. On the day of their flight, there was a heavy swell running all along both county seaboards. The whole coastline was lighting up with breaking waves creating that distinctive perfect V-shape of white water, clearly visible from the air, that acted as a visual demarcation signalling quality waves below to any surfer worth his salt. They passed over the rural farming area that runs to the sea along the north Sligo coast. Stan did a double take; he couldn't believe his eyes. Down below was a fantasy setup of a flawlessly perfect breaking wave. He asked the pilot to double back to confirm that what he was seeing wasn't an optical illusion. The pilot did so, and Stan knew he was looking at something special. He instantly had a bee in his bonnet to find the spot when he got back down to ground level. Stan triangulated the wave's location as best he could from the air and spent the next day or so getting lost on the tiny country roads until he eventually hit the jackpot. He kept his discovery close to his chest, but word started to slip out. As my mother would say, 'It's like trying to put toothpaste back in the tube.' Once the surf discovery genie is out of the bottle, it's impossible to put it back in. In due course, some of the Strandhill crew covertly followed Stan a few times but were spotted by him. He would take them on a wild goose chase around the single-carriageway country roads. They succeeded in staying unseen on the third attempt, marking their direction and progress on the road with paint at each crossroads so they could find their way there and back again. It was like Sligo's very own Hansel and Gretel surfing fairy tale.

My own surf discoveries may not have had the high jinks and drama of Stan's fly by but were no less exciting to me at the time. My last two years in secondary school were 1991 and 1992. During these years, myself and a few of my surfing friends started to get our learner driver licences, which was a major step forward in our quest for waves. My good mate Adrian 'Ado' O'Reilly from Ballyshannon was the first to get a licence and access to his mum's car. My surfing buddies back then consisted of Ado, Seamus 'Shambo' O'Donnell from Creevy, the ever-present Jim Meehan, Damien and Tony Granaghan and Patrick McGloin. We would all somehow squeeze into Ado's mum's car and hit the road with boards stacked high on the roof, all tied down with the Granaghans' baling twine and Ado's ratchet straps that were normally used to secure beer kegs in their family's pub in Ballyshannon. Ado was our documenter. He always brought along his JVC camcorder with him. He has a lot of priceless old footage from those early '90s surf missions. When I've recently watched back some of these tapes, what surprised me was that our surfing still stands up 30 years later and is much better than I expected. The shocking thing was our wet look, gel-infused curtain hairstyles, garish wetsuits and gammy fashion that made us look like scrawny Stone Roses wannabees.

I managed to get my driving licence at age 17 so my mother willingly gave me her car for surf trips. She told me, 'I'll only warn you once not to do anything stupid or show off in the car.' If that happened the privilege of using it would be taken away for good. I was more than willing to be safe in the car. The prospect of being able to travel to waves far outweighed any desire to be a boy racer in her car. My mum's car was a gold-coloured Nissan Prairie bubble-shaped people carrier. The car had a coolness factor equivalent to wearing a pair of Birkenstock sandals with thick woolly green socks. As much as

I appreciated access to her car, I really wanted my own wheels. I eventually got my first car, a battleship-grey, second-hand, 1987 Mayo-registered Nissan Micra two-seater van. The car was tiny, and the experience was like driving an empty tin of beans with a lawnmower AA battery engine. Due to its Mayo reg, I christened the car 'Mo', thinking that was pretty hip. 'Let's go, Mo!' was my muster call. Mo brought me on countless surf adventures on every Irish coast. For most of my own saunters, we would pack the car to the rafters for the journey. On one trip back to Donegal I had myself, the Tramore duo of Dave Blount and John McCarthy plus seven boards all squashed into the two-seater van. Mo, in a real-world sense, was a biscuit tin death trap of a car. It felt every gust of wind and passing trucks made it swerve and rattle. On the plus side, it was a real nuts and bolts car with no computers or any such complication. If you had good tyres, topped up the oil, antifreeze and petrol you were good to go, and go I did.

Easkey on the Sligo-Mayo border was an early haven for the travelling surfer and one of the first places we went when we got behind the wheel. It was an obvious surfing waypoint for anyone cruising along the northwest coast. Strangely, at the time the village of Easkey itself had no local surfers, just like the lack of local engagement in Bundoran 10 years earlier. Every surfer you met in Easkey had travelled there from somewhere else, including us as the young Donegal contingent. On the waves out front, you would find a real mixed bag of surfers from almost every surf community in Ireland. Sprinkled on top was a selection of a few dozen eccentric UK, South African and US ex-pat surfers. This liquorice allsorts of overseas surfers had disconnected from their country's mainstream society in the pursuit of living a quasi-feral existence on this remote piece of Sligo-Mayo coastline. They existed in what looked like a post-apocalyptic, bric-a-brac smorgasbord of kit-bashed trailers, cars, campers and caravans. Barking dogs, numb fingers, flapping canvas and the pungent wafting odour of strong home-grown weed was a complement to the overbrewed Quinnsworth yellow pack tea. It felt very much like a vagrant hippy community that time had forgot. The most well-known of these ex-pat surfers was a Californian lady called Linda Thornton, who was a surfer of merit stateside, hailing from Malibu, California. She lived and surfed in Easkey for over 10 years. Linda once described the waves in Ireland as 'like Hawaii, but better, with more variety of breaks'.

The atmosphere of surfing in Easkey was unfriendly out of the water and aggro in the sea. It was most different from, say, turning up in Portrush or Tramore, where you knew the locals and had a good laugh. The town was such an early magnet for surfing in Ireland but felt completely out of kilter when compared to other Irish surf towns. It didn't feel very Irish in attitude, and with a lack of local surfers the transient surfing groups – universally called the black wetsuit brigade – set the tone. It was the only place in Ireland that you saw a lot of fighting in the water, shouting in the car parks and more than the odd punch-up. Seeing a carload of young Irish cubs like us turning up acted like a red rag to a bull for the cabal of foreign surfers set up camp there. You were seen as a pariah if you were a real Irish surfer. It was so ironic. Down the years, I've had so many run-ins while surfing in Easkey, but I never let any of it put me off.

The waves and coastline around Easkey have a long-standing heritage in Irish surfing, with the ISA head office located there. Easkey is also the area of Irish surfing coastline that got the first international spotlight and exposure abroad. During that period, for any surfer outside of Ireland, if they could name a surf spot in this part of the world, 9 times out of 10 it was going to be Easkey.

Easkey was an odd kind of place that attracted wandering souls, most of them of the lost soul variety. I suppose that's the charm of many small villages and surf towns in the west of Ireland. You can arrive in most small coastal towns in Ireland and you get accepted into the community quickly, with not many questions asked. Irish surfing was even more friendly and accepting in the small surf towns. Bundoran is a different proposition to Easkey, but I've seen that almost immediate acceptance untold number of times in Irish surfing, where someone shows up and becomes part of the furniture in a very short space of time. A friend of mine attests that we the Irish are the most socially intelligent people in the world. The more I travelled and saw how my Irish surfing travelling companions could be dropped into almost any conversation or social situation abroad and getting along no bother, the more I saw truth in that statement. The same is true with folks turning up on our shores. The cut of their jib can get worked out in moments and they are usually welcomed with open arms.

The Easkey area is very different now the black wetsuit brigade of surf agitators are all but gone. Most of the caravans and mobile homes have left or are melted into the grass and overgrown with brambles. Easkey and the surrounding area is still near the top of the bill for travelling surfers in Ireland with its Milky Way of endless waves. The area has now produced a lot of home-grown talent, most notably Cain Kilcullen, who is still regarded by many as the best surfer Ireland has ever produced. The local involvement in surfing in Easkey has nowadays changed the dynamic and demographic of surfers in the water there. The pecking order is no longer overseas dominated; it's now in the hands of the real locals. One or two of the black wetsuit brigade still live and surf there, but under a very different vibe.

The town did play host to one of surfing's original icons. In global surfing, Miki Dora is a name that resonates deeply as a surf founding father, innovator, stylist and agent provocateur of the original 1950s Californian surfers. In the latter part of his life, this most controversial of surfing icons found his way to Easkey, where he lived for a few years. It was on one of these return journeys that I met Dora. His reputation preceded him as a surfing god and devil combined. I was young and new to surfing at the time. The significance of seeing him surf has never really worn off, becoming more important to me the older I get. I watched him ride a massive surfboard with proportions more suitable for André the Giant. Dora told me he would only move his body to catch the wave and for standing up. After that he would stand still on his board in the water and he would let the wave dictate what happened next, putting him wherever it chose. In his own idiosyncratic evolution of riding waves, he didn't see the point of trying to change direction or adjust himself at all. Maybe it was an affront against Mother Nature to him by that stage of his life. He could do no wrong in my eyes that day. It was like meeting the Keith Moon of surfing: he had earned the right to beat his drum or not on any wave however he saw fit. His surfing style was the antithesis of controlled motion and instinctive impulses, two ingredients essential for surfing a wave. It's still the oddest display of surfing I have ever witnessed by anyone anywhere. He certainly left an impression on me that I've never forgotten.

Easkey may have proved a popular destination for the alternative Miki Dora surfers of the world. Having said that, it was a much larger favourite as a surfing destination for the predominantly Protestant East Belfast surfing population. A lot of early Irish surfing was born out of Northern Ireland along the Antrim coast. This group may have been small in numbers by modern Irish surfing standards, a few dozen in total, but they were an important core surfing community in Ireland back then. It's one of the anomalies of Irish surfing that an influential percentage of Ireland's surfers blossomed out of loyalist East Belfast at the height of the troubles many miles from the nearest waves. What's even more unlikely for the time is that most of these surfers chose to come across the border to surf as much as they headed for the Causeway coast. Most of the East Belfast boys stayed living in the city right through the conflict, but they had an almost religious dedication for travelling to the Republic's west coast at every opportunity for the surf and lifestyle on offer. Easkey was also a crowd favourite destination for the hordes of surfers from Tramore in Co. Waterford. I can't think of any other activity that brought together these two 'supposedly' diametrically opposed groups of East Belfast Protestants and Catholic surfers from Waterford, Sligo and Donegal together. It was another example of surfing being the perfect antidote to the worst decades of the troubles. Many unlikely friendships were made and have lasted ever since.

A good friend of mine was Adam Wilson, the Portrush junior surfer who I met at that first contest in Rossnowlagh. Adam was a Protestant lad from Antrim, and I was a Catholic boy form Bundoran. At the time, if it wasn't for surfing there is not a hope in hell we would have met or become close friends. Neither of us cared much about religion back then, or now for that matter, we were all about the surf and that was enough. Surfing was the mechanism that broke down and transcended the boundaries for us and many more besides.

As familiar as surfing made the southern surfers with their northern Protestant counterparts, in some cases there were still some blatant religious and cultural differences between the two. To me, it was the less obvious things that shone a light on those differences the most. I'd become friends with a group of stand-alone surfers from the more staunchly Protestant middle-class areas of Belfast. They came down south to camp, sleeping in their cars beside the waves on the outskirts of Bundoran almost every weekend. They never really committed, socialised or befriended anyone besides me in the town, always staying just out of sight. The green field area they once camped in is now home to hundreds of houses and well within the town limits, but then it was well clear of the town. If you had asked them where they surfed at the weekend they would have said vaguely 'down south', maybe even Donegal but never Bundoran. It would have killed them to admit they had the waves of their lives in Bundoran, that wee Republican town in their eyes.

This group of Belfast surfers were all similar in age to me, but they were decidedly different from most of the other more northern Protestant boys I knew from Portrush and Belfast. Although I was friendly and surfed with them a lot, there was always a conservative, defensive cold barrier to their personality. I couldn't ever break it down and get past it to see what they were really like.

⌒

Later that year myself, Ado and a few of the boys made our first run to Enniscrone, Co. Sligo to surf its rumoured perfect point break that by then had gained an almost mythical status among our group. It was late August, the day of our Leaving Cert results, and the surf was pumping with hot, sunny weather. Most school leavers went on the piss all day, but we went surfing first. As soon as I got my results that morning, we were on the road heading south. The Leaving Cert results are an Irish obsession. Earlier that morning I had received my exam results and passed with flying colours, even managing to get one honours-level A, securing me my first university preference. To be honest though, I couldn't have cared less. I was just delighted to be finished with school and on the road heading south, eyes firmly fixed on new surfing horizons. We met a solitary South African surfer in Enniscrone who was camping at Easkey the night before. He made his way over early when the swell picked up. We watched him on a few waves as we got changed; he was gliding through deep tube rides on minute-plus-long rides. The point had certainly lived up to its rumoured top billing. By the time we hit the water, the South African was hauling himself ashore after surfing all morning alone. He had a smile on his face a mile wide after his solitary bliss. He told us his arms were noodles and his race was run, but he reckoned the point was better than his own country's celebrated wave in Jeffreys Bay. It was a startling thing to hear for four young Irish surfers, as Jeffreys Bay was a legendary wave and recognised at the time as the world's best right-handed point break.

That same summer, we ventured further afield for surf. North Donegal in surfing terms was still mostly a mystery. Up there was like trying to discover the Northwest Passage; it demanded a slew of optimistic expeditions. We knew it was a large area (Donegal being Ireland's second-largest county) and we knew it was full of surf potential. At the time, you wouldn't come across many people on the coast there, never mind other surfers. To the locals, we might as well have dropped down from outer space as driving up from Bundoran with a car full of surfboards. Surfing was totally alien north of Rossnowlagh; if you followed and tracked the coast north you wouldn't see a surfer again until you hit Portrush, Co. Antrim. The islands off Donegal's coast offered another degree of separation and surfing wilderness. Tory Island resembled stepping two centuries back in time, but the waves on offer were of the highest quality. Tory had a much-needed harbour extension in the early 2000s, which put an end to one of the best waves out there, as it now lies under hundreds of tonnes of concrete. I'm just glad I had the opportunity to surf it before it disappeared.

We had some far-out space cadet exchanges and conversations with locals and farmers over the years. When we'd spark up a conversation, telling them we were also from Donegal – 'Bundoran-Ballyshannon,' we'd proudly exclaim – they returned looks like we were taking the piss. Carrying surfboards under our arms did nothing to diminish our oddness in the eyes of the locals. Claims to be truly from Donegal and fellow county men fell on deaf ears. Unless it was an O'Neills size 5 ball under your arm, and you lived north of Barnesmore Gap, you weren't really from Donegal proper. The little pub in Creeslough, in typical rural Irish tradition, doubled as the post office and tripled as a shop serving food, so we always stopped there for an après-surf refuel. It had a no-nonsense menu that was of its time. It consisted of chicken soup, white bread and butter ham sandwiches and a pot of tea. If you wanted coffee, it was a spoon full of milky Nescafé freeze-dried instant coffee. Nowhere in Ireland outside of Bewley's on Dublin's Grafton Street served lattes or cappuccinos in those days, as far as I remember.

The old lady of the house was always very welcoming, and her chicken soup hit the spot every time. After a few visits, she eventually asked us what brought us to the village. We told her it was surfing, and she gave us that sceptical look of reproach. 'Surfing?' she muttered. 'Yep, surfing on the waves down there by the shore,' I said. She replied with a very credible question, I thought at the time. 'Can you just surf in towards shore, or could you also surf back out to sea again?' I think she had seen windsurfing on TV once. I loved her observation; she was as sharp as a tack. We took her out to the car and showed her the surfboards, assuring her that yes, we really were from Donegal as well, although my 1987 Mayo reg did me no favours in that department. She seemed satisfied enough with that. I'm not sure it sank in all the way, as she gave us a withering look for evermore with a slight hint of pity that we were somehow unwell and just let out on day release.

Some of my fondest surfing memories were from those days. We were free as a bird with few strings attached. It felt special to be in such a tiny group of friends surfing in the area, finding unsurfed waves, new surf territory and naming surf spots. With better wetsuits than our predecessors, more modern surfboards and youthful attitudes, we chased and surfed waves that had been previously viewed as unsurfable or out of reach. We made discoveries of waves and surf spots that have now 30 years later spawned into legitimate surf communities replete with surf shops, surf schools and local surfers. I really enjoyed it back then. It felt like we were on the edge of the global surfing frontier, and in many ways at the time we were. I have to confess that my friends and I had a leading role in opening parts of that surfing coast. We kept it tight for a few years, but once that surfing cat was out of the bag that was it, everything changed, as it had in south Donegal years before.

## 10

# World Surfing Championships
# 1992

Depending on which historian you believe, Napoleon may or may not have coined the disparaging phrase 'shopkeepers don't start revolutions'. Let's suppose for a minute that the great French general did utter those immortal words. If that's so, then I'd stand him corrected in the case of my family's propagation of local surfing and major contributors to the Irish surf industry. Our cultivation of the Irish surf industry wasn't so much a surfing insurrection as it was a velvet uprising of neoprene and fibreglass. Broadcasting your own contribution or backslapping is not the Irish way. It certainly doesn't sit comfortably with me most of the time. Nonetheless, it doesn't change the fact that my own, and more importantly, my family's place in Bundoran and surfing in the northwest are an integral ingredient in that history.

The origins of our surf shop, Surfworld, go back to 1990. Calling it Surfworld was an blatant magnification. A world of surfing it most certainly wasn't, but its humble beginning is best viewed through the prism of those scant surf gear times. As the children of the family, we had been involved in the ways of the sea for well over a decade and had been messing with boards and wetsuits for most of those 10 years. My middle sister Annamarie may not have been the most determined water baby in the house. That said, she still possessed a passionate interest in surfing and the sea.

As I've said many times already, access to buying surfing equipment in Ireland was almost nil. The RSC had opened two years before, but it was mostly used for events, summer life-guarding and personal equipment storage, and was run on a club basis for the summer season. It did have a few wetsuits and surfboards available for members to rent. A great facility, no doubt, but not within our reach. The club had little practical use in addressing the ongoing lack of equipment availability on our coast. Annamarie and I asked Mum for a 500-punt loan to buy surfing gear from the UK. Our plan was to sell it in one corner of my mother's gift shop. We had that feeling of, if not us, then who? The UK once again was the only option for getting equipment at wholesale. We used my tried and tested system of looking through the few UK surfing magazines we had, except this time I was doing it all above board and no more smuggling parcels past Mum. We called up a few distrib-utors' numbers and received some positive correspondence. We eventually settled on the Devon-based UK surfing company Tiki as our jump-off point. They seemed to have everything under one roof with their expansive brands. Our initial order was three boxes of desperately needed surfing essentials: one hundred bars of wax; three sets of each size of gloves, hoods and boots; a small, medium and large wetsuit; a packet of surf stickers; and six leashes. That was it. Our order was submitted via a faxed, handwritten form and bank draft.

It was an experiment on a wing and a prayer for Annamarie and me. We hoped there would be a market for surfing in

Bundoran and that it would spread into a wider northwest catchment. The truth behind our setting up of an account and shot in the dark attempt at a first surf shop was to get equipment for ourselves. We desperately needed reliable access to wetsuits and boards. We had been living off the second-hand scraps for years. To get some properly fitting new wetsuits with a steady supply of wax and accessories would be a big game-changer for us and the surfing community in the northwest. I can't convey how extraordinary it was to have access to surf wax. I remember the day we put the box out for sale. I couldn't stop staring at it, thinking how astonishing it was to have surf products in our own shop. Just seeing the wax and leashes sitting there changed so much in the local surfing dynamic. After our family had grabbed their stuff, what was left in the three boxes was displayed in the corner beside the wax and leashes, heralding the new surf section of the gift shop sandwiched between the cassette tapes and stationery. We didn't know it at the time but this simple first attempt at creating a surf business in the northwest was the starting point that has spawned so much throughout the coast and well beyond our family since then.

Around the coast we weren't the only ones. Lahinch Surf Shop was opened in 1989 by Tom Buckley and his family. In Portrush, you already had Troggs run by Ian and Andy Hill from their basement. All three shops were dedicated surf businesses run by local surf families. This is how the fledgling surf industry started in Ireland with only three in the nest. Our surf shop in Bundoran was basic. My mate Jimi Meehan was our first customer, coming in to buy some wax. We sold everything within a couple of weeks, paying back the 500 punt to Mum. With the money earned we opened an account and ploughed the profit back into our second order. This time we doubled everything, increasing the order from three to six boxes. It wasn't an overnight success, but it grew each month and summer on summer. By 1993, surfing had taken over most of Mum's gift shop. By spring 1995, we had converted part of the house, opening a new, much bigger surf shop in what was once our sitting room. That tiny surf corner in the gift shop seeded everything that is the commercial surf industry in the area, which seems incredible to me now when I consider how mainstream surfing has been supporting countless businesses.

For the first 10 years of the surf shop, we spent as much time explaining what surfing was and that, yes, it was possible to surf in Ireland. 'What does a wetsuit do? Does it keep you warm and completely dry or do you get wet with one on?' 'Which way does the wetsuit go on?' 'What are surfboard fins for?' 'What does wax do?' 'Are there really waves in Ireland?' These were just a handful of questions and sometimes jibes you heard all week from almost everybody who walked through the door. It was a line of questioning you would never hear today in our surf shop. Ireland now has over 150,000 people who surf out of a combined population of 6.8 million north and south, with an endless number of visiting surfers hitting our shores from all over the world. Irish surfers are now as sophisticated as any. Technical questions about the flexibility of signature epoxy fins and the suitable litre capacity of surfboards have replaced 'What the fuck is this shop for?' Our early days in the surf shop were as much about changing perception and educating people as they were about any sort of profitable retail. The crazy thing is that our surf shop is just across the road from what's considered by many the best wave in Europe, the Peak. Just 50 metres away at the top of Brighton Terrace you could see world-class 6-foot waves grinding perfectly across the Peak. That's how it was for many years. Bundoran was still in its summertime rough-as-guts years. Our surf shop was probably one of the only surf shops in the world that required two bouncers on the door in summertime.

I'll give you one example of the not so normal surf shop environment that we opened up into. Most surf shops start the day by checking the surf; fair enough, we could do that. Wheeling out boards, signs and beach goods to sit outside the store as a customer lure was unthinkable at that time. For us, it was very different. One July morning I was opening up the store as usual, along with one of our summer staff, a young lad from Ballyshannon called Donal Gallagher. As we came around the corner to the entrance of the surf shop, we heard moans and groans coming from the entrance. It was just before 9 a.m. Three young fellas were huddled over their moaning mate, who was laying on the ground with his head against the shop shutters. The three standing up ran for it when they saw us coming. Not that Donal or I looked in any way tough: Donal was still in school and me in shorts and flip flops looked about as threatening as a shrew. The lad on the ground was reeling in agony. He had been stabbed in the upper leg with a knife, or so he told us. Blood was pumping out of his jeans from the wound. Donal ran inside to ring an ambulance. I asked him again, with shock as much as stupidity, 'Were you stabbed?' He said, 'Fuck, aye, in my leg, mate.' I asked him if was it one of those fellas who'd legged it. He said yes, but they were all his mates from Belfast, so why don't I just 'Fuck away off and ride yer hand.' I neither rode my hand nor fucked away off. When Donal came back confirming the ambulance was on its way, we both sat on him to hold him down. I grabbed a towel from my surf bag, placing it as tightly as I could above his wound to try to stop the blood flow. The young lad was out of his mind with drink, trying his best to get to his feet so he could fight me and Donal for calling an ambulance on him. Luckily for us, he couldn't stand up with the drink and blood loss. The ambulance arrived promptly and took over. Cleaning up a mess of blood from outside was nothing new, but at least this time we knew how it had got there.

A year after offering the first surf products in our shop, my sister Annamarie took another big step in local surfing. In 1991, she initiated the town's first surf club, not surprisingly naming it Bundoran Surf Club. The surf club was a local extension of what myself and my brother, sisters and local friends had been doing in the 1980s. Surf club meetings were on Sunday mornings in front of the lifeguard tower, with afters in our house, although we had to move upstairs after the sitting room became the surf shop. We ran surf club sessions outside of high summer so locals could attend. If we weren't in the water, we would all watch a surf film at home. Sometimes, all the members sprawled on the floor and mashed together on mum's flowery-print settee and flapper trim armchairs. At the meetings, we would give advice to new members and talk about all things surfing in Bundoran. Along with other surfers from town we took mostly children, but some adults too, for their first experience on a surfboard or bodyboard. We used all our own gear, as was the way, pooling all our equipment so we could get 15 to 20 new recruits in the water at once. Earlier in the year, I had completed my surf instructors' course through the Irish Surfing Association in Rossnowlagh Surf Club. It was a new initiative only taken up by a handful of surfers nationwide. There were very few surf instructors in Ireland at the time. At the age of 17 I was young, and truth be told not very experienced in the surfing world, but here among Bundoran's new flock of club surfers I was a wise old veteran. The second year of the surf club we ran weekly surf contests on the Main Beach on Sundays. They proved popular and the members loved it, with all the kids winning some prize or another even if it was just a sticker. Those sessions,

I am proud to report, fostered a new generation of very young Bundoran surfers, many of whom are still on the waves today 30 years later.

The founding of the Irish Surfing Association (ISA) in 1970 was in response to several different surf clubs forming around the coast simultaneously, namely in Tramore, Lahinch and the north coast. This national body would give a collective voice to this new band of organised surfing emerging in Ireland. The ISA followed the path laid down by Kevin Cavey and his 1966 Surf Club of Ireland, pooling their resources and personnel. It wasn't until the Rossnowlagh contest in 1988 that I first became properly aware of and then subsequently involved with the ISA. Brian Britton and Roci Allen were the double act of Irish surfing, between them occupying president and vice-president of the organisation at the time and for many years afterwards. The ISA had the most considerable sway in Irish surfing back then. The sport and participants were a lot smaller in Ireland, plus there wasn't a slew of independent surf schools and surf businesses around the coast like we have today. So, the ISA had much more influence. In Brian and Roci, the association was presided over by two very capable men. This golden era of the ISA under their tutelage overlapped and influenced the beginning of this national surfing boom.

Brian, a Catholic man from Rossnowlagh, and Roci, a Protestant from Enniskillen, told you as much as anything about where and how Irish surfing perceived itself at that time and since then. The ISA was proud of its cross-border appeal as a secular sporting organisation, of which there were preciously few at the time. Brian was the quintessential surfing business man from the Britton brothers clan. At this stage of his life, Brian was only the 'occasional' surfer. Nonetheless, he had dedicated his love for the sport into the development and management of

Irish surfing. Outside of Ireland, Brian rose to vice-president of the International Surfing Association, where in the early 1990s he was the world's first modern-era surfing official to put forward the motion that surfing should be a future Olympic sport. That dream of Brian's has at last come to fruition, with surfing debuting at the 2020 Olympic Games in Tokyo.

Roci Allen could swoon into any surf or attend an ISA meeting without breaking stride. His presence commanded the room, where he always got respect. Roci never seemed to get flustered about anything, remaining James Bond cool. What he said about Irish surfing mattered. For me, Brian and Roci were chalk and cheese, but they complemented each other perfectly. I loved the introduction to the ISA that they afforded me. I will always retain in me so much admiration for both of them.

~

I had surfed at junior level overseas before, but qualifying as part of the Irish team for the World Surfing Championships in France in 1992 was another step up. To surf for the Irish team took dedication and a top-four finish on the domestic circuit. By the 1990s things were changing, with qualifying for the limited number of places up for grabs never easy. Our domestic surfing circuit may not have been of a standard to match the bigger surfing nations but it was still highly contested, and places on the Irish team were coveted achievements that set you apart. Once qualified, the other part of getting to these events, sometimes held in far-off coastlines on the other side of the world, was the financial cost. Under Brian and Roci, the ISA was the best financed it had ever been, or ever would be for that matter. Even so, you had to cough up hundreds and, in many cases, well over 1,000 punts to pay for travel and accommodation at an event. Even today it's a chunk of change, but 30 years ago it was steep. To represent your country, dedication and full commitment was needed not only in the water but from your pocket too.

My mother may not have attended any surfing contests I took part in, but she was always supportive financially. She would commit to half the cost but encouraged me to raise the rest with work, savings, fundraisers and sponsorship, always telling me that if it was handed to me, I would never feel the satisfaction of getting there myself. I would often join forces with Jimi Meehan or any of the other teammates who were keen on a combined fundraising drive. Both myself and Jimi received amazing encouragement from the community in Bundoran and donations from local businesses. I suppose there was certain pride in having myself and Jimi, two young local lads, represent Ireland on an international stage at something no one from town had done before. Local surfing was thoroughly covered in our local paper, *The Donegal Democrat*. The *Democrat* had been for a long time a strong support of local surfing, first in Rossnowlagh and equally so when Jimi and I came on the scene. They really prided themselves in their surfing coverage, putting surfing right up there beside the county's GAA and soccer. They sent a journalist out to spend a few hours with myself and Jimi when we made the Irish team for the first time. Reading back on some of their old newspaper clippings, the coverage of surfing is refreshingly forward-thinking and innovative. The newspaper's acknowledgement of our local surfers on the international stage was an important feature in the growth and acceptance of surfing in the northwest.

I set off for the 1992 World Surfing Championships that September with the rest of the Irish team to the beach town of Lacanau in the southwest of France. Our departure was the morning after the night before that had seen Donegal lift the Sam Maguire Cup for the first time ever as All-Ireland Champions. The homecoming reception and celebration for the Donegal football team took place next door to our house outside the Holyrood Hotel. I revelled with the thousands of other Donegal supporters into the wee hours. Keeping an eye on the time, I eventually only got two hours' sleep before Roci pulled up in his immaculate black Saab at 6 a.m. to give me a lift down to Dublin Airport. Like always, I had set a target for myself at the event. Any World Surfing Championships has the best of the best from up to 51 countries competing in it from around the world. The bigger teams are full of pro-surfers and pro-juniors. With four juniors on each team there was a large field of competitors in the junior men's division. I thought if I could get inside the top 50 under-18 surfers, that would be something to bring home for what was my final year in school.

From an Irish standpoint the team that year was strong. My four mates Dave Blount, John McCarthy, Adam Wilson and Neill Cochrane had also qualified, filling up the junior spots on the team. The Irish team under Brian and Roci had an esprit de corps that made us stand out at those events. The togetherness of the Irish team was always something that other nations commented on. Surfing is a very individualistic sport, but our team moved as one, with management always making sure the whole team and national flag was at the water's edge for every heat. Brian reinforced the deep feeling of pride in representing Ireland and Irish surfing. For someone like me, growing up where I did, open expressions of nationalism had been tempered. I had been raised to feel pride and a deep connection in being Irish. For me, it was the construed symbolism that nationalism presented in Ulster. In the north of Ireland, flags, dates, names and everything else was distorted for political motivations. Even the colours green, black and orange had been taken way out of context and used in the cesspit of sectarianism. Our national flag to some was provocative; to others it had been hijacked by the armed Republican cause. The surfers further south had a normal relationship with our national flag, as I found out. For me, I loved every part of being Irish, including our flag, although I only ever saw the tricolour being uncomfortably paraded around as a banner for paramilitary nationalism. As soon as I represented Ireland under Brian and Roci, I developed a healthy relationship with national pride and identity. It was established at the very core of what the Irish national team was all about. At the time, over half the Irish team were Protestant lads and lassies from the north, with most of them holding British passports. The ISA as governing body was put under severe stress tests right through the worst years of the troubles. The association was in a class of its own when you talk about their ability to hold the north and south together in a cohesive representation. The level of respect and integrity instilled by Brian and Roci in their handling and navigating all the possible minefields of Irish surfing during those times is to be admired.

No account of 1990s Irish surfing would ever be complete without talking about Andy 'Pad' Hill, the son of Irish surfing pioneer Ian Hill. Andy and his dad are responsible for developing the surf scene in Northern Ireland both personally and as a business with their surf shop Troggs. You could exhaust most of surfing's superlatives to describe Andy's Irish surfing successes over the years. My favourite was at that 1992 World Surfing Championships in France. For whatever reason, most of the team had a nightmare in the early stages. Nothing was going right, even though the surf was good, with the big French waves suiting us Irish surfers. Andy drew the World No. 1 seed in his heat: a surfer by the name of Grant Frost, who was part of the always hugely talented Australian team. To add to his global seeding, he was also the Australian No. 1. Andy backed himself and his ability from the moment he saw the heat sheet. He absolutely blitzed the heat in powerful French beach-break waves. Andy is still humble about it to this day, but I remember that heat well. He stormed it from the starting buzzer, getting a stranglehold of the four-man heat and not letting go. He knocked the No. 1 seed out of the main event. It probably wasn't on Aussie Grant Frost's game plan that he'd come up against a fast, stylish surfer from Northern Ireland, of all places.

As a testament to how good a surfer Grant Frost was, after Andy knocked him out of the main event, he slogged it out all week in the round-robin repêchage heats to make it back into the main event again at the quarter-final stage. He went on to leave no doubt that his top seeding was warranted when he was crowned World Champion.

Andy's victory against the World No. 1 energised our ranks. I remember at the team meeting that night we were all buzzing. Roci Allen stood up and said, 'OK, we have beaten the world's best, what's next?' and it brought the house down. I even managed to up my own game and surfed some decent heats before being scorched by one of the USA team. I may not have set the world on fire at the contest, but meeting a junior title contender from the States was a baptism of fire I learned from. On the bright side, I had reached my target of finishing inside the top 50 at a world championships, coming in 48th. It felt like an accomplishment of sorts to take home with me.

At all the international contests, the British and Irish teams moved as one, coming together for social nights and down on the beach. We would often have a warm-up contest against the British before the main event. I loved these contests against the British surfers. It was competitive, but the frank sense of humour, reality checks and self-deprecation of the British team was hilarious. I found the British boys and girls to be the most like us. We were much more compatible with the British teams than we were with say the French, Spanish or Japanese teams.

Both Britain and Ireland were the perennial underdogs at every big contest, even if team placings and individual results suggested otherwise. We were not realistic title contenders, but we could compete with anyone. It got snidey at times from some on the bigger teams. Most of the bigger English-speaking nations that constituted the world's best could accept competitors coming from tiny islands like Trinidad and Tobago. When it came to a surf team from Ireland, attitudes were much more dismissive. Their great-great-grandmother may have came from there, but not a surf team. I think this attitude that the Irish and British surfers were cannon fodder gave both teams a joint cohesiveness and drive. The British team would come down and support the Irish surfers in heats. They may not have been jumping up and down under the tricolour, nor us under the Union Jack when roles were reversed, but the respect, support and friendship between the teams were always there.

## 11

# Irish Mythology: From Swords to Boards

Some popular beliefs state with conviction that surfing in Ireland miraculously materialised on the coast around the year 2000. It's a widespread notion that some Irish millennials frolicked on their first surfing experience on Long Island (or was it Bondi Beach?) and decided to bring their Hollister hoodie-wearing encounters back with them to Irish shores and create Irish surfing. Thankfully, our surfing story has a much older and much richer history than is often assumed. Irish surfing can't be looked on in isolation or set in stone parameters. Much like the global surfing scene, the growth of surfing in Ireland is open to various interpretations and has also been influenced by a multitude of factors through the years.

Every sport will eventually look to discover its genesis, just as Irish surfing has done in the past. There are a few well-written and engaging chronological histories of Irish surfing out there, each one cataloguing as accurately as they can all the important events, personalities and moments throughout its approximately 60-year history in the country, or even before that. Like Kevin

Cavey exhibiting his Surf Club of Ireland at the Irish Boat Show at the Royal Dublin Society (RDS) in 1966, or the joining of all of Ireland's surf clubs in 1970 to form the ISA – a thorough account of our local surf history, from pioneering footholds to what it is today, would span many decades. I am only too aware that my recollecting is from a unilateral standpoint, and that there is a much broader local collective memory feeding into a dominant national surfing narrative.

The further you go back into general Irish history the more blurred the lines become between reality, fairy tales, scientific fact and superstition. History, legend and imagination dilute as myth comes to the fore. So, it should come as no surprise then that even something as relatively new as the origins of surfing in Ireland should cross over into those blurred lines.

As a youngster on shore break of the Bundoran Main Beach and struggling to catch waves up on my Styrofoam bodyboard, I was told a curious story of Ireland's first surfer. The story I heard suggested that fact may have been just as strange as any fiction. By the closing months of World War II in 1945, the Allied forces enjoyed total air superiority over Europe, with squadrons of US and RAF airmen based just over the border from us in Northern Ireland. The fledging neutral Irish government granted an air corridor to Allied aircraft over Donegal out to the west. I was told that immediately after the war ended, as US troops were being demobbed, one US airman stationed in Northern Ireland was an early American surfing aficionado. Before shipping back to the USA, he made a trip down along the Donegal coast to Rossnowlagh and Bundoran, eventually ending up down the west coast. How he had acquired a surf-board we may never know, as 1940s surfboards resembled large wooden canoes measuring 14 feet and upwards. One thing for sure is that he most certainly didn't just pop into Surfworld to rent a board on his way up to Tullan Strand. That would have to wait for another 50 years to become a reality.

It's not an inconceivable story in the search for the Webb Ellis of Irish surfing. I had heard the yarn enough times when I was young to presume there was a smidgen of fire somewhere in among all the smoke. One can imagine in the dying kicks of World War II that a surf-minded airman might have felt a little more relaxed keeping one eye out the window for surf potential dotted along our western approach on the coastline below, while the other eye diligently scanned for the straggling remnants of enemy aircraft and U-boats. I read a lot of *Warlord* comics as a child, so this narrative suited my imagination and memory down to the ground.

One thing we can be certain of from this period of time is that it spawned the first Irish surfer: a man by the name of Joe Roddy from Dundalk, who was the son of a local lighthouse keeper. Joe in his youth was very ocean-minded. He ingeniously built his own surfboard from discarded wooden tea chests, taking to the water for the first time in 1949. The provenance, timeline and effort surrounding Joe Roddy's story are truly remarkable. His contribution as the catalyst of Irish surfing has been excellently researched and documented thanks to Mayo-based Australian-Irish surf historian, Wayne Murphy. Joe's 1949 surfing vintage not only makes him the earliest Irish surfer but also an early surfing pioneer on a global scale, notwithstanding the Hawaiian islanders who had surfing as part of their Polynesian cultural identity for centuries before European colonisation. Joe stepped away from surfing for a whopping 57 years but continued to live a long, interesting and adventurous life that revolved around the ocean in boating and sailing. He settled in Co. Kerry, where he operated boat trips in Valentia for much of his adult life. In his final years, he was reacquainted once again with the sport of surfing in Ireland. He took to waves in Tramore in 2009, and he didn't miss a beat in the water, bridging the 57-year gap with ease. Joe has been rightfully honoured and recognised by the post-1970s Irish surfing community over the years.

From the earliest glass plate photographs of Bundoran to the first film footage of the 1940s and 1950s, the town exudes an authentic old world seaside charm that could have easily jumped straight off the pages of an Austin Clarke poem. The black-and-white images are full of smiling faces, bathing boxes, dance halls, golfing, donkey rides, fairground attractions and daytime dances by the sea; women in their Sunday-best frocks and bonnets oozing civilised sophistication while the men look dapper in their tailored single-breasted suits and flat caps in the style of *Peaky Blinders*. But the Bundoran of my youth had lost most of these traditions that you associate with the seaside. It had become a rough and tacky town, even though many of the local people still held onto a strong connection to the sea.

What has all of this to do with me or surfing? These early images show an ever evolving, bustling seaside town with a fully established mid-century beach culture, with tourists and locals alike engaging in swimming in the surf, cliff diving, fishing, boat rides and waterskiing from the Main Beach to the West End and back again. Bundoran presented a fertile environment for seaside activities and traditions; the town was primed with all the necessary ingredients for the eventual introduction of surfing.

Our limestone coast is littered with reefs, beaches and point breaks that have been shaped, reshaped and eroded by wind, waves, tide and time over the millennia. This weathering has produced perfectly configured natural elements necessary for high-calibre surf breaks. Sea levels abruptly go from deep to shallow, allowing the full force of Atlantic swells to hit our beaches and reefs without losing any power. Many coastlines sit too squarely to oncoming swells, creating waves that break too straight and close out all at once, rendering them useless for surfing. Fortunately, the northwest coast sits at a perfect angle to capture the incoming swells, enabling the groomed corrugated lines of waves to peel down the reefs and beaches. The large variety of surf breaks offered to surfers, from beginner to expert, is unmatched. Bundoran especially excels when it comes to the much sought-after long, hollow and regularly tubing waves that are the holy grail for surfers worldwide. The irregularity of our serrated coast can be seen every day while walking around Rougey coastal path. You can watch the marching swell lines from Aughrus Point sweep into the bay before bearing down on Tullan Strand. From this vantage point, you can easily make out the complex interactions between the incoming swell and bay-wide surf spots it encounters and observe all the dynamics at work. The swell coming into the bay gets corralled into multiple gradients and at angles that would give any linear wave theorist a stinging migraine.

When the rest of the northwest coast is a mill pond, Tullan Strand will always have a surfable wave. The shape of the beach helps to form a bout of surf alchemy, conjuring something substantial from almost nothing. The waves that break from no incoming swell at Tullan are an anomaly that is often written into the dumbfounded faces of the uninitiated as they arrive in the car park. Newbies to the beach often question the logic of how the whole coast is flat and Tullan Strand still has surf. It's a complex process of depth and wave refraction off the cliffs. The rebound creates wedge-shaped cross waves that re-join the initial swell line, doubling or tripling the original, turning knee-high swell into head-high breaking surf.

I've spent much of my life travelling around the world surfing, and the more I see of other foreign coasts the more I know how exceptionally lucky we are on the west coast of Ireland. In the northwest its almost comical how many world-class waves we have squeezed into a small stretch of coast. It should come as no surprise that surfing caught on here on a grand scale. Over the last 70 years, like every other sport and facet of life in Ireland, surfing was not immune to the turbulent social, political and economic upheavals in the country. Surfing's development was also influenced by the increasing global popularity and partici-pation in board sports in general. Huge advancements in equipment – especially for us in the northwest with the emer-gence of warmer, cheaper and more flexible year-round wetsuits – went hand in hand with the explosive uptake in the sport.

~

Ireland's northwest coast is made up of a four-county grouping that includes Mayo, Sligo, Leitrim and Donegal. It's a quartet of wildly beautiful coastlines that have never been industrialised or overpopulated in any significant way. In fact, the sad reminders and human scars of mass emigration are still visible and most poignant throughout the townlands and rural coastal communi-ties all along this Atlantic stretch.

Mayo boasts Ireland's longest county coastline, whereas Leitrim has the country's shortest with only 4 kilometres open to the ocean. Together, the four counties constitute 2,496 kilometres of rugged surf-washed coast. The area is home to geographical extremes and boundless differences in the topography along its beaches, reefs, cliffs and islands. When I write about being a product of my coastal environment, it's this four-county region that I'm referring to. This area – its places, people, customs, history and culture – heavily shaped me as my early stomping ground. It's a region where ancient history sits thickly layered upon itself – a past that co-exists mostly hidden from sight but in some instances often rubbing shoulders with modern life like nowhere else. The countryside and coastline around the north-west still holds Mesolithic, Neolithic, Celtic, Viking and Norman ruins wherever you look. So, it's no wonder really that I was captivated at an early age with antiquity as much as I was with the present. As my mother pointed out to me so often, I 'didn't lick it off a stone'.

Like all west coast surfers, as a young lad I'd become accustomed to surfing in the shadow of old castles, keeps and round towers that litter the coastline. The contrast of ancient and new Ireland was never lost on me, especially being involved with a sport like surfing in Ireland. There couldn't have been more of a contradiction than sheltering in the stone skeleton of a medieval battlement while getting changed into our modern neoprene coats of armour and waxing up our fibreglass lances, as I imagined we were doing in my pre-surf daydreaming.

My family always encouraged me to read up on any subject that interested me and not to just accept the common views on something or accept what I was told to believe by others. I was encouraged to educate myself on subjects, topics and views, to look at them from all sides. Early on, I became really interested in the Vikings, those seafaring masters with swords who left carnage in their wake. What young lad wouldn't find that attractive? I devoured as much material as I could on the Norsemen and their conquests, none more so than Inishmurray island off the north Sligo coast. Inishmurray was the scene of several particularly brutal Viking raids that decimated the monastical population to such an extent that the monastery was abandoned. With my early 1990s appetite for surfing adventure, Inishmurray held the allure of both virgin surf territory and an old Viking hunting ground. With this in mind, I made a few expeditions to find out. Inishmurray, like so many other islands off the Irish coast, proved too harsh an existence for its hardy people. It no longer supports even a small non-monastical population, the last of whom left the island for good in 1948. The place is a mixture of beauty, tranquility and utter destitution. The island's history is clear to see, the story of centuries-long habitation told in ruins like the abandoned nineteenth-century houses, the sixth-century monastery and disused harbour. This type of regression in population is only still visible in a few regions of Western Europe. As for the surf, well, I may have gone to the island originally for some historical enrichment but once I'd experienced the surf I kept coming back for more. Its deep-dark-blue open ocean swells, disorganised and dangerously powerful waves and exposed reef were perfect for surfing and I loved it.

I've always had a deep love of Irish mythology. It had even woven its way into some of my daily surfing life. The famous Bundoran tourist attractions of the Fairy Bridges and Wishing Chair date back to 500 BC, when they were used in ceremonial rituals. There were even some macabre sacrifices, according to some local stories, where animals and humans were thrown into the sea. Today, ironically, we use the Fairy Bridges as a jump-off point for throwing ourselves into the sea. It makes getting into the surf on the main peak at Tullan Strand much quicker and saves you a long beach walk and paddle out, especially at low tide.

One of my favourite historical sights since childhood is the Neolithic Creevykeel Court Tomb on the Donegal-to-Sligo road, which dates from about 4000 BC and has beautiful views of Mullaghmore's coastline. Creevykeel has no visitors' centre or fanfare beyond a small, unmarked lay-by for cars. I guess that's the charm of the area: it's still untouched by industry and population increase in a lot of ways. Nearby Benbulben and Lough Melvin feature unique plant life and fish species found nowhere else in the world. With all this and much more buzzing around in my head as a child, I found Ireland's local history and mythical charms as thrilling as the raging surf out front in the sea.

## 12

# Hy-Brasil

Some surfing moments stick more in the mind than others. When I was a wee cub surfing in the very early 1980s, I hadn't ventured much beyond getting smashed on the main beach waves. It was around this time that Aussie surfing icon Nat Young and pro-surfer Stuart Bedford Brown turned up in Bundoran. I didn't know much about surfing outside of my family circle but some of the older surfers from Rossnowlagh told me who these guys were and how important they were in the wider world of surfing. There were probably more of them in the group of travelling Aussies, but those names are the only two I can remember. As far as I can recall, they were doing a travel piece for an Australian surfing magazine.

They hit town at a good time and scored quality surf in Bundoran and down the coast, but I don't ever remember seeing their published piece. Australian surfing magazines were still two decades away from being available in our local newsagents. While in Bundoran, Nat Young was waxing lyrical about the best waves he had ever seen in his life off one of our coastal islands. I was in earshot of his enthusiastic ramblings, which were repeated in the following years many times among the south Donegal surfing fraternity. Now in Donegal alone you could spend the rest of your life surfing in the county and probably not surf all the waves on offer, never mind the rest of the Irish coast. In addition, Ireland is ringed by hundreds of islands big and small. I've done a fair amount of adventuring over the years to some of these islands, but like everything else you would need another lifetime to get to them all.

As I grew up a bit in the years that followed, I came to understand who Nat Young was and the gravity of the statement he had made in Ireland years earlier. Nat Young was, and still is, a global surfing icon. He was the 1966 and 1970 World Surfing Champion. What he had said played on my mind for years and I had built up his statement about the waves he saw off the coast to a hysterical level. To me, it was the Irish surfing version of the phantom Irish island called Hy-Brasil. Hy-Brasil is an island which is described in Celtic mythology as being cloaked in mist and only visible one day every seven years, but still it cannot be reached. It's the Hibernian lost city of Atlantis, and it is said to sit off the southwest coast of Ireland. So we came to refer to this top-secret surfing spot as Hy-Brasil so as not to reveal its location.

When my surfing had matured enough by the mid-1990s, I felt pretty confident and made two trips to Hy-Brasil. The first trip I took was in in 1994 to sample some of its waves, but it was always during small summer swells. By the 2000s, I decided to bite the bullet and go there when it was under the influence of a code red heavy swell. The boat trip out is something my wife Briohny says she will never forget. Briohny is pretty gung ho and not afraid of much, but for that boat trip out to Hy-Brasil the swell was massive, even though we were in the lee of the island on the sheltered side. The small ferry was pitching from its bow pointing straight up to its stern above our heads with every crest and trough through the booming 20-foot swell cycle. At the helm of our vessel was our own unfazed, one-eyed Captain Pugwash. The skipper was almost a make-believe, old salt-encrusted man-of-the-sea caricature. He had a badly damaged right eye which he informed us had happened years before when a fishhook went through his eye while out working on the boats. Rather than head for home, he put a patch on his eye with the hook still embedded. He worked on and waited with the rest of the crew for the fishing boat to finish its time at sea before returning to port and getting his eye seen to, losing his sight in that eye in the process.

We were the only takers for the crossing that day, and for good reason. Now I've been on plenty of hair-whitening, stormy boat and ship journeys, especially in less developed parts of the world, like the islands off Indonesia's Sumatra region, where health and safety doesn't exist and the integrity of the vessel is a throw of the dice. Although our Irish vessel and crew were perfectly up to the required standard and well experienced and up for the crossing, nothing has ever before or since scared me in the water as much as that boat journey.

When we got to the island, I finally understood what Nat Young had been so animated about all those years earlier. The place had surf so good that it would have brought a tear to a glass eye. Perfect surf breaks were stacked up to the distance, one touching off the next. I can't remember the whole crew that was with us that day, but I do remember myself and one of the boys getting out the back at this one spot that was so good it almost didn't look real. The sets were booming four times overhead, blue waves dredging along the point. Every wave had the speed, power and the ferocious intensity of unin-terrupted open ocean swell. It was an insane level of power and perfection to behold, and we managed to snag a few memorable waves. It was another game of cat and mouse to avoid being smashed to smithereens. Eventually, our luck ran out and we got properly caught in the current as it quickly started to pull us around the island. The ocean moved in a one-way-ticket direction out into the Atlantic, putting us on a liquid expressway for Nova Scotia. To say there was a strong rip is a huge understatement. The whole ocean pulls and pushes around the island, and once you are caught in it, you are powerless to resist. We kept calm and somehow angled ourselves towards the last chance saloon that was a little eddy of swirling water on the corner edge of the reef. The reverse thrusters effect of the eddy offered a one-time-only deal of getting ashore. As we were pulled along, we got lucky and slowed down in the corner vortex. We just got close and shallow enough to grab hold of some kelp, which put the brakes on. We hauled ourselves back onto the reef and dry land, nervously laughing while acknowledging it had been a close one.

I can neither confirm nor deny the location of this wave or Hy-Brasil. As far as my misty memory serves me, it is located somewhere between Bundoran and Strandhill, close to Coney Island.

## 13

# Gabe Davies

I first met Gabe Davies one August morning in 1989. We were both 15 years old and surf-crazy teenagers.

Gabe had driven over from his home in Newcastle on the northeast coast of England with his older brother Jessy as the designated driver. They were accompanied by a group of their zany Geordie surfing mates. The Davies boys had caught the Belfast-bound ferry after a coast-to-coast long haul across England. They first tracked north to Portrush before swinging south to Bundoran for some late-summer surf. It was Gabe's first surf trip to Ireland, and the Geordie boys gorged themselves on Bundoran's surf after the flat summer they had had on Tyneside. I knew who Gabe was by reputation before I ever met him. He had started to make big inroads as part of the British junior surf team. Gabe was also becoming a regular face in the UK monthly surfing magazines, this exposure raising his stock considerably issue by issue. Gabe, along with Russell Winter, would over the following two decades become the most globally recognised UK pro-surfers of their generation. I remember Gabe and Jessy pulling up to Tullan Strand that August morning, when the surf was pumping in town. The waves and beach had that warm early autumnal feel under soft sherbet-coloured morning sky: the sun even at high noon in August starts to cast long, watery shadows on the landscape of dulcet pastel shades, heralding the approaching change of season. The surf that day at Tullan Strand had a bold crayon-green shade at the bottom and shimmering turquoise blue on the top of every Toblerone-shaped wave as they marched in endless lines towards the beach. All set against a cloudless sky offering the Irish 'blue and green should never be seen' contrast to the Geordie boys.

There was a small but powerful southwesterly ground swell running all that week, giving 4–5-foot surf. The previous spring, I had bought another wetsuit; this time it was a new second-hand wetsuit, which was once again at least two sizes too big for me. Kevin Tobin was selling it; my hero worship of him made it worth buying, no matter if the thing was literally hanging off me. The wetsuit had all sorts of new innovations and material incorporated that I had never seen before. Most novel was an inbuilt thermometer on the wrist. Knowing the temperature of the water in winter didn't make it any easier or warmer; even so, the wetsuit's levels of 1980s gadgetry was so cool in comparison to what I was used to. Most of these space-age wetsuit additions were completely redundant to me. The only fancy features that worked were the new style of taped and sealed seams. Sealed seams had replaced the old far-from-watertight overlocked stitching system that left you with red rash snail trail lines all over your body. The new seams were sealed alright, maybe doing their job too well in the water, with an air-filled beach ball buoyancy that made duck diving under the waves virtually impossible. Jessy paddled out to the surf first and said in his Jimmy Nail brogue, 'Whey aye man, me name's Jessy and we're from Nu-cassle, yer not going to sink doon in that suit, are ya?' as I bobbed about, Bundoran's very own Violet Beauregarde, only in all black, not purple, this time.

Gabe and Jessy possessed the air and look of surfers who had just strolled from the waves of Bondi Beach with their mahogany-brown skin, white sun-bleached hair and much snazzier surfing gear than I had. Straight off the bat they surfed brilliantly, backing up the look of boys who knew they had it. For two young lads in my age bracket, they were a lot further down the surfing track than I was. The only thing that gave the game away from presuming they were bronzed Aussies was when they opened their mouths, speaking in their broad Geordie accents laced with unpolished vowels. In the wider world of late 1980s global surfing, it was pretty rare to meet a surfer from the northwest of Ireland, but even less common were surfers from the working-class cities of the northeast of England.

In Ireland, the influence of British surfers is a running theme in the story of Irish surfing. My own development as a surfer was enhanced greatly by exposure to the best British surfers at home and overseas. Their contribution cannot be underestimated, from English surfer Roger Steadman in 1966, who was instrumental in the early days of Kevin Cavey and the Surf Club of Ireland, right through to the current crop of UK surfers. They have played roles in almost every Irish coastal surfing community.

Gabe and Jessy were from the then much more industrialised northeast of England, well away from the Cornish epicentre of UK surfing. The Davies boys had grown up surfing in Tynemouth; their local beach was long sands, with the stomping ground of the city of Newcastle on their doorstep. Tynemouth is pretty sheltered from traditional Atlantic swells; it faces east, towards the Netherlands and Denmark, not coastlines you automatically associate with surfing. To get swell on England's east coast, big low-pressure systems must track north over Scotland, folding around Caithness to push the funnelling swell down the North Sea. It's only open to a tight fetch of swell that is short-lived. So, to surf on the east coast, you must be inventive, flexible with your time and mobile. When swell does filter down the east of England, that coastline has all the necessary geophysical set-ups to produce waves of real quality, especially in winter. The northeast, when it's on, has what many surfers in Britain consider the best if least consistent surf spots in England. It's a perfect example of how illusive, intricate, rewarding and, more often than not, how frustrating surfing can be as a pursuit.

After our initial meeting on the waves of Tullan Strand, Gabe and Jessy showed me the après-surf photos that they had plastered all over the inside of their van. It featured shots of the boys encased in chocolate-coloured tubes along the most unlikely of surf coasts from Sunderland, Middlesbrough, Newcastle and Yorkshire. The colour of the water had that east coast puddle brown, but the waves looked like Cadbury equivalents of their South Pacific cousins. It became apparent very early on that Gabe was a classy product of his environment, and had a cultured level of skill in big, hollow, powerful surf.

My first impressions of Gabe's surfing were that his level showed maturity and experience beyond his years. He had timeless style and an ability beyond any 15-year-old I had seen by that stage. There was not the awkwardness in his surfing so often present in a growing lad not quite finished with puberty. Gabe had the dexterity of a cat, making beyond vertical take-offs look easy. He was stuck to his board every time, with a perfect 50/50 balance of surfing ambidexterity. You see it in the best footballers sometimes when they are equally adept with their left foot as they are with their right foot, always in the right spot to give or receive the ball without it looking like too much effort or wobble. Well, Gabe had that quality in his surfing.

I used to call him the Ryan Giggs of surfing, which pissed him off, as he really hated Man United.

Watching that level of natural instinctive talent was an education that rubbed off on me immediately. Gabe's wavecraft made me think about surfing in much more detail, especially body position. I would watch him fade right to go left on elevator drops, and vice versa, just to get a fraction longer to set up his wave. On a big wave, it's a sublime skill to watch put into practice. With control of minuscule balance adjustments and millisecond timing in the mouth of a steamrolling beast, that is beyond my ability to articulate properly with all the intricacies involved. Surfing at that level is all about feeling; if you think or linger over it for more than a second, it's way too late. I spent years watching Gabe surfing serious waves in Ireland, hundreds of times free-falling down the face of a massive wave, slipping under the curtain like a folded letter into an envelope, or jamming against the grain on bottom turns when all the forces are pushing against you like a moving walkway at 30 mph. Superbike riders do the same thing, planting their knee and dropping the bike going at insane speeds around a corner. Gabe was doing the surfing equivalent of that. He could get so low in his centre of gravity that his whole body would concave inches off the water on bottom turns. His surfing was so perilously on the edge.

He seemed to get better the more difficult the situation was, revelling in the dangerous and complex. To this day, of all the surfers I've watched all around the world – and I've watched more than my fair share – Gabe is still one of the best I've ever seen at getting his body and his board into acute angles; that ability to flaunt Newton's Law of Gravitation for a nanosecond to make impossibly late take-offs under the lip of the breaking wave and navigating through compressed, undulating tube rides.

Gabe's homeland of the North Sea makes Ireland's Atlantic coast feel positively balmy. The Davies boys surfed in water temperatures only reaching 3 or 4 degrees in winter. Gabe surfed a particular wave near Middlesbrough at the mouth of the Tees River that was also an entryway for big commercial shipping and the site of many heavy industries, such as British Steel. Gabe told me about the water quality at this spot, which was thousands of times over the European Union's safe water quality standards for chemicals and pollution. The boys regularly surfed there regardless. Even at this young age, Gabe became a campaigner for the environmental group in the UK called Surfers Against Sewage (SAS). I'm not sure how that acronym would have gone down in Bundoran at the time if they had opened a branch in town. The SAS lobbied hard for cleaner seas and inland water-ways in the UK, and their campaign became the *cause célèbre* for UK surfers. Of any group of ocean-goers, the northeast surfers had perhaps the most legitimate concerns over filthy water. They found themselves surfing waves near the Tyne and Tees River estuaries where water quality amounted to little more than sludgy, slightly diluted toxic waste in some cases.

Gabe and I had a lot in common; we clicked immediately and became firm friends. Gabe had a cheeky Geordie side with a magnetic charm that made him a barrel of laughs to be with. We especially loved big, hollow, left-breaking waves, a type that was abundant in Bundoran and Tyneside, which seemed to seal the deal as much as anything else. This simple fact proved an early indication of the waves that would come to define us in the following years.

Shortly after I met Gabe, he, along with UK up-and-comers Spencer Hargraves and Anthony Storer, signed a professional athlete contract with Quiksilver Europe. Gabe stayed with and was incredibly loyal to Quiksilver for his whole professional career, spanning more than two decades. He is one of only a handful of European surfers to make a full career as a pro-surfer without having to supplement it with alternative jobs or income. Gabe saw it as a job in itself, working relentlessly at his craft in and out of the water. He covered all bases, keeping himself at the top of the pile. Being the epitome of a professional surfer, he was someone I learned so much from in that respect. Gabe's successes and accolades were very broad-ranging and comprehensive. He competed constantly at home and overseas, winning many UK domestic titles, and most notably won the international big wave event, La Vaca Gigante in France, against some of the world's best. He travelled constantly, criss-crossing the globe on surf adventures for his sponsors and appearing in every conceivable surf publication.

Meeting Gabe Davies was such a defining moment for my surfing and advancement into waves of consequence. I didn't realise it then, but having Gabe as a friend and surfing partner would lead to so much for both of us in wave discovery and the journey into big-wave pioneering. You wouldn't have predicted it at the time if you saw us goofing around in the waves of Tullan Strand on that cloudless August morning all those years ago . . .

## 14

# Kelly Slater and World Surfing's New Order

By the early 1990s, global surfing was transforming all over the world. The seismic shift and changing of the guard was being led by a new breed of pro-surfer coming from mainland America and Hawaii. Board design, fashion, wetsuits and what was deemed possible to do on a surfboard were all thrown into question. The faces and fundamentals of progressive surfing had changed beyond all previous recognition. Where once surfing that was prized was all about squeezing in manoeuvres and mercilessly milking every wave to the sand, now in its place came an all-embracing approach of doing less but with much more commitment and precision, with one or two big turns while surfing a wave.

It was the beginning of a new era in surfing, where you needed to be the whole package in big and small waves. Things were advancing so fast that it took surfing culture by surprise, spinning everything into a panicked catch-up. This caused a lot of head scratching in a sport where contest scoring was already so subjective and caused much controversy at every event. These new manoeuvres being performed were so out-of-the-box fresh and futuristic that they didn't even have names or criteria within the pro-surfing judging criteria. If the Dutch were connoisseurs of Total Football, then these young Americans were the aficionados of Total Surfing. Now the emphasis was on skateboard-style acrobatic aerial surfing and full-tilt tube rides.

Skateboarding had started to seep into mainstream America from California during the 1960s. It really came to prominence in the 1970s, when surfers looking for fun and alternatives to surfing took to the concrete for answers. The 2001 documentary *Dogtown and Z-Boys* by director Stacy Peralta is a must watch for understanding this critical period of '70s skate/surf evolution. Here in the early 1990s it had come full circle, with cross-fertilisation between surf and skate complete. Now surfers were being heavily influenced by the vertical rotating aerial antics of skateboarding on display in every halfpipe, concrete bowl and skatepark the world over. Californian surfer Tom Curren was the sometimes-reluctant prophet of 1980s surfing. He was the virtuoso of style in the water during a decade full of garish fashion, questionable style and frantic approaches in the surf. Curren finished the decade with three world titles under his belt. If he was the last decade's prophet, we were all in for a shock with the coming of the 1990s messiah.

The first year of the new decade heralded the age of Floridian surfer Kelly Slater. He was straight out of the Tom Curren school of style but better, much better. Even as a teenager he was freakishly good and way ahead of the chasing pack. What Elvis Presley had done for music, Kelly Slater did for surfing. Elvis changed the music landscape forever. The King didn't invent rock 'n' roll, but he reimagined it with his genius musicality, influences, looks and showmanship. Slater took what was already in surfing and turned it on its head, re-packaged it and presented it back to the world in a new form that was almost unrecognisable to anything that had gone before.

Early reports confirmed what everybody already knew, and that was that Slater was an unstoppable, complete package. Surfing, like so many other action and board sports, is youth dominated. In the contest arena, surf judges reward for innovation and new interpretations of old staples. Through the Slater era this scoring system always favoured the inventiveness of young pro-surfers. So, Slater's continued ascendancy, longevity and getting better decade upon decade was even more startling to watch. He returned serve against a long line of challengers who stepped up. The age of Slater has lasted for an unprecedented 30 years, with 11 world titles and counting. At age 50, he is still on tour, mixing it with mostly teenaged to early twenties surfers on the world circuit. Early in 2022, six days before Slater's 50th birthday, he won the Pipeline Masters in Hawaii, the most testing of all events in world surfing. The Pipeline Masters is the ultimate individual event to win, equivalent to winning golf's US Masters in prestige. Winning one Pipeline Masters can and has defined whole careers. Slater has won eight in the last three decades.

On paper it makes no sense at all. Surfing is one of the most physically demanding and dynamic sports out there. It requires the most complex movement patterns you can imagine that go far beyond golf, for example, for any 50-year-old. In the Pipeline Masters, you are rag-dolled as countless tonnes of Pacific power unload on top of you, pressing you into the shallow reef below. The surfers are pitting themselves against one of the most dangerous waves in the world. For Slater to win this event 30 years after he won it for the first time in 1992 must surely put him in at the top of the pile for the world's greatest athlete. US sportscasters talk of Tom Brady and Michael Jordan; Slater's record has the longevity to match or perhaps eclipse both.

Surfing has now bestowed the GOAT title on Slater. Not in respect to just surfing; that's a given, he is untouchable in the sport. Commentators and experts inside of surfing already recognise him as such, but there are calls for him to be acknowledged as the greatest athlete who has ever lived. The problem with saying he is the greatest across all sports lies not in Slater's achievements but in surfing as a sport. Surfing is a global sport with millions surfing worldwide, but it is still niche in so many respects. Contest surfing is a tiny niche within global surfing. Less than 1 per cent of surfers will ever compete at any level. Surfing is more like skiing, in that it has a specific geography attached. You must live by the coast. Most coastal areas around the world are becoming more expensive by the year, especially in what we consider the western world. This presents a problem and limits the participation of who surfing is available too, with ever increasing attractive ocean-front real-estate now being bought up by wealthy interests. Surfing has financial restraints too, with boards, wetsuits and the necessary travel to improve all costing money. Even a cursory scroll through the list of surfing world champions in all disciplines is telling. Over 90 per cent of all world champions in surfing have come from either Australia or America, including Hawaii. In this tight framework of measuring surfing success it's hard to proclaim a global GOAT. This statistic exposes surfing in much too narrow a spread to be able to select the champion of champions.

For me, Slater has to be seen well outside these parameters: he ruled professional surfing but to me more importantly shaped modern surfing and continues to innovate the sport as a lifestyle 30 years later.

The impact Slater had was profound; it rocked the surfing world to its core. It changed the sport from the upper echelon of the industry to the world order of pro surfing right down to

your weekend warrior surfers heading to their local beach in
Ireland. Kelly Slater was the perfect storm in many ways; he
arrived at the right time and had an arsenal of talent and level-
headedness that was ahead of the establishment.

———

In Ireland, we were far from immune to this new global order
in surfing. The 19-year-old me in 1993 was no exception. We
all wanted in on the act and clambered to see what was going
on across the Atlantic. There had been fundamental changes in
surfboard design allowing you to surf the face of a wave more
like a skateboarder. Never had the similarities of surfing and
skating had so much in common. My mind was blown by all
this new content and how much the goalposts had shifted in
such a short time. I upgraded my own selection of surfboards
(we call these a 'quiver of boards' in surfing parlance). Carbon
fibre was being used in surfboards for the first time. This new
space-age material enabled surfboards to stay incredibly light
while still retaining its crucial rigid strength. You were no one
if you didn't have a carbon-fibre strip or two running down the
centre of your board. (Carbon fibre was an expensive lightweight
material more associated with racing cars than surfboards. If you
couldn't afford to get it in your board, you could draw some
black lines down your board with a BIC permanent marker
instead to give the illusion that you did.)

Boards became wafer thin and impossibly light, with a huge
amount of curved lift in the nose and tail that we call 'a board's
rocker'. It gave the boards of that era their defining banana
shape. These new boards worked well for loosening up your
surfing. Rotating like a spinning top and sliding 180 degrees
when you found the sweet spot was the order of the day. The

speed and ability to spin right round was in vogue and easier than ever to achieve. The downside of overly rockered boards meant they were unforgiving. Very little of the bottom of the board planed at any one time on the surface of the wave. The boards didn't like turbulence, so when you inevitably hit a few sea horses of chop it felt like you had surfed into a limpet minefield on your narrow board. Marginally incorrect weight distribution caused you to catch a rail bogging your board down, losing all speed in an instant and getting caught by the white water.

I liked the new boards, but they felt like you were surfing on one of Aladdin's shoes. Seeing old photos of those boards now I can't help but feel how ridiculous they looked with their preposterously crescent shapes. In comparison to what we are surfing today, they were impractical in so many ways and only suited high-level precise surfers and surfing.

During the summer of 1993, my concentration was now as much about surfing above the lip of the wave as surfing below it on the open unbroken face. It was all about freeing your fins as much as you could to allow your board to pivot as much as possible. 'Fins out for the boys!' was the rallying cry for summer '93. Much like a skateboarder who grinds two wheels above the coping of a skate ramp, blowing your fins free of the breaking lip created the same skater movement, only on water not concrete.

Ireland was also changing. The country was on the verge of an economic boom that ushered in the biggest change to the country since the foundation of the new Irish state in 1922. Ireland would become the darling and envy of global economies for over a decade. There was a national confidence in the air, buoyed by the new standing and international achievements of our football team over the previous few years. It felt like the long overdue good times had finally arrived for Ireland, and in many respects they had.

I was beginning to think outside the box in terms of my own surfing. I was saturated by the new school of surfing coming out of the States. I had the perfect accomplice to bounce off, as my mate, Tramore surfer John McCarthy, had decided to spend the summer in Bundoran. In surfing terms, John 'Mac' McCarthy came off the seemingly endless conveyor belt of top Tramore surfers like his other surfing half, Dave Blount. Tramore surfers in Ireland were universally called 'The Troggs' in my day. You knew they always travelled by the battalion. When they showed up at any Irish surfing contest, the heats instantly got a lot harder. They would arrive en masse to every Irish surfing event competitive or otherwise in the back of Henry and Johno Moore's van, or piled high into Hugh O'Brian-Moran's car.

Mac's hometown of Tramore is a busy seaside/surf town on the edge of the old Viking city of Waterford, which has an incredible maritime history. In more modern times, especially since the 1960s, a vibrant surf culture has sprouted up in Tramore and spread out around Co. Waterford's coastline and into the city itself. Tramore has a lot of similarities to Bundoran, and like Bundoran it was a working-class seaside town. Although the south coast of Ireland including Tramore doesn't get the regular booming waves of the west coast, it has had a thriving surf scene, surf club and is rich with Irish surfing history. Considering its lack of quality consistent surf, Tramore has for many decades, since the birth of Irish surfing, been a production line for top-quality Irish surfers.

Mac has a very endearing quality to his personality. If you have ever met Mac, he is a hard person not to like. He was also very cool and confident for his age back in 1993. He sported a young 'Emilio Estevez' mop of wispy, strawberry-blonde hair with a devil may care smile. He had a double ear piercing in his left ear accompanying a very original funky dress sense. Even though we were peers I wanted to be like Mac, to talk like him and act like him. He wore a cool, loose Clint Eastwood style poncho. I desperately wanted to be the same. I got a pale blue poncho but sadly I looked exactly like what I was, a slightly awkward trying-hard-to-be-cool Irish teenager. I didn't have the roguish style of Mac to pull it off.

At the time, Mac had a board sponsorship from Wave Graffiti surfboards, which were must haves for UK and Irish surfers in the early 1990s. I had wrangled my first wetsuit sponsorship deal from UK surf company Tiki thanks to the owner Tim Hayland, who was known to everyone as Tiki Tim. Tim had founded the wetsuit and board company Tiki in 1963 on the beautiful Devon coast of the southwest. He was a big barrel-chested Devon surfer whose mannerisms reminded me more of a colonial British regimental sergeant major on safari in Africa rather than a surf company owner. Tim and his wife Sue were very good to me, taking me over to Devon the following summer of 1994 for a few weeks to show me the ropes of a surf company. Our family were in our fourth year of the surf shop, and I still had much to learn. Tim put me up in their house and gave me a golden ticket access to all their multiple surf shops, shaping bays and factories. I learned a hell of a lot from Tim; he was a great early business mentor for me. I repaid Tim and Sue for their kindness and hospitality by trying to sneak English girls who worked for him back into his house during the wee hours after local discos in Croyde. I shouted their house down when Ray Houghton scored against Italy in the New York Giants Stadium at the 1994 World Cup. Tim thought I was going to burst a blood vessel.

Through his surfing company, Tim was the first person to

bring wetsuits into Ireland in bulk. He did it of course for financial reasons – he saw a gap in the growing surf market in Ireland – but he also put a lot back into Irish surfing, investing a lot of himself personally. He had the best junior contest in Lahinch every year. The prizes were amazing; as a teenager you would walk away with boxes of surf stuff. He also held the annual Tiki Cold Water Classic in Easkey every year. It was the best contest of the year and always seemed to get great surf conditions. The classic was about as close to an annual pro-contest as there was in Ireland back then. I made the final a couple of times but never won it. I was always very proud to have the Team Tiki stickers on my board. Over 30 years ago, Tim took a chance, signing me up to wear his wetsuits. It was a vote of confidence in me that certainly bolstered my belief in my early '90s surfing journey.

One of the first times Tiki Tim came to visit us at the surf shop he brought along one of his latest surfing buddies, who happened to be Andrew Ridgeley, one half of '80s pop sensations Wham!. Andrew had become a keen surfer since moving to Devon after the breakup of Wham! a few years earlier. We had him and Tiki Tim round our house for tea and a surf at Tullan Strand, where Andrew left me in no doubt that he was able to catch a wave or two. I was mid-teens at the time and only too aware of exactly who Andrew Ridgeley was. I was too cool to admit it at the time, but I had secretly really liked Wham!'s music, even though they were seen as a teenybopper girls' band. Andrew was a super nice chap and had a funny story or two about the 1985 Live Aid concert that I still remember today. I can still see my mum making tea for the buck from Wham! in our old kitchen and my sisters being happy about this particular surfing visitor.

## 15

# Euro Surf '93

Over the summer of 1993, myself and Mac had sent our surfing CV everywhere to raise funds to travel to the Euro Surf event in Scotland. By the dozen we painstakingly printed, cut and pasted photos and a bio of each of us onto every CV with a request letter for sponsorship. We mailed them out to every company we could think of, we were not fussy. It was many years before laptops and a printer could scan and email it all for you in an instant. We eventually got a response from NCF (North Connacht Farmers Co-Op) in Sligo, and they gave us a check for £200. A good start. We were both over 18, so we decided to send a CV to the marketing department at Guinness. Guinness at the time had some fantastic surfing-based TV ads. They had also been the capital sponsor of the Euro Surf in Bundoran in 1985 and had been heavily associated with Irish surfing for over a decade, so we thought what the hell, we'll give it a shot. Lo and behold they got back to us and offered us £300 each for every international contest we went to and as much Guinness merchandise as we wanted – T-shirts, hoodies and hats – but not of the liquid variety unfortunately. All we needed to do was put massive Guinness stickers on our boards. Both of us held that sponsorship deal through to the next World Championships in Brazil as well. To me it was fantastic that a big corporate company was interested in paying you to surf.

We arrived at the ill-fated Euro Surf in Scotland, where every Irish team member was issued with a pair of army-green Dunlop wellies. Add the wellies to myself and Mac having NCF and Guinness stickers on our boards, and we slotted right in with the cows strolling around the contest paddock in northern Scotland. The wellies were a wise addition to our team kit, as the contest site turned to muck in the incessant freezing rain and sleet that October. Mac would put the wellies half on with the two soles sticking out at right angles to his legs like a compound fracture. He called it the wellie walk. He would go up to the swishly attractive French and Spanish team members, talking to them in the thickest Irish bogman accent you could imagine. We'd be in tears laughing at his performance.

Myself, Zoe Lally, Liam Stewart, Anna Marie Stewart and Jim Meehan had left Bundoran for the long drive to the European Surfing Championships in Thurso at the top of Scotland. Arranging to meet with the rest of the Irish surf team in Thurso, we had one stop to make beforehand, and that was to pick up some of the Northern Irish contingent of the team. We drove north, picking up the Portrush shams, as they were known back then, plus Brian Welch in Co. Derry. We all scheduled to meet in Mary's bar and lounge in Magherafelt for tea, soup and sandwiches. (How brilliantly Irish is that as a meeting point for a surf team? I can't imagine the Hawaiian surf team having such arrangements.)

We got the once over just outside of Magherafelt from your local, friendly neighbourhood RUC checkpoint. As we were driving our southern-registered cars and vans packed with young fellas, we might as well have had a flashing light and loudspeaker attached to the roof broadcasting 'Stop and search us!' The RUC just love a car full of southern sons of Ulster. Stern expressionless faces, automatic weapons, tactical body armour and direct questions with little punctuation was the atmosphere at the checkpoint. We were all hauled out and corralled while they searched our vehicles that were filled with probably the last thing on earth they expected . . . surfboards. Dozens of them piled high with stinky, damp wetsuits on top. As they thoroughly searched the vehicles, they also thoroughly questioned us. The RUC seemed more relaxed when they discovered that some of our brethren were the right kind of sons of Ulster, with more pleasing and much less offensive British passports and UK licences. 'So, you are the Irish team, is that correct son?' came the softening but clipped line of questions from the officer in charge. 'That's correct officer,' came my reply, 'and we are heading to Scotland for the European Surfing Championships.' 'OK, son, you can pack up and be on your way.' I'm sure he was puzzled and a bit underwhelmed by our presentation as a national team. His face did look strained. God only knows what he thought of Northern Irish British passport-holding members of the Irish surf team heading off to represent Ireland alongside Republic of Ireland passport-holding surfers from the south. It was certainly a rare occurrence in Irish sport.

We made the crossing to Scotland from Larne and onto the long drive. Some of the team headed for Edinburgh to pick up team gear while we pointed straight to Caithness. We drove for what felt like an eternity before breaking down in the middle of the highlands. We spent a freezing night on the roadside in gales, snow and rain. It was a challenging road trip, so when we hit Thurso the next day, we were thirsty for a pint and a bit of craic with rest of the team before the contest started in a few days' time. The town of Thurso is in the bucolic setting where the highlands meet the majestic surroundings of Scotland's north coast. The town itself was a very drab place back then. It resembled a grey concrete town from the Soviet bloc more than a part of the UK.

The main sponsor for the Euro Surf pulled out at the eleventh hour so the contest site structure and facilities never showed up. The Sandside Nuclear Power Station nearby threw a bit of last-minute money at the event, but I'm not sure it had any effect, because there was nothing added to the bare contest site. Not something you see every day: the European Surfing Championships sponsored by a nuclear power station. 'Only in Scotland,' as they say. The beach directly beside Sandside Nuclear Power Station is home to a quality surf break called 'Sandside' (no surprise there). We surfed 'Sandside' when we were up there, with the nuclear power station with its brutalist architecture in the fore-ground giving quite the contrast. Back then, every now and then the beach would be closed when particles of nuclear material were washed up and detected on the sand. Luckily, it didn't happen when we were there. The local Scottish surfers told us that the water temperature at Sandside was noticeably warmer because of all the 'clean' hot water pumped out into the sea from the station. Maybe it was true at certain times or just an old surfing wives' tale. When I surfed Sandside, I didn't notice any difference in water temperature, and maybe that's a good thing.

The Irish team secured a kit deal with Patagonia, who were strictly a mountaineering company then. They had brilliant wet gear at the time. Now this was 20 years before Patagonia had an eco-surfing division, so the 1993 Irish team could claim to be way ahead of its time. With our Dunlop wellie boots we were a laughing stock to the other nations until the first day of competition, when the heavens opened to unleash rain, hail stones and gales for the entire duration of the contest. There was no shelter, so wellies and wet-proofs never felt so good or appropriate. I roomed with Adam Wilson and Mac in the Overlook Hotel of Thurso. I think we agreed the place was haunted, or maybe it was hallucinations from all the black lung-inducing damp spores we were breathing in.

You know a hotel is really bad when it's got carpet on the walls, as our hotel did. The whole thing was a bit of a disaster, with inedible food to top it off, but it's an Irish surf team trip that resonates with me still. It was brilliant fun, and when you are young you can just brush all of that off. In fairness we were unlucky for that Euros, surf wise anyway, as it didn't turn good until the last day of the event. It was a bad showing by the Irish: we did OK in the knee board and body boarding, but we were all below par and finished in the bottom half of European nations.

Thurso East is the beating heart of a resurgent Scottish surfing scene. It's still recognised as one of Europe's premier right-handed surf breaks. Since then the town has played host to some of the world's best surfers and has had some great pro events up there in world-class surf. The 1993 European final in the end came down to three French surfers, Boris La Taxier, Didier Petier and Fred Robin, surfing against Russell Winter, who was from England. Now Russell is a mate of mine, and of course I was biased for him, but he was robbed in that final and not beaten on talent. Russ was at the time the best surfer in Europe. At that contest, no one came close to him. He went on to become the first European to get on the ASP World Tour and dominated European surfing for the next decade, so he had the last laugh.

~

My favourite Irish contest of the year was always the national team's event, the annual Irish Intercounties Surfing Championships.

It was also in 1993 that our young Bundoran team made up of myself, Jim Meehan and the Granaghan brothers won this contest competing as the Donegal senior team. The contest and social side of the event had always led to a brilliant weekend. It's the highlight of the Irish surfing calendar, with some of the stories over the weekend becoming legendary in the annals of Irish surfing. The Intercounties has been running annually in Rossnowlagh for over 51 years, which is really something, making it one of the world's longest-running surf contests. I won it five times with Jim Meehan and other Bundoran team members. Our inaugural 1993 victory at the Intercounties was covered by RTÉ television on a kid's sports show called *The Grip* presented by Sarah O'Flaherty and a youthful Ryle Nugent. I won the final, getting a wee tube ride in the process, which was aired on TV. It was a big deal for me at the time. It was a great piece on the event, which added to my confidence in front of the camera and set me on a course over the next few years of doing plenty of TV work. Two of the highlights from that time was being asked to do some voiceover work for the Discovery Channel, and when the *USA Today* show came to Ireland I was asked to be a part of it.

At the time, *USA Today* was the most watched morning show in the States. They wanted to do a quirky contrast piece on surfing in Ireland set against the usual Irish staples portrayed in America of Paddy smoking a pipe in a flat cap. I was only supposed to be a small part of the show, but I ended up with a much bigger role, and that was fine with me. They sent me a VHS copy of the show after it aired, and I was happy with it of course. Over the next few months, I started to receive quite a bit of mail in the form of letters from the USA, mostly from girls wanting to be my pen pal, which I was happy about. I responded to most, and in my own head it was my first bit of fan mail. In truth, I loved it.

## 16

# Brazil and the World Surfing Championships 1994

The following year, I continued my good run of form, making the Irish surf team again in 1994. Qualifying for the World Championships in Brazil, it was my first World event competing in the open men's division. The contest was to be held on the famously vibrant beaches of Rio De Janeiro. At 20, I was well travelled for someone my age. I also had a few big international surfing events under my belt. However, nothing could have fully prepared me for the culture shock of being in south Donegal one day, then waking up in Rio 24 hours later.

Because of the attractive location for this World Championships, our domestic qualifying contests for the four open places had been furious. Every competitive surfer in Ireland wanted a spot on this team for Rio. Who doesn't want to go to the Copacabana after an Irish winter? Myself, Jimi Meehan and KT had snagged three of the men's places. As usual, Ireland had a full quota team of four Open surfers, four juniors, two ladies, two bodyboarders, one longboarder and one kneeboarder. We had the strength in depth of a full team to be competitive in every division. The rest of the team members were from Rossnowlagh, Portrush and Strandhill. After a few years of walking the boards at Irish surfing contests, I knew all the team members as friends. The Roci and Brian duet were back as coach and manager, respectively. Our team and most of the other competing nations were accommodated in a swanky, glass-exterior, mini-skyscraper hotel overlooking São Conrado Beach. We had a short daily bus transfer to the main contest site at Barra da Tijuca Beach. The hotel was as big as it was classy, accommodating not only the surfing competitors but simultaneously playing host to an international diamond dealers conference. Not two demographics you would usually put together, unless of course you planned to smuggle diamonds in your surfboards, like Jimmy Slade did in an episode of *Baywatch* the year before.

In today's surfing world, Brazilian surfers are the highflyers, with a commanding grip on the modern professional surfing tour's top tier. In 1994, Brazilian surfers were an emerging force but not a patch on what they have evolved into now. In the 1990s, Brazil had a few surfers on the pro tour who were looked on as snappy, fast small-wave specialists. Brazilian surfers had a passion but were not considered a real threat to the dominance of the US, Hawaiian, South African and Australian professionals. I learned while in Brazil that surfing and football were two of the limited sporting avenues available as a way out of the favellas. Brian and Roci had arranged that the Irish team would surf a pre-World Championships warm-up against the Brazilian team. It was scheduled to take place a week before the championships in a sleepy beach town an hour north of metropolitan Rio called Saquarema. This small event was the first ever head-to-head Brazil v Ireland surfing contest, with the whole weekend being sponsored by Coca-Cola. We arrived at night driving straight from the airport to Saquarema. The next morning, we woke to a hot, humid day drenched with sunshine and offshore waves. I liked Brazil from the first moment I opened my eyes that morning; the musky smell of tropical wet soil and balmy sweet equatorial foliage. The beach was idyllic: warm water, blue waves and a colourful first impression of the rhythmic Brazilian people all around us. We had two days to get accustomed to sunburn, boardshort rubs and surfboard wax friction against your chest before the contest against the home team. That night the beach-side chalets where we were staying was also the venue for a local wedding. The festivities we could hear but not see as they were taking place across the complex in the main function rooms. Our accommodation was block booked for us and separated from the main hotel.

We were warned by management to get some rest, have an early night and for the love of God don't drink water from the tap. Second to that was to not take ice in any drink or eat salads without rinsing them thoroughly with bottled water. With a whole team of Irish surfers coming out of winter hibernation in Brazil for the first night, it was wishful thinking by the management. Astonishingly though, we all turned in at 9 p.m. after our team meal. The toll of jet lag added to the tiredness and sunburn of our first full day of team preparation and surfing in the Brazilian heat left us with red eyes, toasted skin and aching muscles. Sleep was to be short lived, as the bridal party from the wedding had got wind that a surf team from Ireland were staying at the same resort. At 10 p.m. we got a tap on the door. Looking out the window I could see a curvaceous browned-eyed bombshell bride clad in white and her handsome husband outside grinning from ear to ear. I answered the door to a sparklingly beautiful newly-wed couple inviting the whole Irish team to their wedding.

The bridal party assured us that the celebrations were only

revving up. As a responsible senior team member, I woke the rest of the team with the 'good' news. Everyone was dressed in a flash and following the couple across the complex through security. We were treated like returning long lost family members by all the guests at their pulsating drum beat of a Brazilian wedding. I can't say we impressed on the dance floor; our samba moves were wiggles at best, lacking in hip-mania Latin flare. We were however plied with copious amounts of a 'put hairs on your chest' national cocktail of lime-and-sugar-flavoured firewater with a 48 percent tornado twist of alcohol that is caipirinha, at the same time mindful to keep the drinking in check and away from the dreaded crushed ice that is such a vital ingredient for caipirinha. The bar staff were compliant with our odd request of cocktails with no ice, that is until the third team round of drinks, when ice caution was cast to the wind and replaced with the more favourable tone of 'Christ almighty I will have ice, surely!' We had a fabulous night with our warm and generous Brazilian friends. Having all just hit the hay for a second time at 3 a.m., the whole team was awake again in minutes. Now we played a new sport of tag team galloping ceili to the toilets. Every team member came down with the runs or the 'Hershey squirts', as KT called them. It was a rough night and a harsh lesson learned of the danger of frozen water in South America that made our second day in Brazil an edgy one filled with distance-to-toilet calculations.

Every morning and evening, we had informative and high-spirited team meetings that you always felt better leaving. The morning meetings were all logistics and game plans as to who you were against that day and where. The evening meetings were all debriefings on the day and what was up for the next day. Brian would arrive in a whirlwind of faxed printouts. The pages were for any other business at the end of the meeting

Portrush man Ian Hill surfing Bundoran's main beach in September 1964. This is the first known photo of anyone surfing in Bundoran. (*With thanks to the Hill family*)

My Mum, Margaret Fitzgerald, when she was Miss An Tóstal All Ireland 1959. (*Richie Fitzgerald*)

Donegal underage finalists at the Lahinch junior titles in the early nineties. From left to right: Me, David Scallon, Gavin McCrea, Anna Lally, Danny Clarke. In front: Kenny Ward, John Britton. (*Irish Surfing Association*)

Myself, my sister Frances and my brother Joe on the Main Beach in the mid-eighties. (*Karen Fitzgerald*)

Guinness is good for you! Heading to Euro Surf 1993. (*Annamarie Fitzgerald*)

My first sponsor (after my Mum of course) was Tiki Wetsuits. (*Frances Fitzgerald*)

Bundoran surf club in the local Saint Patrick's Day Parade, 1993. (*Annamarie Fitzgerald*)

The first photograph I had published in an international surfing magazine. From Australian *Tracks* surfing magazine in 1995. I was a big Zig and Zag fan too. (*John Frank*)

This shot was taken in 1996, the year I signed my first professional contract. (*Annamarie Fitzgerald*)

Star Wars and surfing was an unlikely combination, but not for me. (*Richie Fitzgerald*)

My trusty tri-colour board was under my feet for years at heavy Mullaghmore. (*Richie Fitzgerald*)

The early years at Surfworld – mid-nineties. (Annamarie Fitzgerald)

With members of the Irish surf team jungle trekking before the World surfing Championships in Rio De Janeiro, Brazil, in 1994. My childhood surfing hero Kevin Tobin with his hands on my shoulders. Left to right: Brian Britton, Frazer Duddy, Colin O'Hare, Ryan Hunter, Peter Donahue, Chris Lafferty, Kevin Tobin, Gavin McCrea, Roci Allen, Declan Feeney. Front row: Niall Cochrane, Neil Byrnes, me and Jimi Meehan. (*Richie Fitzgerald*)

Above: Letting loose surfing Easkey in the late 90's. (*Alex Williams*)

Gerlin Rock looking tropical in winter 2004 with Ian Battrick taking a late drop and me paddling over the back. (*Sharpy*)

Around 2001/2002, riding one of Chris Malloy's specialist Hawaiian Pipeline boards. He gave me the board on the north shore a few years earlier, and it worked just as well on Irish waves too. (*Sharpy*)

Surfing the mesmerising waves of Aileen's, Co. Clare, during the filming of *Waveriders* in 2006. (*Bernard Testemale/Waveriders*)

With Gabe and Joel at the Jameson Dublin International Film Festival for a screening of *Waveriders*. (*Richie Fitzgerald*)

In 2006 Gabe and I were honoured to get to spend an afternoon in Waikiki with Hawaiian surfing legend Albert 'Rabbit' Kekai. (*Richie Fitzgerald*)

Emerald walls in 2010 at home in Bundoran. (*Daveth Fox*)

Deep water sea mount in Co. Sligo – my first wave at Prowlers. (*Aaron Pierce*)

Cows, green grass and blue surf. Just another perfect day on Ireland's west coast. (*Andrew Kilfeather*)

Going warp speed at Mullaghmore. (*Roo McCrudden*)

The beast that is Mullaghmore in splendid isolation. (*Michal Czubala*)

Casual in the ripples at Mullaghmore. (*Aaron Pierce*)

The northwest in full storm rage. (*Andrew Kilfeather*)

With Jimi Meehan, Stevie Burns and Derek Parle in Easkey in 2010, surfing heats against some of Ireland's finest. (*Aaron Pierce*)

Picking Gabe up on the inside at Mullaghmore during the Billabong Big Wave Invitational event, winter 2011/2012. (*Roo McCrudden*)

My last Hurrah on the Irish Surf Team outside Surfworld for the Euro Surf in September 2011. (*Briohny Fitzgerald*)

PMPA point Bundoran, my favourite wave anywhere in the world, steam training down the reef in the early noughties. (*Steve Fitzpatrick*)

Surfing for a Jägermeister TV ad in minus 20 degrees in northern Iceland in November 2014, with Dave Blount, Ben Skinner and Ollie Adams. (*Richie Fitzgerald*)

Stepping out of surfing magazines for a moment and into some lifestyle publications with the talented Kathrin Baumbach behind the lens. (*Kathrin Baumbach*)

My newborn Ella in one hand and my Donegal Sports Star of the Year award in the other. 2012 was a very special year for me. (*Briohny Fitzgerald*)

Left: Generation next. With my two children, Ella and Kai, in Australia December 2021. (*Briohny Fitzgerald*)

Below: Ella surfing a lot better than I was at her age! (*Briohny Fitzgerald*)

with reams of news, sports and entertainment from back home. Brian always handed me the sports printouts full of League of Ireland and Premiership latest news. One evening, Brian announced reading from his printouts that the Eurovision Song Contest just held in Dublin had been another blistering success by all accounts. Paul Harrington and Ballyshannon man Charlie McGettigan had won it again for Ireland, so there was local interest in the victory for us. He continued that there had been a brilliant interval performance by a troop of Irish dancers that the whole country was talking about. Of course, when we got home, we learned the name Riverdance for the troop of Irish dancers. In the seven-minute interval, Riverdance had made Irish dancing sexy forever more. We could have done with some Riverdance hip-loosening inspiration a couple of nights before for our wedding-crashing samba.

Over the weekend, most of us surfed well within ourselves against the Brazilian team. We didn't have any excuse bar the 'caipirinha incident', as it became known among the team. We weren't fully acclimatised either, with a sharp Brazilian team showing no mercy, slicing through our ranks on their local waves. Our bodyboarders and kneeboarder put in a gritty display, but the big Irish talking point was reserved for our best female surfer, Rossnowlagh's Zoe Lally, who won the ladies final. The Brazilian No. 1 Alessandra Vieira, whom Zoe beat in the final, went on to be crowned world champion at the big event in Rio the following week. Mirroring Andy Hill two years earlier, Zoe's performance couldn't be really appreciated until viewed in the context of who she had managed to defeat. This newer, confident era of Irish surfing ignited by the Tobin brothers was offering something more than the plucky spirited display that was expected of the Irish. We were starting to get some good heat results against big names and nations. The only thing missing was consistency.

The prize giving that evening was shrouded in gloom for the home team and local spectators as news filtered through that Brazil's favourite son, Ayrton Senna, had just died in a horror crash at the San Marino Grand Prix. A very emotional minute's silence was observed before medals were handed out. We left for the bus journey back to Rio the next day. I had heard about the Brazilian passion for sport, but seeing it unfold in front of my eyes was very different to watching it on the BBC News. Senna's death for most Brazilian people was a national tragedy, with the government declaring three days of national mourning. This usually beaming city had people crying in the streets. Flags were at half mast, while huge banners and posters of Senna hung from bridges, out of windows and buildings. Everywhere you looked was draped with black flags. It really was something extraordinary to witness.

Surfing as a global sport even in 1994 and up until recent times was saturated with a braggadocio stereotype. The sport itself on all levels had a unfortunate inbuilt chauvinism that portrayed girls as better suited to sitting on the beach in a skimpy bikini while the male wave warriors did battle in the fearsome crashing surf out to sea. I was thinking about this when I was out in Brazil. From my experience, Irish surfing was remarkably free of these attitudes and hang ups towards girls in the surf. Although female surfers were smaller in number than their male counterparts in the early days, they were far from just mere tokenism in Ireland. Irish surfing for most of the last 20 years has been run by Zoe Lally, giving a strong female voice and leadership to the sport. Irish surfing has always produced female surfers of a high calibre. Zoe took this to a new level in Brazil in addition to her 13 Irish titles and international contest experience. Since Zoe, we have seen female surfers like Bundoran's Nicole Morgan, who competed at professional level. Nicole was in Europe's leading pack for many years. Her contemporary, Rossnowlagh's Easkey Britton, re-wrote the book on what Irish female surfers could do in and out of the water. Nicole and Easkey were fearsome competitors, driving each other on. With a cache of national titles already in the bag, both women competed all over the UK on the British BPSA pro tour. The BPSA tour attracted some top-class international female competitors with the cash prizes on offer for event wins. Nicole won the tour in 2005 and Easkey in 2006 and 2009. Easkey has since become a global spokesperson for female surfing, with her talents as varied as university lecturer, published author, delivering TED Talks and introducing women to the sport through surfing on the coast of Iran. I can only say this from my male point of view, but in my eyes women in the surf was part and parcel of Irish surfing. Female surfers got equal billing at events and women were encouraged into the surf. I didn't realise that there was any different attitude until I saw the machismo towards females in the surf overseas.

When we opened our surf shop in 1990, Annamarie was pulling the strings. She made sure we had as much equipment in store for women as possible, which was rare for the times anywhere. Seeing women as equals in or out of the water was the way I was brought up. My sister Frances had taught me how to surf. At home I'd grown up in a mostly maternally dominated household. With three older sisters any notions of male peacocking saw my plumage swiftly clipped back down to size by any or all three of them. On the flipside of that, my sisters were fiercely protective of their wee brother, which I didn't mind one bit.

The team hotel in Rio was leagues above the usual standard accommodation for a surf contest. We were assigned half the bedrooms on one of the top floors. The rest of the rooms were for the star-studded Hawaiian team that included future top professionals like Kalani Robb. We had a few days to get the lay of the land before the contest started. As usual we got down to the contest site every morning to get some practice in. The locals call Rio 'Cidade Maravilhosa' (The Wonderful City), and it was easy to see why as we got to experience more and more of it. There was a huge disparity between the rich and poor everywhere you looked. Brazil, and especially Rio, unlike other less developed places I'd been to, had multimillion-dollar living right up against favellas and vice versa. I had seen similar rags and riches disparity on a surf trip to Peru in the urban setting of Lima and also on the coast. In Rio, it was a much more extreme example. You didn't have to look very far to see the desperately poor majority population. We became friendly with the street kids outside the hotel and on the beach front. Some of them were so tiny and covered in filth that it was heartbreaking to see and put what we were doing in Rio into perspective. We would buy them food, drink and clothes as they spent the day running over and back across the busy roads behind the beach.

For Brian and Roci, they saw these international trips with the team as opportunities for us to see new countries and experience different cultures. While other teams seemed to have little interaction outside the contests, we were given the option of a few exciting excursions during the week.

Brian had arranged for us to watch an evening football match at Rio's gigantic colosseum of football that is the Maracanã. The stadium was a heaving mass of humanity, colour, noise and extremely heated passion. I don't speak Portuguese, but you didn't need a translator to understand what was being screamed and cursed at the pitch. The Maracanã is famous for once holding a record crowd of 200,000, though that had been reduced to a more 'sensible' 100,000 by 1994. By my reckoning it was rammed the evening we were there, with an electric, pulsating atmosphere that is hard to forget.

Our second outing had been pencilled in as the one full day of culturally fulfilling activity. We started with an early-morning visit to the statue of 'Christ the Redeemer' at the top of the Corcovado mountain that towers over the city. After another bus journey we spent the afternoon on a team-building hike through a jungle mountain pass a few hours inland of Rio. We dramatically miscalculated the distance of the hike. At sundown we were still on the top of the mountain only halfway across. It was steaming hot, we had long since burned through our bottle of water and chocolate bar each. We were a sorry sight as the jungle turned the volume up the darker it got. Everything seemed to be either hissing, buzzing or screeching at us in a deafening chorus of monkeys, insects, reptiles, birds and God knows what else. It became every man for himself, sprinting down the rocky, steep and slippery track before our flesh was stripped to the bone by biting insects. About an hour later on our speedy descent, Niall Cochrane and I met a platoon of camouflaged young Brazilian soldiers who were out on night-time jungle exercises. Each recruit had a machete in hand, a sight which instantly wrapped my heart around the back of my spine when I saw them all standing there staring with blades in hand. Our brief conversation with the chap in charge was mostly lost in translation. It was probably along the lines of 'What are you doing up here, you pack of clowns' and 'get the fuck off this mountain as fast as you can.' Our back markers had caught up as the last of the soldiers disappeared behind the curtain of impregnable black and green noise. We eventually made it to the bottom of the mountain pockmarked with bites, scrapes and covered in sticky muck, full of piss-taking giggles at the madness of the day we just had.

Our last engagement of the week before the contest action started in earnest was non-negotiable and compulsory for every team member. Ourselves and our best of frenemies, the British team, were to be guests of honour at a reception held in our honour at an even swankier hotel a few kilometres from where we were staying. We were being hosted by the Irish and British embassies in Rio. City dignitaries and the counsellors' families were all invited to mingle with both national surf teams. When we arrived the pool reception looked like somewhere you'd expect to find Prince Albert of Monaco drinking a martini. The guests didn't disappoint either, with the ladies in elegant evening frocks and the gentlemen all suited and booted and just as polite and engaging as I had imagined they would be. It was a mix of Irish and English counsellor staff with their sons, daughters and invited special guests and friends. There were a few glass-raising speeches welcoming us to Rio by both the Irish and British ambassadors. Our management returned the courtesy by thanking both embassies, staff and communities for their welcome, hospitality and the friendship between Britain and Ireland. Jameson, who were sponsoring the event, had provided the night with enough whiskey to quench the thirst of the Maracanã football crowd. The tuxedoed Brazilian waiters were obviously not up to speed on whiskey servings, which measured less in fingers and more in half pints. It was as if they were serving breakfast juice with each pour. At one stage of the night, I vaguely recall half the British and Irish team ended up in the pool. That was some evening's entertainment.

Our team performed well in Rio, despite the endless distractions of the Rio beach and nightlife. It was the first time I had experienced surfmania. The contest beach was packed with the toned-bodies of Brazilian surf fans every day. We didn't have a standout world-beating heat performance from anyone, but our overall placing of 16th out of 52 teams showed that there had been progress made throughout the ranks of the Irish team. It mightn't sound like a stellar finish, but in a global sport like surfing that had such established countries in the top 20 it was an impressive result for us. I usually have a clinical memory of my heats, especially in big events. Rio is the only international contest that I can't recall any of my heats in useful detail. I did get through a couple of heats in the main event and repêchage combined, hitting the target of inside the top 100 for myself. The open division proved much harder than the juniors I was used to. My lack of concentration could have had something to do with a beautiful Brazilian girl that I met at a meet and greet, as she worked for the event's main sponsor. For me as a 20-year-old, floating around on cloud nine with her proved more attractive than winning heats.

The three weeks the Irish team had spent in Brazil had flown by, and I was so glad I'd experienced a new part of the world.

## 17

# 'Calm waters have never made great sailors'

Anxiety never followed me into the surf. I loved waves: the bigger they were the better. Getting smashed around in huge surf is chaotic and life-threatening; it just depends on whether you embrace that fear or not. Some do enjoy the David v Goliath aspect of big surf, but the vast majority don't. I enjoyed it all: the intensity, the wild unpredictability and danger of it, even the wipe-outs. I loved that sense of a loss of control. Being at the absolute mercy of the sea and getting hammered excited me as much as it scared me. I would always come up laughing to myself and thinking, 'Christ almighty, that was some beating I just took.' My first reaction was, 'I'm going straight back out to get another one and try to make it', but if I didn't, I'd take the medicine willingly. Especially on the days when I'd surf big waves alone; it added another level of intensity and heightened awareness to the whole occasion.

In the scramble that my mind can be in sometimes, I had a large helping of the oddity that is obsessive compulsive disorder thrown in for good measure. If you have never suffered from

OCD, it seems completely bonkers to an outsider. In a way, when OCD is scrutinised from a non-suffering neutral perspective, it seems very peculiar, comical even. In my case, its effects by extension must have made me look completely off my rocker. OCD exhibited in me an impossible to ignore and impossible to switch off repetitive sequence of how I liked to do a task. I always needed to have everything in its place in the right order, or how I thought it should be. Let's just say something as simple as turning on and off the lights or pulling over the curtains, for example. Both are simple everyday autopilot tasks that ramped up to dire levels of obsession for me. I had to do both in the correct sequence that made complete numerical sense to me, and of course it had to be neat and tidy to the nth degree. Any deviation from this compulsion would cause a complete re-start.

Failure to complete, in my mind, would most certainly have led to an end of the world disaster or something truly dreadful happening to myself or loved ones. It was a torturous affliction to live with at times, especially in primary school through to my early teens. Chiefly because I knew how crazy it was and how mad I acted with it, if someone was to observe me in my OCD mode. Thankfully, anyone else viewing or being subjected to my mad ways was exceptionally rare. I became a bona fide expert in concealing it from pretty much everyone. I was a maestro at saying, 'Oh, wait a minute, I have got to run back inside before we leave.' Whereupon I could go about and complete any of the OCD tasks that I couldn't accomplish while others were present, for fear of ridicule and the dread of leaving with unfinished obsessions.

I knew what I was doing looked crazy to everyone else, but it made perfect, real-world structured sense to me. Understanding the complexity of the mind, especially with something like OCD and anxiety, is complicated to say the least for me. I taught myself the mouthful that anxiety was mostly caused by the release of the neurotransmitter Cholecystokinin (CCK). If it could be logically explained in a medical release, then my logical side could combat it. Anxiety and OCD effects and presentation differ greatly from person to person. Prioritising my OCD impulses felt so necessary to me back then. It took me a long time to wriggle free of its clutches. Slowly, I realised that the reality of me turning on and off the lights in the right sequence wouldn't cause a disaster. I know how ridiculous that must sound, but that was how it plagued me. I was extremely embarrassed by it all, but it was impossible to quench and unless you have had it, it's hard to explain how strong the pull is to acquiesce to its addictive demands. As I said, I became an expert in disguising it from everyone, except my mother that is. There was no fooling her, like there is no fooling most Irish mums. My mum was very good about it and helped me hugely with gentle persuasion, understanding and acknowledgment. I think she saw and understood my early connection to the sea as a good thing and a great distraction. Mum was a subscriber to the belief that 'if you believe in nothing, you will fall for anything'. She didn't peddle it in a religious way to me, rather a way to chase your dreams and work hard towards something you want. She saw surfing was my thing and encouraged me to go after it wholeheartedly. While out surfing my anxiety and OCD impulses melted into the background almost immediately.

As the teenage years hit, I'd wake up with a hangover from being out the night before in Hollies disco. I'd realise that I'd went to bed with Ebeneezer Goode ringing in my ears having failed to register or complete any of my OCD tasks. Bleary eyed, I'd get the message and surprise, surprise, miraculously the next morning the apocalypse was not upon me due to my incompleteness of having everything in a neat row and my clothes folded perfectly in the right compulsive sequence. Unfortunately, it was something that affected me greatly until my late teens but it has virtually disappeared since those days. As ridiculous as OCD sounds, when you are caught up in it it can be very physically and psychologically demanding. It has relentlessly oppressive symptoms however you spell it out and, in my case, was most exhausting in my inventive efforts to conceal it. I have never been a great exponent of self-pity. Feeling sorry for yourself was not a family trait of ours, so I worked hard on trying to find a solution to lift myself out of the rabbit hole when I started to slide down.

Many years ago, I had a long conversation with my good friend Colm who has always been ballast for me as I am for him when the chips are down. He is very clever, successful and career-driven in the corporate world overseas. We seldom see each other anymore, but when we do it's always a riot of conversation and some good counsel too. As we were saying cheerio after one of our protracted chats where we had resolved everything and solved nothing by turn, he said to me, 'You know, Fitzie, we are really very similar you and I,' to which I replied, 'Of course we are, misery loves company, don't you know?' I added that I hadn't made millions like him 'yet' and that he could barely swim, so let's draw a line under that similarity, shall we? He continued, 'We have always both been a bit different, even in school, moving sideways at times to a different drum beat than the norm . . . maybe even a wee bit mad, you know.' 'Go on,' I said. 'I already know that too, tell me something I don't know.' He said, 'It's not a bad thing to be a bit different, being normal is boring.'

He continued, 'You know what else, Fitzie? Always remember that 'Calm waters don't make great sailors.' It was a simple phrase, but it was a poignant one to say to me at the time. He knew it would resonate with me, having the desired effect long after he had left on his flying visit. It's six words I've kept close to me ever since.

~

Returning home from the World Championships in Brazil in May 1994, I felt the comedown from the roller-coaster high to a flatness again. It's a dangerous cycle of peak and trough emotions for me. I could easily then after the highs of Rio spiral down quite deep into a personal slump in a short period of time. When I let it take hold, the dark clouds of depression would set in on me and hold me in a vice-like grip. I would wake up some mornings feeling as though the bed sheets were made of lead pressing me down and a wave of dread washing through me. It's a horrible inward torment – and for me it was the incessant worrying and overthinking – to get yourself stuck in. After Rio, I missed the camaraderie of being away with a team, the pride of surfing for Ireland and the buzz of being at the World Championships. I moped around for a few weeks, not quite sure what to do with myself. A couple of years before, I had finished school with a very good Leaving Cert. I had applied for university places in Galway and Dublin and received offers for my preferences of studying English and History. Galway and Dublin to me were on the edge of the surfing solar system, and for the most selfish reasons, I or anyone else couldn't force my stubborn thinking into taking up one of the offers. I took the path of least resistance and did a short two-year course in sports management in the small college in Enniskillen. There was nothing wrong with it, but for me I knew it wouldn't challenge me academically. In my mind, I'd have more time to surf, and I could still live in Bundoran just a 45-minute drive away.

All-important was not missing any good surf. My mother glibly said to me that it was amazing when the wind was offshore and the surf was up, college was not worth attending for free classes and no lectures at all, but when it was onshore or flat it was operating again.

By 1994 I'd finished my short college course and was looking at what to do next. I had my first surf sponsor in Tiki for a couple of years, which was amazing from what I used to. I spent an informative few weeks in the Tiki surf shop and factory in Devon in the baking heat of that English summer, learning everything from surf sales to how to repair a wetsuit correctly. Our own surf shop in Bundoran was easily managed without me, it just took my sister or brother to run it in those days. As much as slotting into a life in the surf shop was attractive it wasn't a real financial option for me back then, not yet anyway. Our surf shop was busy in summer months relative to the number of surfers there were at that time. It wasn't however busy enough to sustain a year-round living even for one of us. My sister Karen, who is closest to me in age, was between jobs and suggested that we should go backpacking to Australia at the end of the summer. We applied for a one-year working visa, planning on being back home for the summer of 1995.

Australia at any time in surf history is a must see. There is not much in surfing that the Australians haven't had a strong hand in. For me though at the time, I had no burning desire to go to Australia, although it was home to my favourite surfers, like Tom Carroll and Mark Occhilupo. I had always seen California and Hawaii as surf capitals I wanted to visit before Australia. In saying that, I loved the brand of surfing that came out of Australia:

it was all about power and fearless surfing. The Aussies had dominated the sport in the 1960s, '70s and '80s, and apart from Tom Curren they were the top dogs. Big surf companies like Rip Curl, Quiksilver and Billabong had all originated in Australia. By the early '90s, the Aussie dominance was slipping, but as a surfing nation they were arguably still the best in the world in 1994.

We landed in Brisbane in early October. I had brought just one board with me. The worst thing you can do as a surfer is arrive somewhere with no board. If you do it's guaranteed that the surf will be brilliant, it's Murphy's Law. Bringing a whole quiver of boards from home seemed a crazy option, like bringing apples to the orchard. Karen and I planned to fit in as much travelling as possible around the island continent. Working would be required; we had some money but not near enough. We pledged to work as little as possible, just enough to do what we wanted. I knew very few Irish people who had been in Australia. The only surfer at home who I spoke to about Australia was Grant Robinson. He had been out there with the Irish surf team in Queensland for the World Championships in 1982. Grant gave me a few pointers of where to go along the Gold Coast and what to avoid. It was long before the modern exodus of Irish Down Under. In my eight months there, I didn't meet another Irish surfer or hear of any while travelling up and down the coast. Australia had so many compulsory surf stops for any surfer. My three must-see surf breaks were Margaret River on the west coast and the sand bottom point breaks in Queensland at Kirra and Burleigh Heads. The Queensland line-ups attracted most of the exposure and focus of surfing in Australia at that time. We bussed straight from the airport to the Gold Coast, checking into the nearest hostel. Within a few hours of landing in Australia, I was paddling out to the famous sandy mechanical lines of Kirra in boardshorts. It was heaven. Kirra was mega crowded that first day, as are most of the popular surf breaks in Australia. I was never put off or deterred by crowds. I felt I was well capable of surfing any of the waves I encountered along the coast. I already knew if you showed basic respect, cop on and exhibited a bit of guile in the surf, you could get your waves even in a swarming crowd of hundreds. The surfing standard all over Australia was out of this world for me to witness. I loved it, watching all ages in the pecking order in the water and every conceivable surf craft being ridden with fluidity and skill. The high standard of the Aussie surfers was inspirating for me. I thrived on how good the surfers were on all different waves and the different surfing styles on display. It was like watching a surf film every time I paddled out to the waves. Where Australia stood out from other surfing destinations I had been to before was that, while other countries may have had surf towns, surf regions and perhaps surf coasts, Australia was a surf nation. Its population were totally obsessed, respectful and engaged with the sea. Even watching the standard local surfers at every break along the coast was amazing for me. Now almost 30 years later the standard of surfing in Ireland has caught up massively, but in 1994 it looked like I was watching a different sport in Australia. The gulf was that wide.

We stayed on the Gold Coast until we had our fill of waves and jugs of poisonously bad beer called VB. It's much too easy to get sucked into the holiday lifestyle and all the night spots along Australia's high-rise sin city beaches of 'Surfers' Paradise'. Eventually you must move on, or you'll end up in a spin that's hard to leave. We headed north to Townsville and Bundaberg, two rough and ready bigger towns where you could pick up fast money working on industrial-sized farms. We entered the time-lapse zombie world of 3 a.m. starts working on a farm in searingly sticky heat, clouded and caked in dust. Our bodies acted as aircraft carriers for squadrons of the repressive army of millions of flies. We worked for a few weeks until our coffers were replenished. Bundaberg was the first town I'd ever seen where the furniture in a few of the pubs was screwed to the ground to stop them being used in a punch up. It still had a real frontier feel for a bigger town, and I liked it. Bundaberg was more of a Crocodile Dundee Australia than the neon Florida slick of the Gold Coast. We blew all our farm-earned money on a week-long chartered scuba dive boat off the less visited areas of the Great Barrier Reef. As we both had our diving qualifications, we got to have a few deeper night-time dives on the reef that were spectacular and spooky. It was the first time I had seen a shark underwater, a black tip reef shark about the same length as myself. It was just as frightened of me as I was of it. It torpedoed off the reef shelf away from me like a rocket into the blackness and out from the beam of my underwater light. Seeing the speed of the shark confirmed forever that if one fancied a bite to eat, you would never outswim or out paddle it to safety. It was not like you saw in the movies, that's for sure.

We re-located to the northern beaches in Sydney after a 17-hour-straight bus journey. I was determined to not end up in Kings Cross or The Rocks in Sydney working in an Irish pub for a few months before flying home. I wanted a different Aussie experience in Sydney, and my MO was to surf and learn as much as I could from this advanced surfing nation. We rented a room in a house with three eclectic local surfers above Avalon Beach. At night, I worked collecting empty glasses in the popular local pub in the Newport Arms Hotel. One of our house mates was a young, arty musician called Mark. He had the talent and the looks and was trying to make it big. The second fella in the house sold advertisement space for an Aussie surf mag. He worked out of the same publishing office as *Australian Penthouse*.

His room was a poor man's playboy mansion, with a blow-up sex doll sitting in the corner. The owner of the house, Col, was a lifelong northern beaches local surfer. Everyone knew Col and he knew everyone; he was a man about town. Being mates with Col meant you met all the real surfing fraternity along the coast.

Through Col I met Derek Hynd. Derek was and still is a cult figure in Australian surfing. A university graduate with a degree in economics, he was no slouch. He surfed as a professional on the world pro tour until 1982, before retiring at age 25 after losing his right eye from being struck by his surfboard. He continued to innovate in the water, surfing with only the use of his left eye. Like Miki Dora before him, Derek Hynd covered so many bases in surfing as a prominent journalist, industry original and film-maker. He did it all with idiosyncratic panache. He was a surfer who may have been too commercial to have been considered a counterculture hero, but he was cut from a different surfing cloth than everyone else. He was curious about Ireland and mildly intrigued to meet the rare species of a travelling Irish surfer. He told me he would swing by and pick me up for some morning surfs. Which he did with a completely erratic timetable of announced and unannounced 'swing-bys'. Some mornings he would chat the whole way to the beach about Ireland, Australia and everything under the sun. Other mornings he wouldn't utter a single word, not even a good morning.

One morning Derek told me we were swinging by to pick up his mate for a surf. His mate turned out to be two-times world champion and one of my favourite surfers, Tom Carroll. I had posters of Tom Carroll doing his famous snap at Pipeline in 1991 above my pillow in my bedroom back in Bundoran. I was beside myself with glee; I couldn't show it though, I had to stay semi-unfazed. Derek's waves of choice were just a short drive north in Whale Beach and Palm Beach, the real-world location of 'Summer Bay' for the Aussie soap opera *Home and Away*. We had a great day's surfing, and in the car park afterwards Tom Carroll wrote his telephone number down on a piece of paper for me and told me to give him a call, though I never did. Spending the day with these two surfing wizards of Oz was a pinch myself surreal moment that didn't sink in properly until I was back in Ireland.

Irish summer was approaching, and our time in Australia was coming to an end. Before I left, I got the sinking feeling that I'd missed something. I hadn't had a real standout surf or seen waves that knocked my socks off. The waves I had seen wouldn't have me running back to surf them again as soon as I could. I had travelled the length and breadth of the coast from west to east and down south. Arriving at Bells Beach in Victoria wasn't the postcard Australia you'd imagine. The water was cold, and the weather had the same inclement unpredictability you'd get back in Ireland, with plenty of winter days in summer. At Bells some of the locals said, 'Nah, mate, the surf's not that good around here, the real good waves are another three hours down the coast.' It was a recurring theme in Australia: it was hard to find those A+ waves. I couldn't shake the feeling of meeting your hero and being a little underwhelmed, which seemed to make no sense. I had surfed some of the most famous waves in the land in Margaret River, Byron Bay and Torquay and some less well-known off the beaten track. I had scored what locals called pumping surf at some of the spots. But in the eight months there I still hadn't seen anything that compared to the quality of the surf we had on the west coast of Ireland. It made me really appreciate what we had on the Irish coast. It was the first long lesson I would learn: that time and time again the realisation that I could travel around the world to far-flung dream destinations but only very occasionally have I ever seen or surfed waves as good as Ireland's Atlantic coast. When Kelly Slater calls Ireland's waves 'a cold-water paradise' you know you have something very special at home. I remember once hearing a boastful, heavy-hitter Hawaiian pro-surfer saying loud enough for everyone to hear that the only place a Hawaiian surfer could surf without going soft was Tahiti. I think you could add a third dimension to that and say the only place an Irish west coast surfer can go without going soft is Hawaii or Tahiti.

Australia may not have taken my breath away like it does to others. I had however really enjoyed my time there and learned a lot about surfing, mainly the reality of just how far behind I was to the standard of good surfers in Australia. I loved the respect the Aussies had shown for their coastline and environment. I couldn't stop thinking how much we could learn at home from this Aussie state of mind. I also couldn't get enough of how much surfing was part of everyday life in Australia. In the public eye and mainstream media, surfing was up there in the national sporting consciousness just like cricket and AFL were. I wasn't sad to be leaving Australia, as I really missed the perfect calibre and power of Irish waves. I thought to myself on the plane home that there were so many other places with better waves that I would go to before returning there again, if ever. Little did I know that within three months of arriving back in Ireland, a crew of maverick Aussie film-makers and some of Australia's best surfers would arrive in Bundoran locked and loaded. Over that summer and autumn, the Aussies in front of our eyes would not only turn Irish surfing on its head but also showcase our waves in such a way that it is still talked about today in glowing terms all over the world.

The Irish section from the culturally ground-breaking 1995 surf film *Litmus* by Jon Frank and Andrew Kidman was the first overseas surf production to contain world-class footage of surfing in Ireland. The Irish footage showed waves that could stand up to scrutiny in any international spotlight. *Litmus* became a global hit, and the Irish section was the centrepiece. The reason it resonated so well with surfers worldwide was that it gave back some soul to surfing, much like Jimmy Rabbitte and *The Commitments* did for music in north Dublin. By the mid-1990s, surf films were becoming formulaic where they were just a few years earlier revolutionary, with short sharp edits set to '90s new wave punk music. It's a widely held belief that *Litmus* saved the soul of the surf film industry. We were just lucky that the Aussies had settled on Bundoran as their destination of choice in Ireland. There was another distinctive shift of before and after *Litmus* in local Bundoran and Irish surfing. What was possible on Irish waves was challenged again, bringing to the fore just how special and peerless the northwest coast is. It changed the way we viewed Irish surfing within the country and how Irish surf was perceived from overseas. *Litmus* really brought Ireland to the global high table of world-class surfing destinations, and gave Irish waves the credibility that we as locals already knew they had. It set Irish surfing on a new, upwards performance trajectory that has continued ever since.

I didn't know any of the *Litmus* Aussie crew of Shaun Munro, Joel and Kye Fitzgerald, Jon Frank and Andrew Kidman before 1995, but Joel swears we are distant relations, our shared surname meaning his family's ancestry is Irish. With his standout performance, Joel was the real star of the show. Another funny thing about *Litmus* is most of the surf footage was taken in Bundoran during that scorching summer of 1995, not during the winter, when most modern Irish surf footage is shot. That year we had three long months of hot sun and pumping surf from the start of June until the end of August. The *Litmus* production crew turned up at the start of August in Bundoran for a maximum two-week stay and they ended up staying three months and getting the worst sunburn in Bundoran that summer. They were bright red and peeling for weeks. They had come from Aussie winter to Irish summer, and were not prepared for one of our hottest summers on record, and they got nuked.

The Aussies were skint, living hand to mouth on a budget of almost nothing, as is the way with any independent film-making. My mum to her eternal credit let them stay in our house for most of the duration of that three-month shoot. Without her, there would be no Irish section in the *Litmus* film. It's true that my mother was so involved and central to local surfing. To leave her out would be a travesty. Some of the big surfing moments took place under her roof and some of it beyond her control, but she was involved, nonetheless. In her lifetime, she has dispensed endless hours of surf reports and surf information to Irish surfers and international surfers visiting Ireland from all around the world. She has sold hundreds of surfboards and wetsuits in our surf shop, which isn't a bad record for a woman who doesn't overly enjoy getting in the water. Neither has she ever stood on a surfboard, caught a wave or put on a wetsuit in her life. My mother fed and looked after the van load of film-making and surfing Aussies. Joel was constantly injuring himself on Bundoran's shallow surf breaks like 3D and PMPA point. My mother had to patch him up daily and molly-coddle him. Joel was like a wounded puppy and cut the shape of an innocent, almost childlike fella. He had such an almost innocent simplicity to him that it always astonished me how he ever got through places like airports by himself. Joel was the prodigal son of Australian surfing at the time.

Most pro-surfers are well below average height; the smaller and lower your centre of gravity the better for surfing. It's a generalisation but it is a most common attribute for professional surfers. I'm not overly tall at 5 foot 11, but I tower above most of the pro-surfers I've ever met. Joel was a big bloke, well over 6 foot and built accordingly. Rather than a surfer he resembled a modern-day rugby full-back. He was fast, athletic and flexible, with that explosive Aussie style of power surfing to spare. Joel's physique and cavalier approach to surfing was a match made in heaven for the challenging heavy autumn swells that we got that year from August on. His surfing was a combination that I hadn't really seen before on Irish shores, at least not at the top-of-pile Aussie surfer level. His fearlessness, and with a skill level to match, was a perfect fit for the heavy, hollow and powerful waves of Bundoran. His surfing was always on an edge, critical positioning, take-offs and turns without a millimetre to spare. He stayed in tube rides until the wave stopped curling over, before he decided it was time to come out into the sun again. It was incredible stuff watching him slowing down and sticking inside the bowels of a wave. Tube rides can be fleeting moments and hard to control or stay in for very long, but here was Joel staying in the tube for the length of a boxer's standing count before re-emerging. His surfing was different in that he was always flirting with disaster on full power pushing each wave to the extreme, but he had the skill necessary to pull it off, unlike others I had watched with loads of heart and courage but not the skill to back it up. He very rarely fell or made a mistake in his all-guns-blazing approach, making it even more impressive. Over the course of a few weeks, he surfed 10–15 feet conditions at many of the waves considered very sketchy in south Donegal and Sligo. I had seen plenty of top-line surfers before, but when it's one of Australia's best young guns, it ratchets up anyone's attention. Here with Joel, I was watching him with my own eyes on my home waves, live and dangerous every day in seriously challenging conditions and in the water with him. The performance wake he left behind him in Ireland lingered for years. It demanded to be matched or bettered by every travelling pro-surfer coming through town thereafter. It also set a bar for me in what could be done on the waves I surfed every day.

The Irish soundtrack to *Litmus* is by a local band, The Screaming Orphans, made up of my Auntie Kathleen's daughters, Joan, Angela, Marie Therese and Grainne. The girls' musical accompaniment to the Irish surfing segment became a fan favourite around the world and projected them onto the global surfing airwaves. Their tracks were recorded in their front room on Sheil Avenue, Bundoran. The quartet of sisters almost seem to be unfairly talented in our already musical family. They have musical brilliance in abundance. All of them can play any instrument and sing anything; coupled with a high energy and overflowing personality they are a force on stage and a dynamite four-pronged attack of fun on land.

*Litmus* was the concept of photographer Jon Frank and writer/director Andrew Kidman. Jon came from Cronulla, another Sydney surfing suburb. It was the dangerous waves of Shark Island Cronulla where Jon learned his craft as an expert water photographer, shooting on its shallow, bone-crunching waves. Watching Jon setting up and in action in the waves around Donegal and Sligo, I learned much about the process of surf water photography, and how he positioned himself to capture the wave and surfer in frame but also how you could surf to get into that frame for the photographer.

Andrew was a former top Australian underage surfer and came to his film project with a pretty clear vision and drive for what he wanted *Litmus* to be. The Aussie boys were young, ambitious and just a few years older than me in their mid-twenties. Andrew modelled himself on Derek Hynd, who featured in and was a writer for *Litmus*. A detail which went a long way in explaining his inquisitive nature about Irish surfing when I met him a few months earlier in Australia. Andrew had a love for classic old '60s and '70s surf movies, and I think he wanted *Litmus* to hark back to that era of surf film. All the crew involved in *Litmus* brought something different to the project. They had virtually no production money, but they had the most important ingredient, and that was an abundance of enthusiasm for their film.

I still have a lot of memories and memorabilia from the *Litmus* shoot. One piece is the original Val Dusty Experiment single-fin surfboard that they had commissioned for the filming trip. The idea behind the board was that they brought it everywhere on planes, trains and automobiles with no board bag or protection just to see if it survived. It did, and it's still there alive and kicking.

Shaun Munro was one of Australia's hot-shot pro-surfers. I liked Shaun, he was a bit reserved, and you could tell he put his thinking cap on. He was well travelled and a bit of a hipster before modern hipsters existed. Shaun only stayed a few weeks, as he had his sponsorship and contest commitments.

Joel's brother Kye came to Bundoran a few days after the rest of the boys arrived, as he was at pro contest down in Newquay, Cornwall. Kye was very different to his brother Joel; he had that alternative look and attitude that reminded me of NBA basketball star Dennis Rodman in his heyday. He would dress very flamboyantly and was quite the apparition with his polished and painted fingers and toenails below a natural mop of bright blond hair that put any 1980s perm to shame. He exuded cockiness and a hyper-confident colourfulness that was hard not to admire.

Joel was hyped as Australia's golden child of surfing and he didn't disappoint, with an incredible pedigree in the surf; however it was Kye's surfing and style that appealed to me the most. He had his father Terry's 1960s poise in spades. Kye's surfing was the most aesthetic I had ever seen, top heavy on angles and soul arches, looping frontside bottom turns like no other. When *Litmus* was released, it was an immediate critical success.

Today the Irish section in *Litmus* lives on as a favourite throughout the surfing world. In Ireland, it is a snapshot of Bundoran and surfing in the northwest at the time. It contains the first water footage of heavy, hollow local waves like PMPA point and 3D with the summer beach crowds frolicking in the background. It's a time capsule for surfing in the town in the pre-boom Legoland-type construction era that was to wash over the coast. The whole film and especially the Irish section has worked its way into adoration levels with a younger 'Insta' generation of surfers that is rarely seen. It's amazing to see all the inspiration that *Litmus* led to. One sad result of the film is that shortly after its release the two main protagonists behind the project, Jon Frank and Andrew Kidman, fell out and have never worked together again.

It was a summer I will never forget: the rarity of three months of Mediterranean-like weather, and for us who surfed the bonus of endless waves and an iconic global surfing film shoot on our shores. I know it stands in the memory of most Irish people who lived through it.

## 18

# Surfing California 1996

In 1996, I was offered my first professional surfing contract. In hindsight, it feels like such a watershed moment for me, something I had projected myself towards as a big goal to achieve. If it was now, I'd be singing it from the high hills and broadcasting it online. Back in 1996, there was of course none of the social media we recognise now, but I didn't make a fuss of reaching that target or becoming the first Irish surfer to sign a professional contract. It wasn't life-changing money or anything you could solely live on. It totalled a couple of thousand pounds a year with performance and publicity incentives and more product than I could ever wear in or out of the water. It was money I could use for the personal expense I incurred when travelling to events as part of the Irish team.

I was on the road. I had got my foot in the financial door with a big company. I had built a strong portfolio in Irish surfing that was beginning to pay off in the way I had hoped it would. Getting a professional contract wasn't easy and didn't land in my lap. I had to put myself out there for it and prove my worth in every way. Surf companies don't just fire money at you as they are notoriously tight fisted with contract renumeration. I was starting to receive an awful lot of coverage in surfing and mainstream media that made for an impressive CV. They say you will never recoup anything close to your true value in publicity, but I was learning how to play that game too. I was still surfing in every contest I could and holding down one of the four places on the Irish open men's team that was always so precious to me. I loved surfing for Ireland more than anything. My new sponsor was more concerned about me building on my coverage in media and magazines than they were about any contest results. An impressive double-page spread in a big magazine was of much more value to them than surfing in a big international contest. Seeing photos of a surfer on big Irish waves was an attractive new departure for them. Even being a European team rider for a big international US surf company was a dream come true and something I had strived and worked towards.

If I tabulated the monetary cost of the exposure and publicity I received, it was always a massive chunk of money. For instance, I remember getting a double inside page of photos and an article in the *Sunday Times* in London during the late 1990s. All my sponsors were visible in the shots with a well-written piece by the journalist they had sent over to Ireland to spend a few days with me. After it was published, I would find out how much it cost to advertise in a double page in the *Sunday Times* by calling them up. The answer would have bought you a new car; it was massive money. I used this tactic of calculating my worth by finding out how much it would have cost in advertising to get the coverage I received per year. Some years it amounted to hundreds of thousands of pounds. It was impossible to calculate it accurately as TV, adverts and film were harder to put a value on than printed media. I would always round it well down, but when it came to contract negotiations, having a ballpark monetary value on what you were worth was a good thing to have in your back pocket. You could place yourself in that big money value, but your financial deal would only be the tiniest fraction of that amount. It wasn't until into the 2000s that I put a degree of separation for myself in these deals by employing an agent to help me broker contracts. Finding an agent to take on the dealings of a pro-surfer in Ireland would have been laughable until 2000. Putting the lifestyle aside, when you look at surfing purely in a sporting context it differs from all others. If you sign a professional deal with a football club you train during the week with your progression being assessed on your performance during the weekend match. I know there is more to football than that, but field sports are set in parameters that are a lot easier to understand than trying to do the same in surfing. Only a small percentage of the global interest and money in world surfing is based on the pro circuit or professional surfers. Suffice to say that only a miniscule number of surfers in the world are at any given time good enough to compete in that tight money-earning bracket of the top 32. You see surfers who make a much better living as a professional outside of that, as a free surfer or big-wave specialist.

Since meeting Gabe Davies in the late 1980s we had both made a conscious effort to spend a few weeks during school years and later a few months surfing together every year in autumn-winter or early spring in Ireland. From Gabe, I continually learned about the hustle you had to employ to keep yourself relevant and to keep alive a never-on-steady-footing world of a pro career. Gabe was a full-time pro, whereas for me it was at a much lower level. Nonetheless, watching how professionally Gabe handled himself really helped. Gabe was always a few steps beyond me in ability, equipment and approach. That suited me fine and gave me some-thing to chase and aspire to when watching him surf, seeing a new style of board he had or how he approached a tricky wave. The first generation of Irish surfers had laid down a trailblazing marker on many of Ireland's known waves. For us, we saw the second layer of Irish waves just begging to be surfed. Surf breaks that were just out of reach of the equipment and ability of some of the early pioneers. The coast was pockmarked with tantalising offshore reefs, slabs, inaccessible waves and ones that had previously been deemed too dangerous, too hollow, too shallow or just outright unsurfable. When Gabe and I got together, it was these waves that we obsessed on. Some were unsurfed and some unknown. A few surf breaks that are now household names to surfers in the northwest hadn't been discovered back then. It was still a few years before the introduction of jet ski-assisted surfing that would open up the 25-foot-plus realm. This was a new technique in which you used a jet ski to pull or tow the surfer into a wave that was moving too fast or was too big to catch by paddle power alone. Until then, Gabe and I paddled and explored as many waves as we could. We would work out the wave's limitations and ours along with it. If we felt we had a certain wave dialled in at say 6–8 foot then we would talk about how it would be on the next 10-foot swell. What tide, swell direction and wind would be best. Mentally Lego blocking up to the next level by putting another few feet on what we knew. Then we would enter into a discussion about what board would work best on a bigger day. It was a slow progression that was punctuated with some major leaps forward. Some progression we predicted for ourselves; more often than not that progression came out of the blue, blindsiding us to more possibilities. As soon as we worked out one break up to a certain size, we would readjust our objectives going at it again.

In 1996, I qualified for the World Championships again and this time they were to be held in the surfing mega-capital of southern California. I had probably foolishly always held California in such a dreamy aura in my mind. It was a common tendency of mine to build somewhere up to a level of unrealistic expectation. Whatever way you looked at it, to be part of a big surfing event in California was a billing to whet the appetite of any competitive surfer. It was a coast and culture that represented Americana at its most brash: Malibu, Surfing USA, LA, and maybe a chance to see the Hollywood sign.

The Irish team departed a week early as was the norm to get acclimatised to the lay of the land, or more accurately the sea off southern California, before the contest started. Arriving in California would prove a different adventure for any Irish team I had been on before. We were to be accommodated for our first week by the Irish-American community around Los Angeles. It sounded amazing. We all had a good laugh on the plane over with flights of fancy bouncing between team members of an Irish-American success story family like the Kennedys or John Ford's descendants picking us up in their Escalades and driving us to their mansions. We knew that was never going to be the case, but for some of us we couldn't have guessed that the reality would turn out to be so far at the other end of the scale. I think our team staying with host families was a necessary cost-saving strategy, although the offer for us to be their guests was made by the Irish diaspora many months in advance. We would be met at the airport by our host families, with individuals splitting up but re-convening every morning at the contest site. It felt like an odd thing to do as a team, landing as one cohesive unit at LAX and then dispersing into the sprawling mesh of the metropolis that LA is, especially at night.

Where you ended up seemed to be a lottery, with one or

two dodgy fixed tickets in the draw not left to chance. A few of the pre-determined winners on the team got families with nice beachfront condos or houses. Most ended up in tiny flats in the middle of urban concrete jungle LA, a very long way from the sea. As a senior, I was assigned two junior members to watch over as the three of us were grouped together for the same accommodation arrangements. The two teenaged boys I had were David O'Donnell and Colin O'Hare. I knew both boys well, as they were from just down the road in Strandhill. Now they must have put something in the Sligo water with this batch of Strandhill giants. The two boys cleared 6 foot 3 even as mid-teenagers. At home they came from an equally tall grouping of young Yeats Country surfers. Collectively, we called the Strandhill boys 'the 7-foot surfers' a name that still sticks today. As tall as they were, both boys were fantastic young surfers, and this trip to California wasn't their first rodeo. They were from an exciting generation of Irish juniors with a new confidence in their ability that were coming through the ranks. On paper, Colin, David and I seemed to draw a lucky straw with our family set-up, but the reality was anything but. I had been in the USA plenty of times before, but it was all east coast, so this was the first time on the west coast for all three of us. You know when you arrive from a long-haul flight landing in a strange city in the middle of the night that all you want to do is have a shower, something fresh to eat, a cup of tea and toast maybe, and a good night's sleep.

The family who picked us up seemed initially very nice but a bit too much on the airy-fairy side of things, telling us they would take us on a whistlestop tour of some of the sights on the way home from the airport. It was night-time but their generous sentiment of a spot of sightseeing excited us; we were in California after all. We presumed our noteworthy detours would be something like the Hollywood sign, perhaps. We quickly worked out that they thought they had inherited three Irish jackeens with one hoof still stuck in the primordial soup. By the manner in which they spoke to us, it became apparent that they presumed we had never seen tamed electricity at work, flushing toilets, paved roads, streetlights, food you didn't catch, skin and butcher yourself, or sand and salt water before. They had an Irish surname and claimed to be proud Irish-Americans. Their almost immediate braindead line of questioning should have set my alarm bells ringing. At first, I thought it was a joke before quickly realising to my horror that they were serious. Their image of us and Ireland started and abruptly ended in the year 1847. To them, being culturally Irish in America revolved around Lucky Charms, Irish Spring soap and the fighting leprechaun of Notre Dame college football team. I whispered to the boys to just answer normally and for God's sake don't say anything too cheeky or laugh in their faces. The boys couldn't have been more mannerly.

Our sightseeing tour consisted of them driving us up and down indistinguishable residential roads showing us traffic lights and what a Walmart, Barnes and Noble and Taco Bell looked like from the outside. They eventually stopped in a dark, deserted beach car park. Most beaches are off limits at night in the LA area. They told us however that there were no law enforcement officers in the area and that we could get out, and jump the wall copping a feel of the sand under the fence if we liked. Both boys had the shocked and confused gaze of a goat in a thunderstorm. Neither David nor Colin said a word, but as the grown-up I had to pipe up (bearing in mind we had been driving around for hours at this stage) pretending to be impressed. I said, I don't want to offend you folks, but we are really very tired and would love to stretch our legs, have a shower, get changed into clean clothes and get some rest. They looked a bit flabbergasted at my insolence in not wanting to view the exterior of another massive Costco, but they took us directly back to their house. We were chuffed when we pulled up to a nice big house not far from the beach. Each family had agreed to get their Irish team members down to the contest site in Huntington Beach early each morning. As he turned off the engine, the dad said, 'OK, jump out and you can get yourselves and your luggage into our campervan.' I thought that's fair enough, they don't know us from Adam so sleeping in their driveway in a campervan was a perfect set-up. The host family were under no obligation to provide us with food or entertainment. They just gave us somewhere to sleep at night and got us to the beach for the day, and we would make our own way back in the evening on the team minibus. The dad continued that we would be staying in the campervan down on the beach, which still sounded good. Probably out of tiredness or cluelessness on my part, we all bailed into the camper. No shower, no food – you'd swear we were crawling with black plague fleas the way they herded us in and away as fast as they could. We weren't allowed inside their house, and they told us there were toilets down at the beach. The dad jumped in and drove us on another mystery tour selection of different beaches to show us more of what a beach looked like. We still hadn't eaten or showered when I interjected again, saying with a bit more force this time to just take us to the location that they were dropping us at. We were too full of that classic Irish suffer-on-in-quiet-desperation-don't-make-a-fuss-of-yourself-at-any-cost mode. It was David's turn now; he decided to stick the knife in by saying we all lived by the beach at home, we know what sand is and we were keen to get some food and sleep. The dad told us it was too late for food, everywhere was closed at this time down around the beach, especially in the off-season.

We arrived at our final destination with bursting bladders. Having had no say on which beach we were left at, our home for the next week turned out to be the car park at Brookhurst Beach. It was 5 kilometres along the coast from the contest site at the citadel of surf that is Huntington Beach. I haven't been back there since, but back in 1996, Brookhurst Beach was a thin stretch of unattractive hard-packed sand that backs onto a multi-lane freeway. Across the road was an imposing power station with a standing army of massive, long-legged buzzing steel pylons and an industrial area. Between us and the beach was a concrete storm drain. Maybe the whole place looked and felt very different in high summer, but it was nothing short of a dystopian film set when we were there.

The dad dropped us off before being picked up by his wife, who we never really saw, only the back of her head and voice in the car. He took the keys of the campervan with him, afraid that we would drive away. He told us the battery had power that lasted for about 45 minutes of light. He also said he'd be back in the morning. We never saw him or our host family again. The campervan was dank, damp and had a musty smell. It was a sizeable RV but was rammed with all their family's personal effects and junk. It had three wet sponge mattresses for us to sleep on, boxes of their shoes, papers and clothes, folded piles of old curtains, trikes, bikes and big plastic containers of their kids' old toys. California dreaming it wasn't, but we had a laugh at how shit our situation was and our grand tour of foot-paths, sets of lights and the modern miracle of plumbing. To make it even worse the beach car park toilets and showers were shut up at the end of summer. It was off-season, so the car park was completely deserted by day. We were the only vehicle in this massive parking facility, but at night it was different.

The Brookhurst car park turned out to be an attraction for

all kinds of weirdos cruising and doing burnouts in their cars while pumping their music. The hanging about went on most of the night, with lots of shouting, buying and selling. I made an initial attempt to be friendly, but it went down like a lead balloon. That first night was pretty scary; we didn't sleep at all. We worked on a plan for when someone tried to break into the camper, we would hit them hard and run like hell for the freeway. We had a long night of ne'er-do-wells skulking about the camper that night and every night for the next week trying the door and banging on the side telling us to get lost.

Brian Britton had poached a surf coach off the French team, convincing him to come over as a full-time paid national surf coach for Ireland. His name was Peter Cook (or Cookie, as he came to be known), a wee, always smiling, quick-witted, machine-gun-fast-talking Aussie man with a fiery personality, and he suited the Irish team down to the ground. Peter had coached surfing in Australia at national level before taking the wheel of Europe's best: the French team. He proved to be a fantastic addition to the Irish set, singlehandedly taking Irish teams to places they hadn't been before, and adding that critical element of consistency in performance. Cookie had a very energetic and different view of Irish surfing. He was a great tactician and understood surfing inside and out. While we saw Irish surfing success as something of an occasional anomaly as rare as a lightning strike, Cookie with his winning mentality saw that we had incredible surf in Ireland with a rapidly developing surf scene and standard, so why couldn't we compete with the big dogs? Cookie had been parachuted into Irish surfing, taking the reins at sprinting pace with little time to settle in and get to know everyone. Luckily, he was in place for management of the team in California.

That first day by mid-morning, Peter Cook and Brian Britton

arrived down at Brookhurst with food. Cookie was ripping about the dispersal of the team and the predicament we had ended up in. Little could be done until we got to the team hotel at the end of the week. We told him we were grand and that it wasn't a big deal. We joined up with the team for the day's prep. Despite our nightly car park siege, I had a really good week running up to the championships. We surfed the waves in front of the contest podiums. We had a very memorable day's surfing at the famous but immensely crowded waves of Lower Trestles. I couldn't get enough of those high-performance waves; they suited my surfing. The peaky long waves had a feel of some of our less threatening and more playful northwest reefs at home. Huntington Beach is surf city USA on land, but it is often criticised in the surfing world for having below par surf. During the world's event there we got plenty of sizeable waves on the beach. The shape and breaking form of Huntington were far from perfect, but neither I nor anyone else could have complained about the surf we got for the duration. The team hotel was another odd one in that, unlike in Brazil and France, it was located well inland. The journey to and from the event was on specially chartered buses. So, surfing outside the arranged time on the beach wasn't easy, as there was no walking from the accommodation. I saw my first heat sheet the day before, and I had drawn the US No. 1 seed. Cookie had prepared us well in the team training weekends at home. He took me through a heat strategy based on the conditions and likely scenarios of needing a score, of holding a score or guile in jostling for position as the clock ran down. We talked about all outcomes. My confidence was high, especially as I felt the week of acclimatising to Californian surf had been my best lead-in to any event. It was another strong Irish team across the board, with my mate Dave Blount as one of the other open surfers.

We had for the first time the addition of two Irish passport-holding Californian pro-surfers in our ranks. It was always a controversial decision to include foreign imports into your national team. It is something that you see in almost every sport nowadays. I saw the inclusion of the two well-known Irish/American pro-surfing brothers Joe and Terrance McNulty as a necessary addition. The brothers had come across to surf in some Irish qualifying contests, and they had a genuine desire to surf for Ireland. This Californian team's event was open to full-time touring top 44 ASP pro-surfers for the first time. Most countries laced their teams with touring pros. The French had become the shrewdest in employing surfers from outside of France. Most of the French team were not born and raised in France. Their countries of origin included Morocco, French-Polynesia and Réunion Island. France had already become a headquarters for the global surf industry now they had realistically become the first European country challenging surfing's big four nations in the water. Surfing in France had leapt forward in less than 10 years, overtaking the old powerhouse of the UK and all other European countries. I know Brian had similar ambitions for Ireland with the addition of the McNulty brothers. His view was that a rising tide lifts all boats. The powerful US team had the star-spangled surfer Taylor Knox, who was one of the most recognised surfers in the world. I was glad to see the McNulty brothers on our team; it felt like we had heavy artillery to call on.

The parade of nations through Huntington and the opening ceremony was enthusiastically received by the thousands who lined the streets. The US and Irish teams seemed to get the biggest cheer of the day from the Californian crowd. Beyond our first week of questionable sleeping arrangements in the Brookhurst car park, I was loving everything else about California.

The next morning the contest was on. I had gone to bed brimming with measured expectation that I was good to go. I had a shallow interrupted night's sleep punctuated with excitement that quickly turned into rising anxiety. The next morning, I woke up plagued with fits of panic and an inner turmoil that I had manufactured for myself from nothing very substantial. I let in imagined worst-case scenarios, locking that and everything else into my head, magnifying it way out of proportion. What if I couldn't surf? What if my boards didn't go under my feet? What if I couldn't get my bloody feet on the board? Worst of all, I had a night full of my dreaded recurring vivid nightmare. The nightmare was always the same: me falling off a massive cliff backwards into water, no one hears my screams, I don't feel the impact but suddenly I'm in the water boxed in on all sides by a steep grey-walled quarry staring back. I can't stay afloat in the deep cold water; it's like treacle, I'm trapped in it, I'm running out of time and breath . . . and then I wake up in a sweat just before I go under. For a few moments, the vestiges of the nightmare in my mind feel scarily real. It's odd, as I have no fear of water, but I don't like the idea of falling or feeling claustrophobic. All of this and more had coalesced, taking up stubborn residence in my mind. It was no one's fault but by breakfast my usual considered pre-heat rationale had become arbitrary, and by the time I reached the contest site my internal surf accounting had bolted south for the Mexican border. I had replaced confidence with a spluttering panic that only I knew was happening. I had become a dab hand at never showing any obvious outward signs. I kept it all to myself. I just couldn't get out of my own head. Most of what worried me was concocted and imagined, but that didn't really matter, I just let it get on top of me before the heat. I wanted to do well or at least give a good account of myself at this contest. I was physically there at the water's edge waiting for the paddle out, but my head was somewhere else; I couldn't winch it back onto my shoulders.

Coming up against the US No. 1 in any sport is always going to be a challenge. I had drawn top seeds before, but the other two, a Canadian and an Argentinian in the four-man heat, were there for the taking. I never got off the starting blocks, instead taking all my baggage into the heat with me. Paddling out I had committed a mortal sin in letting anxiety hitch a ride into the surf with me for the first time ever. I fell off five waves in a row. My fitness was there, my wave count was good, but I just couldn't string any of it together. I've always been good at compartmentalising at times of pressure or stress, sticking something to the back of my mind until the task at hand is done. Nothing worked that morning. I felt bogged down in my mental molasses like I had never surfed before with my head cast to the wind. The surf conditions were good, my equipment was spot on, I'd no excuse other than getting in my own way.

The final buzzer couldn't come quickly enough to put me out of my misery as I had been combo-ed by the other three competitors. I felt sick getting a horrendously low score and finished last in the heat by a country mile. Walking up the beach through the watching crowd of hundreds, all the faces were looking down from the pier as the booming PA called out my Paddy last result. Cookie, being the professional coach that he was, didn't flip out. I knew I had underperformed, letting myself and the team down. He didn't have to say anything. I never minded losing a heat if I surfed to the best of my ability or went down fighting, but I had been demolished not surfing anything successfully. I knew I was better than that. Cookie said all the right things to me on the beach and at the team meeting later that evening. I had a second chance the next day in the repêchage round. It wasn't the end, but no more safety net. The next day and my next heat came around fast. Despite my best efforts and Cookie's wisdom to reset, the rot had set in and history repeated itself. I had an even worse heat than the day before, only this time it was in lower tier 2 repêchage. I should have advanced through that second heat, not easily – there are no easy heats in a world championship – but I should have had a good run in the reps, earning vital points for the team. Instead, I finished fourth again. Embarrassing. Two flat lasts, and on day two I was out before some of the divisions had even started. I contributed nothing to the team placings. My nightmare had come true. I had drowned in the treacle. I felt gut-wrenchingly disappointed and burning angry at myself. I never tried to blame anyone or anything else when things went bad. In the past, I could use a defeat or disappointment as motivation to come back better in the next heat or next wave. This time, I was out of the event so fast it was a 1-2 knockout combo in just over 24 hours. So many other surfers at home had competed to get on this team. I had secured a team place, but my showing was pathetic. I felt like an imposter with no rightful place on the team or at a big event like this.

I had a loyalty to the Irish team above all, so as soon as I could I re-engaged to support the other Irish surfers in their heats. Being down at the water's edge in full voice was a characteristic of the Irish team at all events. I stayed involved in all team preps and meetings. It was a bitter pill to swallow, but sulking about it never helps. My contest was over. I couldn't throw a tantrum and change that now, I could only learn from it. By the end of the event, despite my roasting, the Irish team had put in a stellar performance overall. Terrance McNulty had made it all the way to the second-last day in the round of 16. Joe McNulty surfed in two divisions, the open and longboard, which is a superhuman effort of logistics, concentration, discipline and fitness. He made it to the semi-final of the longboard. Joe's individual world placing for Ireland was only managed once previously by Brian Tobin 10 years earlier; however Brian's record stands, as he was in the open division. One of our bodyboarders broke into the top 10, finishing 9th in taking a heat down to the wire against the World No. 1 pro-boarder, Brazil's Guilherme Tâmega. The success of the Irish team in California was due to a combination of Brian Britton's ambition in taking on Peter Cook as coach, Cookie's new approach, and professionalism in the set-up. The McNulty brothers were the cherry on top of a confident Irish team that was reflective of the growing popularity and rapidly rising standard of surfing in Ireland.

## 19

# Costa Rica

When I got home from California, I felt all surfed out, burned out on everything to do with surfing in a way I had never felt before or since. The last few years up to 1996 surfing had been all-consuming in my life, just how I wanted it to be. It was a case of be careful what you wish for. I was young but I had got so caught up in surf goalsetting, developing myself in big waves, competing, becoming professional and the surf shop, that I'd lost sight of the fun side of surfing. I've always had plenty of drive and enthusiasm in me for something I want to achieve, work or surfing wise. I'll go at it for however long it takes. My problem is taking time to relax. I'm not very good at taking it easy. Lying about is something I can't do; even if I feel horribly sick, I'll force myself into feeling better by getting up to do something, anything, productive. I was failing to stand back from surfing, relax and appreciate it a bit more. The result of that drive was starting to make surfing a chore, which wasn't a healthy road to go down. Viewing surfing as a burden goes against the grain of what it is all about. For the next three months I didn't surf, I took a complete break. I played five-a-side indoor football most nights in St Patrick's parish hall. It was a completely different set of friends from surfing, it kept me super fit and I really enjoyed the rootless local banter with the boys and men playing each night. The one surfing thing I did was to stay focused on what was our growing surf shop. I was behind the counter every day and enjoyed the wintertime leisurely pace of the shop. You had time to chat to everyone. All the local surfers would come in, including my mates ribbing me for not surfing, telling me I was a prima donna. The surf shop was the local hub of surfing; we had all the regulars in and out every day. Half of them had never surfed but they just popped in for the craic and chat, which the shop had gained a reputation for, especially in the quieter months. My mate Jimi, with a wicked smirk on his face, told me I had become the priest of that parish.

I hadn't forgotten my abysmal run at the World Championships. It picked away at me every day. I called up my sponsor's Euro-team manager and offered to give back the money and told them I would understand if they wanted to cancel the contract. In all honesty, I felt too embarrassed to even have it. I thought there are a million kids in Australia, Brazil and America who would leave me for dust in surfing and were much more deserving of a pro deal. Here I am with a professional contract and I couldn't do better than two equal lasts. I was secretly hoping they would agree to end it. They re-iterated that they didn't base their deal with me on contests and didn't care if I stopped competing altogether. They just wanted to see me free surfing on big Irish waves when and where I could. It felt good, but I couldn't shake the notion that I was a phoney somehow. I was relieved that my professional contract was with a company we didn't deal with or have an account with in the surf shop. I'm not sure our wee surf shop at the time would have swung any deal-making with a global surf brand. Even so, I wanted to be clear of that nepotism in my personal surfing career and dealings.

I had a good mate in town called Mike Smith, a laid-back, mild-mannered Protestant fella from East Belfast. Mike started surfing on the Antrim coast before living in Devon for a few years, which really enhanced his surfing. He came out of the East Belfast 1980s surf/skate community. Mike had a skateboarder's style in the surf, and I credit him as the first Irish surfer who could regularly land aerial manoeuvres. After his stint in Devon, Mike had relocated to Bundoran. His being a few years older than me was no block to us becoming good mates. Both of us had talked about doing a trip together for a few months after Christmas. Our criteria was simple enough: somewhere hot, with good waves and where the pound stretched a long way. We settled on Central America. Our plan was to bring a two-man tent, boards, backpacks and we could sleep in or on our surfboard bags as we camped our way along the coast of Panama, Nicaragua and Costa Rica. It was the kind of trip with no real planning, no contacts, no bookings bar the flights and no real idea of where we were going – a trip that would scare the bejesus out of me now. Back then at that age, I was a lot braver and more carefree than I am now. I had stayed with Mike in Belfast a few times. His dad worked as senior prison warden at the Maze (Long Kesh) prison. Their house was a normal enough Irish house except for bulletproof this and bombproof that. His dad's car had extra steel on the bottom, and bulletproof glass. He would check underneath the car every morning in case of a device. Besides the pretty shocking ordeal of security measures, Mike's family were normal. Like so many folks I knew in the north, they had no interest in religion, fighting or sectarianism. They were always warm and welcoming to me. His dad loved to chat about music and claimed he had once played the saxophone with Belfast boy Van Morrison. I never had any reason to disbelieve him, as he was a good musician. As for Mike being a compatible travelling surf buddy, he was easy-going and a smooth, experienced surfer who proved to be the perfect companion. Growing up where he had, I knew he wouldn't freak out if the going got tough on the road at any stage.

We landed in San José, the capital city of Costa Rica, right in the centre of the country, to punishing heat and humidity. Sporting brilliantly white mid-winter Irish skin and being about half a foot taller than most residents, we stood out a fair bit. We had both crash-coursed in Spanish before we left Ireland. Languages are not my strong point, but I was amazed how quickly I learned passable Spanish and how much I picked up in a few months in Central America. We had been warned that the Coca-Cola central bus station in the city centre was a pick-pockets' free for all, with a mesh of pokey streets and low corrugated roofs full of street urchins around the station. The name of their game was for some kid to grab your bag and fire it up onto a roof, with their accomplice waiting to run off with it across the buildings. I had one friend who had surfed in Costa Rica before and that's exactly what happened him on the first day; he lost all his luggage bar his surfboards. Luckily, Mike and I were switched on and didn't lose anything.

If you look at Central America on a map, it's a thin stretch of land that for a surfer offers coast-to-coast access, from the Caribbean Sea on the east to the Pacific Ocean to the west. The best way to find out surf information on a country at the time was to get hold of the surf guide. I had mail ordered the surf guides to all three countries from *Surfer Magazine* in the USA. A surf guide is a bit rich for what they were. It was 20 pages of photocopied paper stapled together, but crucially they had the all-important surf information. Costa Rica was well-known in surfing, and it got a steady stream of US east coast surfers to its shores. As a country, Costa Rica had set an exemplary standard in abolishing their military in 1948. They re-directed their defence expenditure towards health, education and, more recently, re-wilding and environmental issues. As popular as Costa Rica was in the mid-1990s for surfing, when we got there surfer wise it was still a country with big swathes of empty coast. We took an eight-hour bus trip from San José to Dominical on the west coast. It was a bumpy journey on mostly unpaved roads. Dominical looked like exactly what it was, a tiny scattering of dwellings hacked out of the side of the steaming-hot rainforest. There was a small Red Cross camp in town. The owner of the land it was on – I still remember his name, Bernardo – had a side hustle where he rented a strip of grass adjacent to the Red Cross for US$1 a night. There was no accommodation, although I'm told the whole place is a big beach resort town and surf centre now. Back then, Mike and I were the only takers, and set up our tent on the scrub. There was a flow of families in and out of the Red Cross station. It had one tap and one dribbly outdoor shower hanging from a metal post, which we were told we could use. Costa Rica was a feast for the eyes and ears, full of tropical colour and beauty. Dominical felt pre-historic; with the smell of steaming earth, it was a place where you'd expect to see dinosaurs lumbering in and out of the leaf-heavy canopies. The surf looked class and we were paddling out within a hot minute of arrival. There were no other surfers out in the water. The sea temperature was a roasting 82 degrees and my skin went all pruney as if I was in a hot bath. I have never been in a sea more alive with creatures. Fish and God knows what else swarmed under the surface with constant splish-splashing above it. More than once, I had something collide with my board or body as I waited for a wave. On land was even hotter; the life and noise from the rainforest was more spectacular than anything I had experienced in Brazil or northern Queensland. Above it all, the howler monkeys reigned supreme in decibels as the jungle's DJs. They never stopped roaring and shouting. In the morning as we unzipped the tent, it was as if David Attenborough had dropped off another exotic animal for us to look at. Iguanas sunning themselves and rhinoceros beetles that looked fake they were so big became our most common companions as front-door morning guests.

We could buy bottles of water and squares of madeira cake at the desk in the Red Cross shack. Beyond that there was only one place to eat with a big evening meal. A local lady who never gave up her name had her house set back a few metres into the jungle. She had a generator and would cook in her tiny kitchen and offered an evening meal to anyone. She had a massive satellite dish as big as her tiny, wooden house. For $2 for us both, it was eggs, refried beans, chicken or omelettes and orange juice. I can be a creature of habit when I need to be, so eating the same thing at her house every night never bothered me in the slightest. There was a small army of wee children running about. The smallest toddler hid under her dress, but I never saw a father. She was a big woman and would crack eggs, cut and cook with her right hand while her left arm supported a newborn breast-feeding baby under a light scarf thrown over her shoulder as she cooked away every evening. Her gaze was never off the TV in the corner. Its small screen showed overacted Spanish-language soap operas for the entire time we were there. Her kids looked healthy and happy, and although she never smiled, laughed or really acknowledged that we were there, she wasn't grumpy either. She always called out after us 'mañana' (tomorrow), to which we replied 'Sí, gracias', saying it a few times as we walked away. After dinner it was back to the tent and that was that, unless you fancied a pitch-black all-out assault by bugs outside.

We travelled around the coast a lot and scored some memorable empty waves, sometimes for days on end. The famous right-hander at Witch's Rock was top of my list. Costa Rica rewarded us for crossing rivers or hiking miles along the coast to remote beaches. We surfed by ourselves most of the time, but despite that we sought out even more remote locations that felt like they had been transported back to 10,000 BC. The waves at Tamarindo and Playa Langosta were our favourites, with just a handful of American surfers around. We stumbled across one wave near there that we got for a week straight in brilliant conditions. Only once did we see a jeep with boards on top pull up. We stopped catching waves immediately, so it didn't look that good from a distance. The jeep drove away, and we started catching waves again. Our ambition let us bite off more than we could chew. Thinking we could cover three countries' coasts in a two-month spell was foolhardy, especially the way we were travelling. What I knew about Nicaragua was that the war between the Sandinistas and the Contra rebels had ended a few years before, in 1990. The country was still a bit on the wild west side of things, but Mike had bulletproof glass in his house at home, so how sketchy could it be? The stories of volcanic black sand perfect beach breaks in Nicaragua were alluring. We surfed just over the border and stayed a few nights in an abandoned and subsequently converted jailhouse. The holding cells had been turned into accommodation by an enterprising local chap. He told us that when the war stopped the jail doors were opened and all inside were let out. He had just taken over the building, as no one else seemed to want to claim it (that was his story anyway). He had put new mattresses on the bunks, installed new light bulbs and unlocked the cell door, and that was it. It was 50 cents a night and we got eaten alive by bugs in the rooms with glassless barred windows and no mosquito nets. Before we left our jailhouse palace, we heard commotion one evening, the voice of an American lady crying outside. We went out to investigate and were met by a bedraggled-looking American couple who were on their honeymoon. They had been driving their rented jeep along a remote jungle road up on the hills above the coast. The border was unclear and unmarked. We did see a few pick-up trucks with armed bucks in the back, never sure whether they were a quasi-military local police or bandits. Anytime you see shams in the back of a pick-up with machine guns, it's a good life lesson to avoid them like the plague. Mike and I had a Central America plan, and that was that we never wanted to look like we were worth robbing. We didn't wear watches or carry around bulging wallets or expensive cameras around our necks. We came up with ingenious ways of hiding our passports, return tickets and dollars when we were out surfing. Our tent was always exposed, but in saying that we didn't lose anything and were never threatened, robbed or pickpocketed. The American couple had been confronted by a few men with guns who stepped out of the jungle and told them to get out of the jeep, which they did. The gunmen stepped in and drove off. The couple had lost all their belongings, money, luggage, passports; all they had were the T-shirts and shorts they were wearing. They were panicked and distraught after walking down through the jungle to the coast. We told them the next bus would be in the morning, as they needed to get to the embassy in San José. We gave them $200, which was more than enough to get them there. We weren't flush with money, but even if we wanted to spend money we couldn't. We were staying in remote coastal areas with no facilities. I felt sorry for them; they looked like one of those spirited adventure couples you see wearing matching bandanas and hiking boots. Doing nothing for them wasn't an option; it was a shitty thing to happen on their honeymoon of all holidays. They were thankful to us and made the bus the next morning still in an awful state.

We headed back towards Dominical. On the way we met a friendly American surfer who had bought an old double-storey shack on the beach and was going to convert it into a guest-house. He had a satellite phone with him and told us we could use it. We paid him $10 each for a quick call home. It took about 10 minutes to connect, but seeing as it was my first contact with home since I left eight weeks earlier, I knew I was overdue to touch base. My mother's voice was one of relief in hearing us on the other end of the crackly delayed line. She was vexed, saying that together with Mike's parents they thought something awful must have happened to us. It took my mum a while to forgive me for not calling home earlier. Most of the places we stayed at in Central America had no electricity and certainly no phones. I know Nicaragua and Costa Rica are full of surf resorts now. Costa Rica has become a real-world leader in progressive national thinking and eco-tourism. In surfing terms, I am glad I saw it at that time, as much of its coast still felt well off the beaten surf track. At age 22, it seemed dramatic and a bit self-indulgent even to want to have a pull away from surfing like I did. Surfing is usually the tonic that people use to defuse themselves, and here I was before Costa Rica seeing surfing as a slog and to be avoided. I had become much too wound up with navel-gazing the next step of my personal surfing ladder that I had rarely paused for thought. That trip with Mike to Central America stripped it all back to its very basics of boards, tent and hunting for waves in absolute remoteness. On the journey home, I felt re-invigorated and back to a healthier, less narrow appreciation of surfing.

## 20

# Euro Surf '97 and the Malloys

I first encountered the Californian trio who were known the surfing world over simply as the Malloy brothers in 1996. I met Chris, the oldest brother, first when he unexpectedly popped into our surf shop in Bundoran one day. I knew exactly who he and his brothers were, the three of them part of the Taylor Steele Momentum Generation. Taylor Steele was a trailblazer of surf film-making. He featured California and Hawaii's brightest young stars in his surf 'rockumentary' films – a new wave, California punk version of surfing set to a soundtrack of bands like Pennywise and Offspring. This group became collectively known as the Momentum Generation, and they were about as famous as it was possible to be in surfing.

Chris said to me after initial pleasantries, 'Hey man, do you surf?' After I said yes, he continued, 'Do you know of any good left-handers in town?' I said yep, I love left-handers, let's go surf, so we did. The brothers were the darlings of surf films and print, making a name for themselves every winter in Hawaii. The middle brother Keith and youngest Dan were tackling the pro tour, with Dan jumping in and out of high fashion as a male model for designer brands. In surfing, Dan had recently won the biggest pro junior event in the world, the OP Pro junior at Huntington Beach. Ireland became a regular surf destination for the brothers when they were back in town in early autumn 1997 as part of a new surf film they were featuring in. From first meeting the Malloys, for the next 10 years or so I would step in and out of their lives as a friend in Ireland, Hawaii and California. Their effect on me wasn't a deliberate wave of their influential wand, rather it was just by the sheer act of being their mate and being welcomed into their world. I couldn't help but be influenced by them in a positive way and also, I have to admit, a little bit awed by the life they led.

If you have never heard of the Malloy brothers, they were much more than just career pro-surfers. The three boys came from an Irish-American family whose business is in ranching. Their grandmother was an Irish emigrant from Sligo, and there was Irish on their grandfather's side too. You could see their Irishness at their home ranch: the odd cracked shamrock mug, a harp pin on a bridle and an old dusty tricolour on the top corner of the stables. When I met the boys first, they were top pro-surfers for Billabong USA. They were involved with and on every surfing publication imaginable. Keith was on the world pro-tour; Dan was the young gun and Chris the oldest was a standout in Hawaii and the leader of the pack. The Malloys were the best example of multifaceted surfers I had ever met. They had their pro careers, but they were also designers, producers and film-makers. They had grown up on a ranch that was all about riding and breaking horses, roping cattle, shooting guns and drinking beer with Mexican ranch hands, and as young boys, riding in local rodeos was a big part of their lives.

Rightly or wrongly, I suppose I've always considered myself

outside the stereotypical surfer cast. Don't get me wrong, I love to surf, but the perceived surf lifestyle can be very limiting, and it's something I've never prescribed to. I enjoy so many other interests, activities and sports away from surfing. I'm not one to stand around whining if the wind blows onshore for three weeks. It's for this reason I think that I got on so well with the Malloy brothers. The Malloys let me step into their world, where they knew every pro-surfer and so many Hollywood and music stars. They were always introducing me as their good friend from Ireland and I was always accepted as their equal. When I was in their homes in California or Hawaii, their surfing mates were the most elite names imaginable, like Kelly Slater and Shane Dorian. Most of these pro-surfers I'd only ever seen on TV winning the US Open of surfing in front of 100,000 screaming fans, or on the cover of a magazine with a beautiful Hollywood actress under their arm. The situation I found myself in with the Malloys and their big celebrity friends took me a while to get used to.

The Malloys involved me in many of their projects, including the film *Thicker Than Water*, but when they called me one day and said they were coming over to make the new Bruce Brown movie *Step Into Liquid*, I knew it would be something much bigger than normal. Bruce Brown is a famous surf film-maker most well-known for the iconic surf movie *The Endless Summer*. The Malloys, the production crew and Bruce's son Dana Brown were coming to film a segment in Bundoran. The plan was to centre the piece around the Malloy brothers surfing and inter-acting in the northwest. Long story short, they ended up filming kids from my brother's secondary school (where he was a teacher) having a surf lesson from me. I thought the surf lesson footage would be a fade out to another scene or a few seconds at the end of a segment. I had no idea that it would be the main backbone of the whole Irish section and the sentimental heart of the film.

~

On returning from Costa Rica that year, I felt fully recharged and ready to get stuck into surfing from all angles again. Making the Irish team was my priority, turning over a new page from my double-whammy failure to launch in California. I had the coming summer to look forward to, as the surf shop was getting bigger and more legitimate as a profitable undertaking every year. Most important to me was that Bundoran was to host the European Surfing Championships for a second time that September. I knew the Malloy brothers were returning to Ireland in the autumn and I'd get a chance to chase some big early winter swells with Gabe for a few weeks after the championships. I had a lot to work towards. I did, however, make sure I stopped every so often to have a system check for surf overload, learning to relax for an evening and surf without an ulterior motive, just for the pure fun of it. My top priority was to make the Irish team again for the Euros. I had been 11 years old the first time it was held in town in 1985. Now it was a much bigger event and I'd get a chance to surf in it at home if I could manage a top-four points finish on the contest circuit. The selection events were running at the end of March through April and May, with the team announced in the first week of June, giving Cookie and the management team a three-month run-up with scheduled team-specific training weeks and weekends.

Qualifiers were held all around the coast, in Tramore, Lahinch, Strandhill, Rossnowlagh, Portrush and Bundoran. Competition was fierce for places, with much larger attendances than normal for a chance to surf in this home international. Surfers were coming out of the woodwork at home and overseas surfers with Irish citizenship coming over to compete. Attending every qualifier was essential, as your points were tallied at the end of each event with the highest tabulated combined scores making the national team. As it turned out, I had a brilliant run at the contests, getting enough points to qualify first for the open men's team with a contest in hand. Brian Britton, Roci Allen and the ISA had been working behind the scenes for a few years to put this event together. It was to be Brian's magnum opus. Guinness had come on board again as the capital sponsor, with Tourism Ireland and a host of secondary sponsors jumping on. There was a new corporate energy for Irish surfing that I had never seen before. Irish team gear was designed and sponsored by UK clothing company Saltrock. The whole two-week championships was to be very well financed and planned to an inch of its life. The Irish team was invited to Dublin for the launch of the contest at Guinness HQ. It was another flashy event that I really enjoyed. My Brookhurst car park mates Colin O'Hare and David O'Donnell, along with Rossnowlagh's Anna Lally, were all on the Irish team. Before the grand opening, we were asked to do a photo call for the press on Sandymount Beach. Sandymount is not an Irish surfing hotspot but it's a beach nonetheless. We suited up with boards in hand, running in and out of the water together as if we had just experienced the surf of our lives, with the Poolbeg chimneys standing to attention over our shoulders. The photos appeared the next day in most of the national newspapers, along with corny puns. I didn't mind one little bit; it's all part of surfing, with the build-up to the contest having grabbed more national attention than anything Irish surfing had before.

Three weeks before the big event I fell ill and ended up in hospital for 12 days. I had no choice but to drop my place on the team. The Irish surf team doctor had given me the benefit of the doubt for a week or so, but he delivered the bad news with just over a week to go before the contest started. I'd be in no shape to compete, which I already knew but didn't want to admit to myself. I wasn't pushed, and was given the respect by Irish surfing to relinquish my place on the team. I had contracted a serious strain of salmonella, which in its most basic form is just a bout of food poisoning. The strain I got was so serious that I nearly died from it. After I got out of hospital, I had many visits from the health board staff as they were keen to find the source of where I'd picked it up. They were most concerned about how badly it affected me.

Missing a European Championships in my hometown was gutting; I felt inconsolable as the opening day approached, I remember being so upset. I was 23 years young with an ambition dashed. To surf at a home international is an opportunity that only comes around every 10 years or so. That's when good friends and family count. In a strange way the disappointment I felt in California the year before was worse. Maybe that experience had given me a bit of steel, and within a few days I had compartmentalised my disappointment. I had lost what felt like half my body weight and all my muscle tone needed for surfing. I was still unwell, and surfing would have been just impossible even if I still had my place on the team. In fairness to Brian Britton and the rest of the Irish team, they included me in everything, even though I was as weak as water. Brian made sure I got the full team kit and let me carry the Irish flag through Bundoran during the opening and closing ceremony in front of the home crowds. I'll always remember him and my teammates for that. My mum, as she always does, managed to say the right things to make me feel better and to push on; she knew how important this was to me. Later that autumn when I felt suitably recovered, she booked a week's holiday to the Canary Islands for just her and me. We stayed in a great place, ate good food, lay by the pool and I surfed my brains out. Mum is a class act, and a surf trip with your mum is the best one. To help me recover, I was put on a course of steroids to build me back up. I hate taking tablets at the best of times, but in truth it was three years before I felt fully back to myself. I hated the idea of being a hypochondriac sitting around thinking about how sick I was and trying to recover. 'Just rest' was never me. I think in life sometimes, if you tell yourself you still feel sick, you will stay that way. It was mind over matter with me. I refused to be ill. Stubbornness is something I have in spades, and I suppose it can be turned into a virtue sometimes. So I got up and got going as soon as I could.

Euro Surf 1997 in Bundoran turned out to be a big success. The surf lay flat for the first week, but the competitors were bathed in hot, sunny weather. When the surf did hit, it came just in time to run the event in four-to-five-foot pumping foot waves on the reefs. I cheered my mate Gabe on, even though he was surfing for England, and he reached the quarter-finals. The Irish team surfed well throughout. I was a bit too ill to stand and watch for too long, but I made sure to watch Enniskillen's Grant Robinson win the masters division for Ireland. To have a European champion at a home event was a very special moment in Irish surfing, and I was delighted for Grant.

When the dust settled after the Euro Surf, I did some re-evaluation. I had two crappy setbacks at big events, one of which was out of my control, but I felt like I'd run down a dead end. Surfing for Ireland was still a priority, however. I didn't know it then, but I wouldn't surf in another contest or represent Ireland again for the next 14 years. It wasn't a forced hiatus from contests, it was more that big-wave surfing had wedged it out of place in my view. I had some memorable big-wave moments between 1995 and 1997, receiving lots of attention for the waves I was surfing, which went down well with the sponsors. My partnership and friendship with Gabe was going from strength to strength. We had opened a few doors in waves or wave sizes that hadn't been touched in Ireland before. We never stopped our ongoing conversation about all the unsurfed potential we still had in front of us, and how we should double our efforts in exploration and surfing along the coast. Gabe had his own professional career to think about. His world revolved around travelling the globe for his sponsors from his new home in the south of France. He wanted more than anything to surf on the west coast. Gabe committed to it, saying he would sacrifice exotic trips and sponsorship commitments just to get the Irish waves we had been staking out.

Before the Malloys left that autumn, Chris said to me to come out to them in Hawaii that winter. 'Rich, you will love the waves,' he said. I couldn't refuse. I was welcome to stay for the season and use their boards in their extensive rack. Who would turn that offer down?

# 21

# Hawaii

M y wife often says of someone with a bit of a swagger that they 'have tickets on themselves'. By the winter of 1997, I had a few surfing tickets on myself. If you are confident enough to strut, you must also be prepared to stumble and even trip over from time to time. The Hawaiian Islands offer plenty of opportunity to an aspiring surfer to do both. Hawaii looms in the consciousness of every surfer, with visions of grandeur and notions of ability beyond a local hero status. The mid-Pacific Islands are considered the Mount Everest and the spiritual Mecca of the sport of surfing. A trip to Hawaii for any serious surfer is as much a pilgrimage as it is about catching waves. The fabled North Shore of the third-largest island of Oahu is surfing's ground zero and the sport's ultimate proving ground within the island chain. It's a tiny speck of volcanic rock in the middle of the vast Pacific Ocean, home to the planet's most isolated city in Honolulu/Waikiki. Every winter the island becomes jam packed with the world's best surfers flying in from all corners of the globe. Over-exuberant surfing tourists mix with the local surfing population about as well as water does with oil. The whole season is frantic with hyper-focus, surf rage and friction on this tiny melting pot rock of surf mania. The island is known locally as 'The Gathering Place'. For surfers it humbles many and gives you a stiff shot of truth serum as to where you are on the international surfing graph.

You don't have to be one of the surfing faithful's flock of pilgrims or a cocksure, young gun pro-surfer to visit and surf the Hawaiian Islands. Many casual surfers visit the islands just to sit on the sand to witness the carnage, bravado and barrels that Oahu's North Shore dishes out every season. Seeing it all unfold live in front of you is worth the trip alone, even if you don't paddle out. If you are inclined to surf but don't fancy the pounding waves of the North Shore, you can always sip a piña colada after dipping your toe into the waters off the islands' softer south shore alternatives, like the *Magnum PI* soundstage of Waikiki. I was always pragmatic about going to Oahu's North Shore for the first time. I knew it was somewhere I wanted to go to test myself, and if anything, I was late to the party at 23.

Surfing uses the moniker 'the 7-mile miracle' when talking about the North Shore due to the high density of powerful waves on its tiny stretch of coast. Of the eight main islands that make up the Hawaiian archipelago, Oahu is the centrepiece, forming a large part of the 'Aloha' depiction we all have of the islands. The island chain is plonked in the middle of the Pacific Ocean, the result of the movement of the Pacific tectonic plate over a mid-ocean volcanic hotspot. It is an incredible place to witness the continuous volcanic creation of new land, but also its disappearance as older islands slip back under the ocean, over eons of time of course and not in real time. All the main islands have surf, but Oahu's is the Big Daddy.

It's always been such a magnet for surfers over wintertime as it gets long-ranging storm systems and open-ocean swells marauding down from Alaska to the north. In summer months, it gets hit with south swell charging up from the bowels of the colder, deep southern regions of the South Pacific. Most swells have travelled thousands of miles through uninterrupted deep ocean and arrive with incredible power before abruptly slamming into the islands, creating massive surf all along the Hawaiian coast. Like all mid-ocean islands there is no absolute rule in the sea of where, when or how swells should arrive. So, the Hawaiin Islands can get swell from pretty much any direction at any time of the year. Oahu offers an extensive smorgasbord of waves on all sides. Being a small island, if the wind is bad on one side you can easily travel to another coast in less than an hour to find more favourable offshore conditions, making it the perfect surfer's paradise.

My loose arrangement with Chris Malloy in the surf shop in Bundoran meant I arrived just before Christmas in Hawaii. I landed in Honolulu at night after a 35-hour journey from Dublin. At Heathrow airport on the way over, I met up with *Carve Magazine* photographer Mike Searle and some of the tiny group of UK surfers who were Oahu bound. We drove straight to the North Shore that night, but in a cloud of jet lag confusion and night-time disorientation I failed to find the Malloys' house.

The English contingent let me sleep in their rented car that first night. I woke up after three uncomfortable hours of sleep in the passenger's seat. Still feeling zonked out, I meandered my way bleary-eyed up the nearest sandy lane to the beach. I was greeted by 6–8 feet of blue Pacific power. There was nothing better to wash away jet lag and the anxiety of unfamiliarity I was feeling than the magnificent booming sound of turquoise waves smashing down and draining away on crushed white coral sand.

The blast of heat and musty smell of evaporating tropical rain off warm asphalt hit my nostrils. Although I'd come across it before in Central America and Indonesia – that strong aroma of tropical soil, decaying earth, foliage bountiful and balmy – the whole setting felt so alien, as I had just stepped out of the Irish winter two days previously. I caught a hold of my meandering self and found the Malloys' house shortly thereafter; fortunately it was just a short distance away. The three brothers were still in California, but their housemate Jeff let me in. He was a gentleman, a real 'stars and stripes apple pie kinda guy' who was very kind to the tiny contingent of two Irish and British surfers on the island that year. Jeff was a Flight Attendant for US Southwestern Airlines, with Captain America blond hair and college sports jock good looks. He had a mouth full of perfect white teeth that in Ireland would have required planning permission to go to the dentist. We returned Jeff's automatic friendship and good deeds towards us by calling him 'Jazzy Jeff the Air Hostess', which he didn't appreciate, but we never let up.

Jeff was and still is a hell of a good surfer and outdoorsman, who found a second career years later as a photographer, writer and adventurer for Patagonia, where he still is today. The Malloy house sat in the middle of the action at the heart of the 7-mile strip. It backed into the beach at Pūpūkea just down the sand from Pipeline and Backdoor, the heart of the whole Hawaiian surfing experience. The waves out the front of the house had one of the least appealing names in all surfdom, Gas Chambers, which that season amounted to no more than an almighty close-out shut down. Ninety-nine per cent of all breaking waves at Gas Chambers that season were unsurfable due to the shifting sand, or rather the lack thereof. On the plus side, it wasn't very crowded, as most rational surfers preferred their bodies with skin on.

If you had time and proximity to Gas Chambers, as I did, to get to know the wave intimately, it produced moments of surfing magic and fleeting glimpses of perfection. During the day when the tide was just right, it would open up and give you 60 minutes or so where it would peel left and right over a serrated blade-sharp reef two feet below the surface. You had to be on it, because as soon as the tide dropped out too low the peeling wave would go into hiding again and be replaced by an all at once collapsing wave above the knives-out reef below. It was a shallow spot even by North Shore standards that year, so wiping out there was sketchy and getting dragged across the reef left me with plenty of deep cuts and gashes as mementos of the trip. Gas Chambers became my go-to wave that season. It lived up to its reputation, with plenty of uneven chambers and caves under the water, leaving me with more than a few chastening experiences with close outs. In surfing terminology, a close out is when a wave shuts down all at once along its whole length, offering very little open face to surf. If you straighten out on a close out, you get rear ended by a juggernaut, and if you punch through the wave face you risk getting sucked back over the falls and dragged across the reef. The shallow walk in and out was like having a game of barefoot hopscotch on broken glass, but growing up in 1980s Bundoran meant at least I was a dab hand at après-nightclub broken glass avoidance. For me, Gas Chambers typified the conflicting brutal paradise that the Hawaiian Islands offer on land and sea.

The Malloys' house was also within walking distance to Pipeline, Backdoor, Off the Wall, Rockpile and beyond; every day, after I'd had my fill of near-death experiences at Gas Chambers, I would be looking for more thrills. At that time, you would get a small crew from the UK to Hawaii every year, including Gabe Davies, Russell Winter, Spencer Hargreaves and a host of bodyboarders. The Irish at the time were unheard of on the North Shore. Fellow Irishman Dave Blount had decided to make the pilgrimage that year too, and along with Dave we were the total Irish representation. A couple of years before my first trip to Hawaii, my mate and Irish champion Andy Hill had spent a season on the North Shore and showed me photos one day as we chatted in his surf shop in Portrush. They were of him surfing Pipeline. Imagine that, an Irishman successfully surfing Pipeline. Talking to Andy that day on the Co. Antrim coast gave me an extra incentive to go to Hawaii and see exactly what I was made of in surfing terms. I knew I wanted to have a certain amount of big-wave experience before making the voyage, so a couple more winters surfing Bundoran's reefs was in order before I went to Hawaii.

Dave and I opened our Hawaiian account on triple-overhead-sized waves at Laniakea, which is a real belter of a racetrack right-hander. Nothing like jumping off the deep end, but we were more than ready for it. Laniakea is the surfing equivalent of the Formula One straight section at Monza. You stick on the DRS and gallop down the line as fast as you can. When surfing Laniakea you must stick tight to the wave face, all the while hoping not to lose grip and spin out on its towering turquoise walls. When the surf is big at Laniakea, it is not a wave on which you want to open up your surfing with expressive turns and creative manoeuvres. Especially not that morning anyway, and not at that size. The Hawaiian coast is one of the most heavily localised surfing areas in the world. Almost every wave has traffic in its pack and a pecking order of serious local surfers. I have found on my travels to most countries across the globe that most of the surf localism is less hurtful as a bite than it is loud as a bark. In saying that, showing respect to the locals goes a very long way. That morning in Hawaii was not the time to test any of my conclusions about localism, especially on our first outing, so we didn't mess about. We were all business.

What a venue it was for our opening surf. Dave and I got some class waves that morning, the full-on Hawaiian experience. I can still remember charging down the line on thundering triple-overhead waves and watching Dave do the same. Laniakea was stacked with perfectly spaced waves lined up like the folds of an accordion out into the Pacific. After two hours we were cooked and paddled in. We assessed our maiden Hawaiian effort in the car park, recounting our heart-pounding big waves, and we concluded that essentially both of us had a successful Hawaiian surfing baptism.

As we quietly recalled and reviewed our individual waves, we were approached by two big local Polynesian lads. The two of them had been the alpha males in the surf that morning, ruling the roost on every set of waves that came through and calling the shots on who went on what wave and who didn't. Dave saw them coming first and said to me, 'Fitzie, it's too late to run, we're fucked.' We were sure we were in for a knuckle-sandwich welcome from these lads. They lumbered up beside us and said in their thick Hawaiian accents, 'Where you from, bra?' 'Ireland,' came the answer in unison. 'We ain't never met no surfers from Ireland, bra.' In the end, they gave us a massive aloha handshake and were very complimentary on how well we surfed big Laniakea on our virgin outing.

In surfing terms, myself and Dave were at the bottom of the food chain in Hawaiian line-ups. I didn't mind that feeling of being the absolute underdog with no seeding in the pecking order. The low billing always gave me burning desire when the surf got big. Dave and I had nothing to prove to anyone, but at the time we were both probably the most established Irish big-wave surfers, so we had something to prove to ourselves.

It was a board-breaking bonanza for me and Dave right from the get-go. We especially found the strip of waves along the

Pipeline and sunset stretch of beach broke boards like toothpicks; it became our surfboard graveyard. I paddled out one morning on a new, unused 7-foot pintail surfboard duck-diving my first wave at a place called Off the Wall. The board was pulled from my hands and flushed out between my legs. I was hog tied by the leash as the board got sucked backwards into oblivion. That was it for my new board: snapped in half, never to be used in action.

Luckily, the Malloy brothers had told me to use any boards I wanted at their house, so I extended that offer to Dave. The Malloys' house offered the Willy Wonka's Chocolate Factory of surfboards. There was every size, style and colour of board you could imagine. Board racks out the back were stuffed to over-flowing, piled high under the house, in the garage, in the bedrooms, boards everywhere. Now Blounty and I dipped our sticky fingers into that pot with aplomb. In fairness to the Malloy brothers, they were sound as a pound to us, as a new quiver of surfboards can set you back thousands of dollars. I snapped one of Keith's favourite big 7-foot boards at a wave called Seventh Hole on a big day. I lost control at the top of a substantially big hollow wave and fell arse first from a height, hitting the board 'people's elbow' style, with my tailbone taking the biggest impact. I broke the board in two and ended up walking like John Wayne for a few days. At the time I thought I'd broken my coccyx, as I went numb and came up for air in agony.

We met up with Jon Frank and Shaun Munro, who I knew from the *Litmus* shoot three years earlier. Jon was living in not much more than a broom cupboard he had rented under some-one's house behind Sunset Beach, such were the rewards for one of the best cameramen in the business. Shaun was in Hawaii for the contest season with his Aussie mate Boogs VandePolder. Boogs had just appeared on the cover of *Surfer* Magazine riding a Hawaiian beast of a wave. The cover shot propelled him into the spotlight that year. Boogs was a solid, no-nonsense Aussie power surfer from New South Wales. One day, I went along with Boogs to check a few spots around the coast as a really solid swell was wrapping around the island, so some lesser-known spots were on the menu that day.

We came to a spot called Hammerheads, which looked like big 10–20-foot waves by our best estimation. There was no one else out, so it was impossible to gauge it and judge scale. The wind and swell were running a cross offshore chop, and the water had a brackish orange hue from all the recent rain and the red clay run-off. The combination of nasty-looking water coupled with the name Hammerheads didn't have me brimming with confidence that morning. It's never a good idea to surf in murky run-off water for health reasons, but also because of sharks, especially bull sharks. We waxed up our boards and paddled in regardless, the waves breaking way offshore with intermittent big sets.

Boogs at the time was a considerably more experienced surfer than I was in big conditions. He proceeded to paddle about 100 yards further out than me. I stopped further in because I thought I was bang on the take-off spot. To me, Boogs was heading for the shipping lanes. I squeezed in a few medium waves and wondered at the madness of Boogs sitting way out in the open ocean. Of course he was right, as a really big set came swinging out of nowhere and caught me inside with my trousers down. A good battering was dished out to me. I was ecstatic that my leash or board didn't break under the pressure as the swim back to shore would have been a mammoth task. The water was full of sticks, branches and bits of junk from the run-off. I learned another valuable lesson that day. If the waves are big at a spot you have never surfed before, sit way off until you see a big set break and then triangulate your best positioning. I kept going after a heavy pummelling and ended up having a memorable surf. I got a few massive waves; well, they felt massive to me surfing them from way outside until they petered out on the brownish-orange water on the inside. It was like surfing in warm carrot juice with bits in it. That surf still stands out for me as one of the oddest big-wave sessions I've ever had. The weird water colour, the fear of hepatitis or other nasty ailments from dirty water, the threat of sharks, the rips, the freakishly big out-of-sync sets, the large number of tree trunks and amount of storm run-off in the water all added to the unlikeliness of having a good surf. That it turned out to be a watershed surf for me only highlights the beauty and attraction of Hawaii; even at its ugliest it can be memorable.

The Malloys took me under their wing when they were on the island, and they were generous in all respects. In a sport that lends itself too often to a culture of me, myself and I, it can be an extremely selfish and individualistic lifestyle that you lead. It's all about you catching the best wave for yourself. The Malloys bucked that trend, being exceptionally open and kind to me and the rest of the Irish and UK crew I was with that year. When Blounty and I eventually left the North Shore, we went home with more boards than we came out with.

I had preconceived ideas of what Hawaii was going to be like and found for the most part it lived up to my expectations. It had all the tropical beach perfection you could wish for: Waikiki/Honolulu on the south shore were full of flowery Hawaiian shirts, bikinis and tropical cocktails. Every type of surfboard under the sun was visible in the water. Locals and tourists frolicked around enjoying the area's soft rolling waves. Oahu's rural North Shore vibe has plenty of 'keep the north shore country' bumper stickers on show. It can be a contradiction among the beauty and perfect surf that there is a serious heroin and methamphetamine problem. One of the only take-away lunch spots back then was called Kammies, which was run by a very patient, old Japanese family. A daily visit to Kammies required wearing some sort of footwear to the kiosk, essential if you wanted to avoid stepping on discarded hypodermic needles and drug paraphernalia.

On my trips to Hawaii, I've never really discovered the true sense of what being Polynesian on the island was. Maybe the only exception has been through their culture of surfing. It is, after all, where the sport started. I was a bit naïve. The very fact that I was a surfer from the northwest of Ireland standing on a beach in Hawaii told me all I needed to know about Hawaiian culture and how it had influenced and filtered its way to the coastal fringes of Europe and into seaside towns like Bundoran.

I've been back to Hawaii a few times, since as much as any visit to Hawaii is a barrel of fun it is also an intensive course in surfing waves of consequence. One morning while in the Malloys' house I was snapped awake by excited, raspy voices and the sound of booming surf just beyond the bedroom window. Like I've said, the Malloys always treated me as an equal, which is all well and good until they pulled me from my slumber at 4 a.m. to tell me that Waimea Bay was on. The call came down the hallway to quicky grab an energy bar and some fruit for breakfast, as they already had a 10-foot board strapped to the roof for me ready to go. 'Get up, Fitzie! Grab your stuff, let's hit the road.' Waimea Bay is at the end of the North Shore and is Oahu's premium big wave. The place makes and breaks people, boards, careers and confidence. It's a very serious big-wave surf spot. I had my head pressed against the car window as we zoomed down the Cam highway trying to catch a glimpse of the surf through the trees and buildings in the darkness before the dawn hour. The boys were amped, saying it would be really big and perfect (like that was a good thing), and if we paddled out just at dawn, we might beat the crowd for the first hour or so. I was feeling nauseous, trying to think of a legitimate excuse not to paddle out. I needed to think of something unequivocal as an excuse that would get me out of surfing with my dignity intact. But it was too late for any back-pedalling. I couldn't come up with anything in time. The reality was, in surfing terms, I was not their equal. I was good but nowhere near where the standard of the three brothers and their mates were.

When we arrived, the surf wasn't as big as expected. 'Thanks be to Christ,' says I, but it was still sizeable and had proper Waimea sets breaking out the back. At a big-wave spot like Waimea there is an incredible amount of water moving around; Mullaghmore does the same thing. There is a large pecking order in the Waimea line-up, with a lot of jostling for position. A haole (non-native white boy) surfer like me had no hope of ever getting a wave at Waimea. We suited up wearing shortie wetsuits, as a thin layer of neoprene protection is an asset worth having at Waimea even in the tropical water. As we paddled out, I had the feeling that blood was draining from vital organs and butterflies with razor-blade-tipped wings were in my stomach. I was on my way out to surf the mighty Waimea Bay. We made it out the back and after a long wait one of the boys paddled for a good set wave as he was in the slot and had priority. He said to me, 'You paddle too, Fitzie, and just take off. Don't look back at me, just paddle for your life and take off.' The ploy worked and the wave was left to him by the pack. He took off with me on his wing a few metres further out. I paddled with my heart beating fast. I gave it an extra blast of three or four paddle strokes as I didn't want to get hung up in the strong offshore wind. Getting sucked over the falls into oblivion wasn't the start I was looking for. The extra paddling is like oversteer in a car that makes sure you take the corner, but you are forced to make sudden re-adjustments. My over paddle made the drop down the face a little later and more critical than it needed to be. The speed and beyond vertical face of the wave felt incredible; my fins were engaged with just the tail of my board in the face as I dropped in. When you feel the wind in your ears for a few moments on the drop, you know you are on a big wave. The spray in my face blinded me, forcing me to act on pure instinct for a second or two.

Once I knew I had made the drop, I put my foot down. Waimea is a short-duration wave with an unnatural concentration of power packed into every inch of water in the wave. It requires you to launch for the shoulder, getting clear of the cascade of exploding white water behind you. That first wave felt like I had just surfed the biggest wave of my life as I kicked out in the channel. I managed to catch a couple more with the boys running interference for me in an effort to keep me near the front of the surfing peloton. Eventually, I made a silly mistake, cutting across the inside of the wave during a prolonged lull, trying to cut out metres in an area called Pinballs to shorten the distance on my paddle back out. I was caught short by my inexperience when a big set loomed, feathering way out the back before breaking long before it hit me with still enough power to vacuum me up on the inside. The walls of white water dragged me to a forced introduction to the famous Waimea shore break. I got washing machine tumbled, chewed up and spat out onto the sand, dragging my 10-foot board behind me to safety. I couldn't help but smile, and so ended my first day at the Waimea school of ecstasy and agony.

People would always say the biggest adjustment to your surfing when going to Hawaii is the power of the place. That spookily enough was the one thing I found comparable. The transition to the power of Hawaiian waves was no different to the power of the waves I was surfing at home in Ireland. The strength and intensity of the Hawaiian waves are very similar to Ireland's northwest, only 20 degrees warmer in wintertime.

~

It was around this time that I started to get some high-profile exposure in surfing media outside of Europe. I had been paddling into some solid waves in Ireland and I had a good winter in Hawaii. I had been invited to a big-wave surfing event on the island of Madeira a couple of years before. Madeira was a relatively late discovery in world surfing terms, but it had some of the best big-wave spots in the northern hemisphere. On the back of this invite to Madeira, I received a notification to tell me that I had made the waiting (alternatives) list for the most prestigious big-wave surf contest in the world, the Quiksilver Eddie Aikau Big-Wave Invitational in Waimea Bay, Hawaii. Eddie Aikau was a 1970s lifeguard and big-wave surfer at Waimea Bay who during his career performed over 500 rescues. He is a revered figure in surfing, as he was tragically lost at sea in an attempt to reach land to raise the alarm when an ocean-going canoe he was crewing got into trouble during an island to island expedition. The contest is held in his honour every year. It only runs a couple of times a decade as the wave conditions to green light the event must be extreme, and often a whole winter season's swells don't reach the enormous wave height needed during the waiting period. My invite confirmation arrived from the organisers. It really was quite something to open up that envelope. I had no clue whatsoever that it was on the cards for me. To this day, I'm not sure of the mechanism and people responsible for that invite. I was humbled, terrified, excited and confused as to why I'd get an invite. The invited competitors totalled 55 for the event, and they are selected from the best big-wave, Waimea Hawaiian specialists and top pro-surfers in the world.

That 55 also includes 10 surfers in the standby list in case any main invitees pull out. I was told I was the first European to be considered for the event. Even with this privilege, I always only had an outside chance of competing. Many surfers would have had to drop out, and I was not top of the Alternative 10 list, but that didn't matter to me. It was the fact I'd even been considered for it that I found incredible.

Unfortunately, the contest didn't run the year I got the invite. The surf during the Hawaiian waiting period didn't reach the monstrous height required. If by chance it had gone ahead and I had got the call, I wonder if I would have accepted. I had answered the RSVP-style letter saying I was available, but if push had come to shove, would I have gone or wilted? Would I have been up to the task at the time? On reflection 24 years later, I think I would have been way out of my depth, but the truth is I'll never really know.

I feel I was a lucky man in the way I was finally introduced to Hawaii, its waves and its complex but colourful culture at the end of 1997. It will always be somewhere I can look back on, as a place where I felt surprisingly relaxed, confident and full of self-belief when it came to big-wave surfing. I didn't feel fazed by the challenge. I didn't hold back at all, and went for it. Hawaii, and in particular Oahu's North Shore, took me to another level and helped point me in the direction of where I wanted my surfing to go.

## 22

# Mullaghmore 2002

The year before the release of the 1991 Kathryn Bigelow film *Point Break* we started hearing reports (even in Ireland's northwest) of its production through the surfing rumour mill, magazines and word of mouth from travelling Californian surfers. This was a time, of course, before every bit of information and movie spoilers were available at the swipe of a thumb.

*Surfer* magazine in the States ran a short article in one issue about two of California's best and brightest young pro-surfers who were in the movie mix. Their names were Matt Archbold and Dino Andino, who were well known in the surfing world at the time. The two surfers had secured a dream gig and pay cheque as the surfing stunt doubles for Keanu Reeves and Patrick Swayze.

It seemed like we in the surfing world had access to an exclusive club that knew the inside track for the upcoming film. More news came down the rumour mill that Hawaiian lifeguard and big-wave surfer Darrick Doerner was being paid $10,000 to wipe-out deliberately on a huge wave at Waimea Bay in Hawaii as part of the movie's finale. At the time, the sum of money seemed enormous to me, as did his risk of death. Who in their right mind falls off a giant wave on purpose? Hawaii, by way of movie magic, was to stand in for Bells Beach in Australia. I watched the film when it was released. The actual surfing footage was pretty good, but for some unknown reason the editors had flipped the footage of Matt Archbold back to front.

Big tent-pole movies like *Point Break* were important for surfing, as they projected the sport into mainstream consciousness. *Point Break*, love it or hate it, was a cultural movie moment, and with its slew of quotable dialog it rightfully earned the title of 1990s guilty pleasure classic. The film undoubtedly encouraged people all over the world to try surfing. If I'm honest the film was a cheesy favourite of mine back then and still is today.

Gabe and I made a pact after our season in Hawaii. We had witnessed and surfed some big waves, coming out the other side without the usual shell shock that Hawaii can cause. We knew there were waves in the northwest of Ireland that matched the waves on the North Shore. Some of them we were surfing at the time, especially PMPA point, our very own Pipeline in Bundoran. We pushed each other with a small core of local surfers at PMPA during every swell. Mullaghmore, however, was our real focus, and by 1998/99 we had made it priority number one.

As the 1990s turned to the 2000s, me and Gabe would get the opportunity to work on many productions, big and small, in TV and film. In the early 2000s, I would meet and surf with Dino Andino of *Point Break* fame, surfing doubles in Bundoran as part of the short-lived and ill-conceived rebel pro-surfing tour.

When I first met Gabe, he was well beyond me in surfing terms; he was capable in waves of any size and for the first few years it was a master and apprentice relationship in the water.

As the years rolled by, I started to find my feet in bigger surf and develop improved techniques to claw back the gap between us ever so slightly. I still had that burning desire to get better with every surf. I became forensic about it, analysing every detail of equipment and where I was going wrong. I approached it from all sides. If I wasn't surfing I'd train, going on long hard runs no matter the weather. It always cleared my head and gave me my best ideas and most direct thought processes.

I would always push myself on runs in both time and distance, all the while milling in my head where I wanted to be in surfing over and over in my mind, willing it to happen, visualising it. I would say to myself, 'Why not, why not me? If I put in the hard work, it's possible, it's going to happen.' I really believed that, and it became very emotive for me.

I'd break down techniques frame by frame, visualise myself surfing big waves from take-off to kick out, slowing it down and speeding it up in my mind. Running over every situation and scenario that might present itself, good and bad, and how I'd deal with it. Any time I got a willing volunteer, I'd ask them to video me on the old camcorder, even in poor conditions. I'd come home, pop the tape in the VHS player and pick apart all my waves, my body dynamics, board positioning, speed or, more often than not, the lack of it. Everything in slow motion, while constantly pausing the action. I'd rewind and look again, being critical of myself. I'd try to detach myself with a spilt personality of good cop/bad cop histrionics, scolding myself with commentary where I'd gone wrong but most importantly the 'how' to make it better. I find it's easy to critique myself or someone else in surfing. Highlighting what's going wrong is the easy part; finding solutions is the harder assessment. I obsessed where I should be better. I looked at my surfing as a scrapbook. I had my own style and ability, but if I saw something in another surfer I would apply it to my scrapbook, filling in the pages year on year.

I would always finish off my training runs with sprints up and down the sand dunes on the beach, but with one big difference. If you are surfing big waves and you get hit, the air gets knocked out of you on most impacts or squeezed out of you with the pressure underwater. Surfing a big wave can be fast, and if you fall the impact and release of kinetic energy can be hard enough on impact alone to do damage. Then the wave gets hold of you and pulverises what's left in your tank. You very rarely get the chance to take a full breath before being sucked under into madness. It all happens fast and violently. So, to practise breath training by taking a big gulp of air and then seeing how long you could sprint flat out was futile. For me, I would exhale all the air in my lungs and then see how long I could go flat out, sprinting on empty. In the pool, I'd do the same thing: my starting point was again when my lungs were on absolute zero screaming for air, burning inside. Then you go and swim a length underwater with your eyes closed, or front crawl speed widths on the surface. By the end I'd be seeing stars and feeling faint, but I got control of that natural urge to gasp for air. After a lot of practising and training, I developed an ability to keep going with a good lung capacity and a mental strength to stay calm for a period of time without air. It's as much psychological as it is physical, teaching yourself not to panic or more important not to waste precious seconds panicking. My years of breath training led to me holding my breath well beyond 2 minutes under water. Conditioning was key, learning how to control myself served me well in many sticky situations, with one incident standing out above them all for me.

It was the wintertime in the early 2000s in Ireland's northwest. By this stage, Gabe and I had been surfing together for about 15 years, with bucketloads of experience in chasing and surfing big waves under our belt, including a few years at Mullaghmore, most of it alone. We had a shared vision of what we were doing and where we wanted to get to in the future, setting targets and ticking boxes along the way. That day, the ocean was in the throes of a violent winter storm. Angry and disorganised, the sea full of white horses with bitterly cold miserable weather only a degree or two above freezing, with wind chill bringing it well into minus values. The coast was being raked by hail and sleet storms galloping across Donegal Bay from Killybegs. The surf was big, which was a plus, but it was on the margin of being surfable with gale force, cross-onshore west-southwesterly winds. Almost everything was going against it as a workable surfing day. The Sligo and Leitrim mountains behind Mullaghmore were covered in snow, making the water temperature plummet due to the freshwater run-off from swollen rivers and fields. Every time a low hail cloud passed, it turned the sea black and reduced visibility to just a few metres.

We had of course been out on plenty of big waves of this size before, but on this day the sea conditions were desperately bad. We both went through the same preparation routine, checks of equipment. We sweated the small and big stuff well in advance of days like this when the North Atlantic gets vexed. That's what all the training and preparation is for, so you are as ready and as confident as you can be. We phoned Malin Head coast-guard station to let them know we were leaving the harbour and how many we were, a party of two, as was the norm on days like this. We relayed our estimated time of return, informing them that we had a phone, flares, life jackets, swim fins, etc., on the jet ski. I knew some of the staff working at Malin Coast Station, and they understood the craic with us, telling us to be safe and sensible, but they had long since stopped trying to talk us out of it.

When we got out there, we realised that the waves had a much worse case of cross-chop morning sickness running through their face than we had anticipated from land. I've always enjoyed the crazy, stormy, piercingly cold days that nobody else wanted a piece of. When Ireland gets horrendous wild winter weather, it always feels that extra few per cent more hardcore in Donegal Bay than anywhere else on the west coast.

The days we were most ready for were when the Met Office issued a severe weather warning, advising people to stay indoors and only travel if absolutely essential. Days like that usually mean massive surf if the wind plays ball with its direction. Heading into that environment you become about as switched on as you will ever feel when you are risking so much. Gabe and I would laugh to ourselves not in arrogance but at the pure insanity of it all. Actively wanting to put yourself in harm's way with extremely limited options for escape takes a certain mindset to get yourself tuned into. It's one of those basic instinct frames of mind: you either are that type of person, or you are not.

We kept some of these early sessions low key for fear of grandstanding as much as anything, not that anyone was watching or taking notice back then. That said, we didn't want to openly fly in the face of authority and ignore their weather warnings. We would get giddy like two schoolkids at break time blabbering away, slagging each other, and giving each other dead arms, with nerves, anticipation and adrenaline taps turned to the maximum. We were dizzy at the prospect of what we were about to do. Running through our plan for the session would bring all those emotions into line for me, and I'd feel quite calm, confident, placid almost, before we set off beyond the safe embrace of the harbour walls.

Gabe was good to have in my ear. He'd say, 'You've got this Rich, we've got this. We are well able for it, we are going to get some epic ones today . . . this is where we are meant to be, this is for us to be the first to tackle days like this.' No matter how big it was, Gabe always said to me whether paddling or tow surfing in Bundoran, Hawaii or anywhere else, 'Rich, you've been out in bigger days than this before, so no worries, you'll take it in your stride.' Gabe would have been a great commanding officer in another life. We had that sense that we were going into conditions no one else wanted anything to do with on land or sea. You would drive out the N15 Bundoran to Sligo road and people would be struggling to shut the front door of their houses with the wind and weather forcing cows and sheep into sheltered corners. We'd be heading out to mountainous freezing seas to go surfing. It seemed preposterous.

That day was painfully cold; I was already cut through to the bone by the biting wind chill. Before we got out beyond the harbour near the top of the headland, my body was trembling. Beyond the headland we could see double-storey-house-size waves breaking with explosive power, eating themselves alive before detonating on the rocks below the bluff. It was a rough ride out to sea once we left the shelter of the harbour, the jet ski struggling for traction and being buffeted with each new pyramid of swell.

My lips were numb, but we were used to this side effect. It ended up that you couldn't form words after five minutes out to sea. My inability to speak didn't matter much with the wind, engine noise, breaking waves and hoods on. We had long since learned through trial and error to mostly communicate using hand signals. When we were on the jet ski, we had developed our own set of signals for yes, no, wait, 1st, 2nd, 3rd wave, help, come get me or stay where you are, I'm OK and so on and so forth. I went on the tow rope first and I said to Gabe, 'I'm freezing!' I was shivering uncontrollably and laughing too at the pure raw, savage craziness of the day with no other souls out and about. No one in their right mind was anywhere near the ocean or the headland. We knew back then over those years that we were the only two surfers in the country or anywhere in Europe at that time out in conditions and waves of this size. There was something in that for me and I'm sure for Gabe too. It's the fatal attraction, the on-the-edge-of-oblivion-exclusivity of it all I suppose.

Gabe whipped me into a few big ones, mostly off set waves and avoiding the biggest ones for starters. I surfed them well and with confidence and got some circulation going, so it felt like my body was coming back to life a bit. My eyes were burning after the first wave. In conditions like this, your face ends up with windburn like your mid-winter white skin just got a blast of desert sun. The take-off on the waves that day was like falling down a 30-foot flight of stairs strewn with debris, there was so much flak on the face. Trying to keep control with the liquid roof of the house pitching after you, and that was just the first section. We swapped out and I towed Gabe into some ugly, angry waves bigger than my first salvo. Most of Gabe's waves looked to have more right exploding against a lighthouse in a storm than to be surfed. We swapped out again after 30 minutes so that neither of us got hypothermia driving the jet ski. We were both in the best wetsuits imaginable with neoprene overcoats, boots, hoods, gloves and thermal polypropylene under-neath. It all added up to thousands of Euros of kit, but no wetsuit in the world can stop that kind of cold when you are constantly getting wet and exposed to wind chill.

I told Gabe to get me on a set wave even if we had to wait a wee bit out the back. 'I want the first wave in the set,' I said, which was usually the biggest with the least turbulence in the foreground, having no bigger breaking waves out front to mess up the surface with air boils and foam or changing the depth of the water to be even shallower than it was.

You must wait outside the breaking zone treading in the freezing water like a water-skier holding a slack rope about 15 metres behind the jet ski. Gabe switched the jet ski engine off and we waited, getting swirled around by the movement of what felt like the whole Atlantic Ocean pulling us in every direction. Within five minutes a big set came rampaging across the bay. You can tell waves are properly big when they start to present way out to sea. When it's big enough from our sea-level point of view to obscure St John's Point (some of the tallest sea cliffs in Europe) and Killybegs in the distance, it indicates serious stuff is on final approach. Donegal Bay is a pretty deep stretch of water, with little continental shelf. The drop-off is steep, so a wave has to be very substantial to stand up in deep water in the middle of the bay like that. I knew it was a make or break set, and Gabe was going to stick me right on the spot on the biggest one, of that I had no doubt, he wouldn't hold back. Gabe got me right on the money, in early and at the right speed, the wave pitched up and started to horseshoe as it slowed down, sucking the untold tonnes of water off the reef as it reared up behind me hitting the shallows, sending a clear signal that it was about to throw out in a massive cylinder.

It was in the 35-to-40-foot face range, a whopper of a wave by any standards. It drew hard off the uneven reef and rock slabs. I pulled into its mid-face, avoiding a straight drop down the face and bottom turn that would have been suicidal with the chop. It engulfed me in the tube, the thing was huge from the inside so who knows what it looked like from the outside. I felt like I was inside a giant cylindrical Duracell battery with its opaque copper colour. That's all I remember. I must have been launched by a cross-wave chop running up the face. Hitting a big pothole and being buckarooed over the handlebars of your bicycle while freewheeling down a big hill gives you the same sensation. That feeling of 'Oh shit, I've no control, this is going to hurt.' The next second I was bouncing around like a bingo ball inside a drum until I penetrated the internal face of the wave and got sucked up and over the falls.

If you have ever dreamed you are falling off a cliff, well, that's exactly what going over the falls on a big wave feels like. It's a nightmare being pulled over and down a big waterfall, plus you get the almightiest physical clattering. It's something few people realise about big wipe-outs, just how savagely violent and physically punishing they can be. The possibility of broken bones, ripped sockets and muscles, cuts, bruises and the fear of hitting the bottom are ever present. Luckily, I've avoided major injuries in my surfing lifetime. I've only ever suffered minor to medium cuts, bruises and a few broken bones.

That wipe-out was completely black for me. Absolutely disoriented, I hit the bottom hard. I was being trashed around like a rag doll. I would always try to curl up in a ball to avoid breaking an arm or leg from the sheer force of water. As hard as I held on in the foetal position, my arms and legs got prised open and pulled into unnatural angles in the underwater whirlpool.

The force of air and water under pressure being pushed down is hard to describe. You are absolutely at its mercy. A fly in a tornado isn't far off. I described it once in a magazine interview over 20 years ago as being like someone standing 30 feet above you and pouring an Olympic-sized swimming pool down on your head.

I made it to the surface to be greeted by one of the most terrifying sights I had ever seen. The waves in the rest of the set were well spread out and lining up on me. My wipe-out had pushed me over further to the impact zone. Stacked up in front of me now was the rest of the set of 4 or 5 waves bearing down on me. I couldn't have been in a worse position. Gabe was way out in the channel on the jet ski and couldn't do anything anyway. No vessel, aircraft or person in the world can help you in situations like that. It's the loneliest, most terror-stricken place to find yourself. Shots of pure fear ran through my veins as I tried to come to terms with what was about to happen. I had only a brief moment to compose myself before the first one hit the rebound, with the impact of the white water from the breaking wave going way beyond the height of the original wave face, so I knew what was coming. I remember thinking to myself, 'Well, if this is it for you, if this is how it ends, you don't have anyone else to blame but yourself. You asked for this and here is the consequence.' Talking to myself in the third person before all hell breaks loose is a common recurring trait that I have. There is no team to back you up, no support, no place to hide or take cover, you can't even move or change position. Gabe was my first and last line of defence, and he was out of the fight.

That second wave of the set hit me like an enormous liquid guillotine landing square on my body. The impact instantly blew me into the air, my breath knocked out of me, and launched me forward. I free-fell for a moment and got pulled down deep, squeezed and then mercilessly tossed around. I was gasping for air, lungs screaming, but I had taught myself that, no matter what, you don't take a gulp under the water, or you are finished. I came to the surface in bits.

For as long as I can remember I have always had this mad internal debate going on in my head, especially during times of duress when fear or pain is involved. I seem to have a conversation with myself in the blink of an eye, but to me it feels like it goes on for a long time when I'm at it. I say to myself, 'You think that hurt? You have no idea. Wait until you see what's coming next, I'll show you, so harden the fuck up and get on with it.' It's an odd way to think or process difficult situations but it makes sense to me. I become aggressive with myself and very focused, which can come in handy. I've always had a high pain threshold, or rather an ability to switch it off for a while at least, and that applies to nasty wipe-outs too.

Gabe could see that it was time to make his move. Driving a jet ski in those conditions is a demanding test all in itself. Once a big wave has broken and peeled off, the walls of white water continue to cascade towards the shore. This surge eclipses everything in its path, pushing vast amounts of turbulent water in and pulling it back out again, rendering you powerless against its might. Every jet ski rescue we performed for each other was inside the surf line in the white water where no one wants to be. The aerated water and foam produced by big waves can often be a couple of feet thick. It can make swimming or even staying afloat on the surface extremely difficult, as aerated water loses buoyancy. For small watercraft like jet skis, it can make the engine cut out. It just sucks in air and coughs, slowing it to a standstill. You would frantically bounce the jet ski from side to side to try and get the engine to kick in again. The jet ski was our ark; if it failed, all was lost. Unfortunately, the sea is full of discarded plastic, fishing line and all sorts of rubbish which gets churned up during storms. If you got a piece of plastic bag, entangled seaweed, fishing line or rope sucked up from below, it wrapped around the shaft and choked the engine, so you'd have to be fast to dive under and use a knife to cut the blockage free. In doing this, you only had seconds before a wall of 30-foot white water hit and engulfed you.

Gabe showed outstanding bravery and skill to come in so deep with the jet ski and haul me out the second he got an opening. I wouldn't have made it out without him, I had zero left in the tank. It was still before the days of sleek impact vests and the now commonplace inflatable vests that use pressurised air to shoot you to the surface like an aircraft ejection seat. On that day, such equipment was still more than 10 years away from coming on the market.

~

Of course, Gabe and I didn't just jump from surfing Tullan Strand back in 1989 to Mullaghmore in 2002 without putting in a long apprenticeship to get there. We had spent the majority of the 1990s concentrating on paddling into the biggest, hollowest surf we could find. The generation of Irish surfers before me had opened many doors and explored the coast as best they could with the equipment and standards of the time. As the 1990s rolled in, Gabe and I had decided to expand on what had gone before. Waves like Gerlin Rock (G-Spot) in Leitrim were untouched, and PMPA point in Bundoran had been surfed before but only rarely and not to any substantial size. Both spots featured waves from rumours rather than reality, so we made it our mission statement to surf PMPA and G-Spot to their limits, whatever those were.

It entailed a big leap into the unknown for us, covering new ground daily and going from swell to swell in different conditions. We were good to our word: PMPA is now considered one of Europe's finest left-handed barrels and G-Spot is considered by many international surfers to be the equivalent in Europe of the famed Tahitian wave of Teahupo'o. They may have been just one level under Mullaghmore for intensity, but we pushed what was possible on these Irish waves at every opportunity. Much of the foundation and style of how marquee waves like PMPA point and G–Spot are surfed now is owed to Gabe's influence and how we approached those waves in the early years.

I had a different mainstream exposure than Gabe in the media at home and abroad. I did as many articles, interviews and pieces to camera for surf publications as I did for general media. If our early-2000s big-wave antics went mostly unnoticed, by the mid-2000s we were creating a real buzz about big-wave surfing in Ireland. I'd have phone messages and emails backed up from publications all looking to speak to me or Gabe or both. That sounds pretty cocky but it's true. I downplay it but that constant media attention was there for many years. There is a big differ-ence between confidence and arrogance, and we tried to stick to that. So over that period, through good and bad experiences, both Gabe and I had become very savvy when it came to dealing with media attention and our handling of the publicity. We did make mistakes, but we learned from them and moved on a little bit wiser each time.

Our focus in the water became more and more centred on Mullaghmore. In the late '90s I took Tom Curren out to look at Mullaghmore on a massive day, with 30-foot-plus waves, on one of his first trips over to Bundoran. It was breaking perfectly, but he said, 'No thanks, that's a tow-in wave', which is just as well, as I would have had to paddle out there with him. Curren was pretty taken aback by Mullaghmore; not that I needed it, but it was reaffirming to get the rubber stamp from the master himself. I'd been watching that wave for my whole surfing life. Big waves can break so fast, propelling you at speeds of up to 30 mph depending on the length of the wave. In trying to paddle into a wave like that, the fastest paddlers can move is about 5 mph going flat out. The wave will simply pick you up, move through you, and you get left behind. A few years earlier when I was on the North Shore I was watching maniacs using jet ski-assisted towing to overcome the speed problem and to surf waves that were too big to paddle into, which puts surfing waves like that into perspective. It hit me like a lightning bolt that day: that's the answer, and it was another one of those moments in my life. Now I'd seen it in action live, my head was racing with possibilities.

At the time most people, even in the surf industry, had no clue about tow-in equipment or how to get hold of what we were after. Gabe, through his contacts in France, managed to get a proper tow rope, rescue sled and basic clips and fasteners, all necessary for us to move forward. We were inexperienced and green when it came to tow-ins. We had no one to ask or follow, we were trying to work it all out ourselves, and no 'How to be a big-wave tow surfer' manual existed. We got hold of some heavy-duty tie-down marine-grade straps which would prove essential in the future to prevent flooding the ski if and when we managed to get a jet ski. I bought two wake-boarding impact vests that would have to do as flotation aids and offered some protection around your ribs and back.

The main obstacle to overcome was getting a jet ski. They were expensive, and we couldn't afford the £12k initial outlay for a two-stroke ski. On top of that we knew the jet ski would need all sorts of essential modifications, but who would do them for us was another hurdle to jump when that time came. Gabe's brother Jessy was heading to Hawaii the following winter and Gabe asked him to keep an eye out if he saw any tow boards for sale. If he did, he was under starters orders to grab one and to bring it back for us. It makes me laugh now that we were so naïve in what we needed. For us, just a tow board, in fact any tow board, would do. It felt like I was back in the 1980s and clueless at the start of my surf journey with my brother and sister. Again we were not fussy; we just wanted to get going. Jessy came through for us and brought back one of the tow boards that had been used in a big session at Log Cabins the year before. He had spotted it second hand in a surf shop in Haleiwa. The set-up suited us: it was laid out with foot straps for right-foot-forward surfers, which Gabe and I both are. In comparison to what boards look like now, our first tow board was a pre-historic relic. It was needle thin and narrow, a 7-foot 6 pintail almost as pointy at the nose as it was on the tail, like a lance. It served us well but was not manoeuvrable on the face at all; once you set your line you were locked in. It was the first tow board in Ireland, and by some miracle we never sold it on as we moved beyond it up the board ladder and added more boards to the quiver. I still have it now.

I had fished off Mullaghmore Head in a fishing boat a few times. We had paddled out there on small-wave days that we thought were enough just to get a look at the conditions, taking off on inside waves. On flat days in summer, I'd take my snorkel, face mask and spear gun and go spear fishing off there just to get a look at the reef and rock. I wanted to get an up-close look at what I was sure would be my future big-wave arena. It was something I had done for all the local surf spots I went out on: I liked to view them from under the water. It was a good and bad idea to see what was under the surface at Mullaghmore: the bottom is full of dark grey slabs of rock, deep gullies, caves and drop-offs; the whole area is a massed jumble of collapsed stones. It's almost as intimidating from below the surface as it is from above on a big day. It's been said that nature doesn't do straight lines; certainly nothing is straight or orderly about Mullaghmore below the waves.

A few years before I had met a young film-maker from Dublin called Joel Conroy. He had just returned from Australia, where he had been working as a crew member on a reality TV show. Joel was now attached to a pilot event that was to be the beginnings of a rebel surf tour breakaway from the established ASP World Tour. Some pro-surfers supported the rebels and jumped on, but many didn't. The rebel tour was fronted by my old early-morning Sydney surf taxi driver Derek Hynd and backed by Red Bull. Bundoran was chosen as a venue for the new tour, and this first visit was a reconnaissance dress rehearsal mission for the kick-off of the rebel tour the following year. I had been asked long before this day to get involved with them for local logistics and contacts, etc., which I did initially. I was also asked to join this recon trip that was hopping from one European surfing hot spot to another. A couple of months before the crew arrived, I jumped ship on the project and told them I wasn't interested. It was a big decision on my part at the time, one I didn't take lightly, as there was a lot of money and talent behind the venture and some great opportunities and doors opening possibilities. Their modus operandi was to make a new pro tour all about getting perfect world-class waves rather than just the same old famous locations with a lot of mediocre surf. In an ironic twist, the current CT 'Dream World' Tour is pretty much what this breakaway tour was trying to achieve back then.

The reason I pulled out was that a lot of the ideas were fantastic, but the application was non-existent. From the outset, the whole thing was a mess and descended into comical chaos. It was in the middle of this crew that I met Joel. He had just come back from Australia and was recrited into this rebel tour. Joel was a keen surfer and a smart, bohemian, artistic Dubliner, and we clicked right away. I remember when I decided to leave the project, I called Joel to tell him because I liked him and thought it was the decent thing to do. I remember saying to Joel on the phone, 'I'm sorry, I'm out mate. I don't like where this is all heading, and it doesn't feel right.' He responded, 'You know what Fitzie, I am doing the exact same thing', and he left too. We had come to the same conclusion independently.

I stayed in contact with Joel for the next few years. I told him in early 2001 what Gabe and I had planned to do, which was surf big at Mullaghmore. He told me to keep him in the loop, that he would love the chance to come up and shoot the footage of those first sessions.

We rented an ancient jet ski with a big No. 2 sticker on the front. I think it was an old racing ski from the late '80s. It was tiny and completely unfit for purpose but it was a case of beggars can't be choosers. Like years previously, we kit-bashed equipment into what we needed for Mullaghmore. Joel was good on his word and came up to Bundoran to film some of our preparations, training and first sessions at Mullaghmore. Joel turned the footage of us into a 45-minute-long film called *Eye of the Storm*. It did the film festivals in Ireland in 2003 and won the Stranger Than Fiction Documentary Film Festival in Dublin that year and screened on RTÉ TV soon after.

With Joel's film under our belts, it gave Gabe and I some ammo to look for a sponsor to try and get a newer jet ski that could be used properly at Mullaghmore. The wee rented ski we were using was sketchy in every way possible; with the engine conking out without warning it was an accident waiting to happen. In 2003, Joel introduced us to a fella called Philip Goode, who was then head of Red Bull in Ireland. This was 20 years ago, when Red Bull was not what it is today. He liked what he saw in what Gabe and I were trying to do at Mullaghmore and agreed to pay £6,000 towards the total cost of £9,000 for a new jet ski. All we had to agree was to have Red Bull logos on it. We got a lot of coverage for Philip and Red Bull over the next couple of years. Philip was a cool cat and ahead of his time with this kind of sponsorship. He also got us Gath Helmets and sailing life-jackets that looked great, but we couldn't really use them. Gabe and I went in £3,000 each and we had the first proper tow jet ski in the country, which was a big moment for us. Philip was moved up the Red Bull food chain to European level within a year or two. He told us our deal with Red Bull would continue. But the fella who took over from Philip told us Red Bull had no future in extreme action sports like big-wave surfing in Ireland and discontinued their association with us. We kept the jet ski but our short time with Red Bull was over; it was back to financing it all ourselves.

Gabe and I didn't let it affect us. We spent a lot of time day and night around my kitchen table, in the water and on the boat quay wall trying to work things out. Stuff like rope length, communication with each other, hand signals, speed when towing, pick-ups, fins, board lengths, board type, weight, how to get the straps right, literally hundreds of things we had to work out by ourselves. We had no other crew to bounce off or learn from. We used to train a lot out at Gerlin and big Tullan Strand; we would just run and run the ski through every condition we could. I'd drop Gabe on the beach at Tullan on a big, messy stormy 8-foot surf day just to practise navigating our way in and out to the beach on the jet ski to pick each other up, trying to avoid the avalanche of white water but also learning to punch our way through it. Gabe came up with a really effective way of standing on the jet ski to blast through white water without getting KO'd.

We took as many precautions as possible: we took flares, a radio, a phone in a waterproof pouch, swim fins and a knife to cut any flotsam and jetsam free that got stuck in the impeller.

Especially on the big days, our most important rule was DON'T LOSE THE JET SKI. We had no back-up, no safety net, so mistakes like flooding the ski or letting it get caught by a wave and wipe-out was unimaginable in our position for those first few solo years. We would have backed ourselves on swimming in, but anyone who has surfed Mullaghmore and finds themselves board-less and without ski or back-up out there knows it's a hell of a situation to find yourself in. Since then, I've seen a fair few skis go over on big waves there, and it's a horrifying sight.

I remember the jet ski sprung an oil leak and conked out once. Luckily, we were out of the impact zone out the back, waiting for a set when it happened. I had to paddle to shore and run through the fields. Gabe's wife Lauren was waiting on the road and we drove back to town, bought some oil and I paddled the wee drum of oil back out to the ski, which had drifted a lot with poor Gabe on board out on the high seas.

At the time Lauren would act as our beach marshal onshore; she had a phone and knew that if we lost the ski and were in trouble, she would call for coastguard rescue. Fortunately that never happened, but it came mighty close more than once. Lauren would be the only person watching from the road above Mullaghmore. How things have changed now.

It took three years to get our first real surf at Mullaghmore in waves of substantial size. It was complicated, as apart from our tow board everything else felt held together with Sellotape and superglue. I had paddled a few small days out there but with nothing over 6–8 foot. Our first proper session with the jet ski was in 15-foot surf as the tide crept in. It was a great moment for us both, in the way we had crossed that particular finish line only to open up a multiverse of bigger waves. It had been a combined effort over many years. As we expected, getting to that point was really only the start for us. We had got our first taste of what was possible at Mullaghmore, and we wanted much more. We reckoned the sky was the limit: Donegal Bay is a massive body of water, 22 miles across at its widest, and Mullaghmore can theoretically hold any size of waves. The bigger the swell gets the further out it breaks, and I've never seen it close out.

The tow-in surf scene had grown at a fast rate internationally, with new boundaries being pushed all the time. Gabe and I had garnered a fair share of attention from media in the UK, Ireland and overseas. Most of it was good. We were a tricky proposition to journalists only too keen to come up and write a piece on what this Irish big-wave surfing revolution was all about. It was all new and not seen before in the country or continent for that matter. I think some journalists struggled in where to place us. They weren't quite sure whether we were a quirky lifestyle piece, a straightforward sports story, adventurers or a novel curiosity. In truth, we were a mix of all of those things and something more. Early images weren't the crisp digital photos and footage you see today; most of our sessions went unrecorded, but in saying that we were producing some startling never-before-seen images coming out of the northwest. Some of our content was picked up all over the world. It's often said that it's not a good idea to be first, you can be forgotten about and it's easier for those after you to build on it. There is some truth in that; we were way ahead of the curve, but I wouldn't swap those days for anything.

There was a bit of snobbery in some quarters within surfing; an almost disbelief that this little surfing outpost in the north-west of Ireland was leading the way in European big-wave surfing with two surfers from the UK and Ireland holding the reins and knocking on the door of established norms. Some of this haughtiness was aimed directly at myself and Gabe. We didn't fit neatly into the required surfing typecast from the right countries. Some snide things were said, and it all got back to us eventually in one way or another. Surfing can be a bitchy sport. I tried to just concentrate on what we were doing, brushing off the negative comments as begrudgery. Most people, especially locally, were delighted to see our success. Our antics at Mullaghmore really raised the profile of the local area and Irish surfing as a whole.

At the time, footage and photos started to emerge of a big-wave spot in France near the headquarters of all the bigwig surf companies. The wave was called Belharra. It was then and still is today a legitimate big-wave spot and it garnered much attention. Gabe was closer to all the razzmatazz of the Euro surf scene. We weren't surfing Mullaghmore for the coverage, but we didn't shy away from it either. What we were building in big-wave surfing terms had a financial price tag. Apart from the personal effort, it cost a lot of money to get all the kit we needed, well in excess of 20,000 Euros. That would be a big outlay even now. It's a balancing act: if you get coverage, which we were, it has a financial value and can be used very effectively to attract sponsors. We knew this from the outset and were determined to push ahead ourselves no matter what support, sponsorship or not.

Gabe was one of Quiksilver's go-to European pro-surfers so he had all the contacts within the industry. He always told me that he never felt completely integrated or accepted as the solitary Brit in a sea of continental pros on Quiksilver's books. Gabe had brought our proposition to Quiksilver and others very early on, as far back as 2000, to see if any of the surf industry were interested in coming on board with us. We were looking for not only financial help but an ability to acquire equipment, advice, expertise, the loan of equipment, any sponsorship really.

We were open to working our way up and proving our worth in what was all a new surfing landscape. The answer we received time and time again was that's great fellas, but we don't have any marketing budget for this at all. That's fair enough, we thought. At the time, Gabe lived mostly in France and surfed Belharra. He knew it paled in comparison to Mullaghmore and was a very different beast to what we were surfing on the Sligo coastline, but it wasn't a case of ours is better than yours. We genuinely felt fair do's to the Belharra crew and more power to them, but what was happening on the French Atlantic coast was being rammed down the throat of European surfing as if nothing had come before or could compare to Belharra. There was more than an undercurrent of desire to establish Belharra as the next big thing in global surfing. Surf company money and resources that spared no expense were being thrown at Belharra; suddenly there was no shortage in the coffers of the marketing budgets with their floodgates wide open.

For comparison's sake, let's say Mullaghmore and Belharra are both big dinosaurs. Mullaghmore is a Tyrannosaurus rex while Belharra is Barney the purple dinosaur, both big dinosaurs no less but vastly different creatures. Mullaghmore could bite your head off, whereas Belharra was more likely to squeeze you to death over-enthusiastically while giving you a big cuddle. There was almost a glee among some within the surf industry that said, here comes Belharra rebalancing the powerbase of European big-wave surfing to its rightful spot, while downgrading a much less fashionable Irish west coast spot and relegating what was going on in Ireland to the past tense as an unwanted, short-lived insurrection. If it wasn't happening in France, Hawaii or some such destination with big globally recognised surfers, which Gabe and I were not, well then, it couldn't be happening at all. Gabe and I knew we were on the right track and on to something very special with what we were opening up in Mullaghmore. We kept our heads down and didn't deviate from our course or targets we had set. It was disheartening at the time, especially for Gabe, as we couldn't squeeze a penny or helping hand out of the surf industry to acquire the equipment we desperately needed, while they were firing out all sorts of support when it came to the continent. As time would tell, Belharra faded from the spotlight pretty fast and Mullaghmore's growing reputation only solidified, as word of the monster waves off the northwest coast began to spread internationally. Mullaghmore in time became the go-to European big-wave surf spot.

The waves at Mullaghmore take no prisoners, and there is no negotiation when you find yourself in a tight spot out there. My own state of mind and fitness levels had to be right and running in parallel with everything else we were doing and putting in place to conquer its waves. My own personal physical and mental strength when it came to big waves was really the most important element for me, especially in the early days when we didn't know what to expect and it was all virgin territory we were pushing into. I've always been an early riser and seem to get all my best work done in the morning hours, getting up long before the sun so I could get stuck into an hour or two of physical and mental preparation. Repetition and muscle memory is crucial for improving in surfing; do it until you can do it with your eyes closed was my mantra. Surfing is different because no two waves are the same: you can surf a 2-foot onshore beach break one day and 6-foot offshore reef break the next, so comparable repetition is hard to conjure up on a daily basis. In saying that, I set about working on a style of surfing that I could apply to any conditions and any board I was riding, within reason. Sportsmen and women get motivated by different things: what makes them tick is diverse. For me, it was always confidence based. How I felt confident was through fitness and preparation. If I didn't train and feel flexible, I surfed poorly no matter what the conditions. It was as much the internal psychological battle as it was the physical effort for me.

Not every hotshot surfer is going to make it as a professional contest, lifestyle or big-wave surfer. That's just down to a numbers game with a dollop of luck thrown in and a personal ability to make it happen. If you look at other sports like football or rugby, they are full of academy rejects; it's a conveyer belt of broken hearts and broken dreams. Surfing is a very individual sport like skiing, skateboarding, tennis or golf. The pitfalls in pro-surfing that I see more than in any other sport involve life after professionalism. Like no other sport, many successful pro-surfers who have had good careers end up on the scrap heap, penniless and without a skill set to go beyond it. Pro-surfing is very badly paid, contest earnings are a pittance in comparison to other sports, even sister sports like snowboarding attract much higher contracts and contest purses. Now there are surfers like Kelly Slater and Mick Fanning who have made millions through successful careers at the top with smart investments outside of the pro-tour to back their careers up. There are only a tiny handful of surfers in every generation who get to that level of financial security after retiring. Of the millions of surfers in the world, only about 50 of the pros in contest, big wave and lifestyle are making enough money from the sport to call it a proper pro-career. That is a minuscule number when compared to professional sports elsewhere.

## 23

# Ireland in the Spotlight

Driving south towards Dublin one Friday evening in 2000, I was really struck by the number of cars heading in the opposite direction with surfboards strapped to the roof. Every west-bound bunch of cars crawling out of the greater Dublin area seemed to have at least one with a surfboard racked. It's not as if the popularity of surfing in Ireland in the new millennium had snuck up and taken everyone by surprise. With our surf shop, I'd had in many ways the best view in which to see this surfing growth. The numbers heading north and west in the weekend surfing exodus from the Dublin suburbs was still a surprise to me. If surfing had exploded in Ireland in the 1990s, it went supersonic for the first decade of the new millennium. In every way, surfing continued to grow in Ireland throughout the financial good times of the 2000s.

In 2000, I was contracted to a French surf brand called Oxbow. It was a company that surged in popularity at the time. Their big international surf star was none other than superhero looka-like Laird Hamilton. The previous winter, Hamilton had surfed what was to become known as the Millennium Wave in Tahiti.

A wave of such proportions that made him look like a mini figure surfing in a tropical snow globe. Hamilton was no contest pro-surfer, he was more a surfing Adonis with superhuman aquatic exploits who had already gained legendary status in the surfing world. He is widely credited with re-introducing and popularising modern SUP'ing (stand-up paddleboarding), which is now seen in every river, lake, harbour, beach and ocean around the world. It was his Millennium Wave, however, that propelled him into the stratosphere. He became a must have at American institutions from *Sports Illustrated* and shaking hands with US presidents to opening corporate expos for Mastercard and luxury supercars. In the early 2000s, Laird Hamilton was everywhere.

In a testament to how Ireland was viewed in surfing, Hamilton's European press engagements were located at the resort of Inchydoney Island, Co. Cork that summer. As the Oxbow surfer in Ireland, I was invited down to the big weekend. There was one surfer in the UK sponsored by Oxbow. His name was Sam Bleakley, a laid-back, intelligent surfer and master longboarder whose timeless style hearkened back to a bygone era. As the Oxbow representatives for the UK and Ireland, Sam and I were to float around the fringes of the press weekend in case we were called upon.

As it turned out we were not needed for anything. The weather was roasting hot, and we had a fantastic weekend with Hamilton and the Oxbow crew. Watching Hamilton perform an endless two days of press interviews and seeing his professionalism throughout was impressive. Every glossy magazine from *Men's Health* to *GQ* were there plus a host of Irish media interest. I can't say I became good mates with Hamilton over the weekend, as we were both too busy for much downtime. He always had his professional veneer up, which made it feel like I was hanging out with Captain America. We did get to play 12 holes of golf, with my score being somewhere in the region of 100 over par. Eating morning and evening meals with Hamilton and getting two gym sessions and a beach run with him showed me a lot of what it took to get to his level. I was just at the start of my tow-surf-big-waves-above-20-feet career, so it was a good eye opener to see his downtime training, which was more than my maximum.

Between 1998 and 2002, Gabe and I were surfing to our limit in big waves, pushing hard and orchestrating ways that would get us to the marquee conditions and waves we wanted to get to. It was a journey that needed both skill and equipment upgrade to surf what and where we wanted to. While all my efforts were dedicated to that task – with big-wave surfing at Mullaghmore being the ultimate prize – something else came into my world, the how and why of it I'm still not quite sure. I was never too shy to jump at media opportunities. From 1990 to 2000, I had done a roomful of media. Most had been worthwhile, but inevitably there was some cheesy print media and TV that I regretted doing. If you don't have these experiences good or bad, you'll never learn, so that decade had taught me a lot.

By 2000, I had become more shrewd and pickier through experience with what media I agreed to. I stopped jumping at everything that came my way. These years heralded the big time for reality TV. I was contacted by a researcher at Channel 4 who wanted me to be a judge on their upcoming reality show called *Faking It*. One episode was a surfing piece based in Cornwall. They would take an absolute beginner and train him for a few months on how to surf. Then put him into a mix of intermediate surfers on waves at a Cornish beach. As a surfing 'expert', it was up to me and a panel of three other experts to pick out the novice from the surfers in the water if we could. That was the premise in a nutshell. I accepted the offer to be on the show, spending a few days filming in Cornwall. When *Faking It* screened in November 2002 it was a smash hit.

I've heard it said many times in our modern online world that you should never google yourself. It was something I have never done until recently. Googling myself turned out to be a useful way to check some details on media I had done over the years. I discovered that I had a Wikipedia and an IMDB page, two things I never realised I had. The thing that struck me was that of all the things I have done, the reality show *Faking It* sits at the top of many Google searches for my name. I enjoyed doing the show, but in the grand scheme of things I wouldn't put it anywhere near the top of the pile, but that's the way it is in Google world.

In Bundoran by the early 2000s, the town had gone through an almost complete facelift, with some good and some ill-conceived Celtic tiger Legoland building additions. The town felt in ways like someone in the Donegal County Council drafting office had taken planning inspiration from North Korea. The beach front (promenade) is a shining example of something that was done right during this period. It had been pedestrianised and paved with securing rock armour along the walk to stop undercutting and erosion, which greatly enhanced the shore-front experience. This new beach front was about to play host to the biggest, most high-profile surfing contest in Irish history.

By 2001, Irish surfing had some of the healthiest coffers in its history, and it was sending ever more successful and well-funded teams overseas to compete. The northwest was seeing more and more international and Irish surfers on its shores every week. Short-term rental holiday homes all along the coast were fully occupied on most weekends with visiting surfers from overseas and Ireland's east coast.

On a global scale, surf companies were also at their pinnacle. Quiksilver was the big-hitting industry leader no matter what way you looked at it. Quiksilver had Kelly Slater as its flag bearer. He was miles ahead of anyone in the history of the sport. Slater was proving to be a cultural and sporting sensation, fuelling surfing and Quiksilver's success.

I was involved early on when the idea of the Quiksilver World Masters being held in Bundoran was suggested. I acted as a liaison and local coordinator, advising and joining the dots for everything from accommodation and night-time entertainment to the contest venue itself. I signed on in a volunteer capacity for those roles, which seems a bit mad when I think of it now. You only learn from your experiences. I wouldn't say 'mistakes' in this case, not wanting to sound disingenuous as I enjoyed the event and would do it again in a heartbeat. Back then I wanted to be involved regardless and we owned the surf shop in town, plus I was totally immersed and completely engrossed in everything to do with surfing, and this was a big event that was about to hit our shores.

Quiksilver's man in Europe was an Australian called Phil Jarrett, who I met with several times in the year building up to the event. Phil was and still is an articulate man with integrity and a lifetime of experience in surfing, writing, publication and working at the upper echelons of the surf industry. I liked Phil's personality and found him to be easy to work with throughout. The premise for the Quiksilver Masters was to bring together all the past surfing world champions and global standouts for a contest and social gathering that helped to keep companies like Quiksilver connected to its roots.

It wasn't a vanity project, but neither was it the cut-throat world of pro-surfing; it was something in between, something more refined and dignified. It had as much to do with legacy and surfing philanthropy as it did with surfing heats, and much credit must be given to Quiksilver for running events like this. The opening of the event took place in Dublin with the competitors making their way northwest to Bundoran shortly after, with a few days of free surfing taken into consideration before the contest proper. I've had some heart-pounding sessions in the big Pacific power of Hawaii's North Shore. I've won a few tight heats in European Championships and got that feeling of crossing the line out in front. All those surfs have been individually seared into my memory for the rest of my life. So too has the surf I had at the Bundoran Peak on the eve of the Quiksilver Masters. The waves were idyllic and glassy, 4–5 foot, with a golden sunset. In the surf that evening was a fairy tale line-up of the surfing world's past champions. I watched three-time World Champion Tom Curren from California split the Peak and go right, while two-time World Champion Tommy Carroll from Australia elected to break left. The atmosphere in the water was electric. The next morning, we were greeted to a 3-foot choppy, broken swell and a conveyor belt of northwest onshore winds that stubbornly stayed in place for the whole event.

The surf didn't turn up like it can in Bundoran and conditions were banal at best for the remainder of the week, but at least there was surf at the reef for the whole event. The lack of world–class surf for the contest was a disappointment but inconsequential to the spirit of the event. I won't give you a minute by minute, heat by heat breakdown of the contest, but every match–up was thrilling. Ireland was awarded two wild card surfers for the event and it was left to me to nominate two Irish senior masters to represent the host nation. I was 27 at the time, so I took the decision seriously and had a good knowledge to make it. In the end, it was an easy choice for me to make but not an arbitrary one. I suggested local surfer and two-time European

Champion Grant Robinson and Waterford's Henry Moore, both of whom were still competitively surfing heats and charging big waves in Ireland. So, Ireland was well represented. Some of the heats like Garry Elkerton v Martin Potter and Tom Curren v Derek Ho were wallposter dream match-ups to watch take place on my home surf spot.

Australian legends Mark Richards and Gary Elkerton took top honours at the final bell. I got to know Gary over the event, he represented that brand of absolute raw Australian power surfing that you just don't see in modern surfers. Gary endeared himself to the Bundoran locals instantly with his big personality, and most critically he understood when in Ireland, he stood his rounds at the bar with the local boys. He chatted to everyone like he'd lived in town his whole life, and knew all the boys by name within half an hour. For me, I was delighted for him when he was crowned World Masters Champion in Bundoran, as he had been one of the world's most influential surfers but had been bridesmaid a few too many times. He surfed all his heats in board shorts during the contest including the finals. Not bad for a Queenslander in Bundoran in September.

The socialising and night-time events were as good as the action in the water. The best memory I have was on 1 September. The contest was having a forecasted lay day or two. Ireland was gearing up for our big World Cup 2002 play-off showdown against the Netherlands in Dublin that evening, and U2 were playing a massive concert at Slane Castle. Many of the competitors were keen to go to Slane to witness U2 at home. The U2 concert was completely sold out a year in advance even though Slane Castle is a gigantic open-air venue. Miraculously, tickets became available at extremely short notice. One of our local group had a long-time friendship with Larry Mullen going back to Italia '90. The U2 drummer is a die-hard Irish football supporter. I never asked how or where the U2 tickets came from, but on reflection it's safe to presume that connection was the source.

U2 rocked the foundations of the Slane Castle and its estate, where they played to over 160,000 fans over two nights. Ireland's Liverpool alumni Steve Finnan combined with Jason McAteer on stage for the televised World Cup match to send the country and Slane Castle erupting into hysteria. I recall mahogany-suntanned Hawaiian surfing gods, Californian three-time world champion style masters and Australian surfing icons being engulfed by an inundating sea of Irish jubilation as soon as the ball cruised past Van Der Sar in the Dutch goal for the Ireland winner, all before Bono took to the stage.

I had one of the veteran Australian pro-surfers tell me afterwards that in all his years around the world he had never experienced anything in sport or at a concert quite like that night in Slane. How the whole crowd reacted and how the entire country celebrated in unison for days afterwards had him speechless. I knew what he meant: to Irish people it was normal but blanket national passion like that doesn't happen in all four corners of the world. Ireland was still at a time when the country stood transfixed for big crunch sporting matches. The whole population was glued to the screens, with the only people on the streets being tourists and pretty much all cars on road during big games had foreign number plates. You still feel drops of that magic from time to time, but it's not what it once was.

The Quiksilver Masters in Bundoran left behind countless stories and thousands of memories for the people who witnessed it over those 10 days. With the international surfing spotlight very much on Ireland and my home town it was a special event to experience.

## 24

# Frances

Ten years in age separated myself and my oldest sister Frances. For me as a child and the rest of the Fitzgerald kids, she often crossed over into a second in command of our family. Being the youngest wee cub of the house, I especially felt the benefit of her older sister/motherly role more than anyone. There is a great comfort in having a squad of older siblings. You feel protected and content in the knowledge that you have a mini army in front of you constantly watching out for you while teaching you along the way. My early memories of Frances are all from an elevated perspective. She picked me up constantly and I saw the world from her point of view as if I was a biological 1970s 'GoPro' camera at her shoulder height. She constantly had me straddled on her hip as the ultimate accessory. When I look at old photos of that time, I think I was her real life 'Baby Born' doll. I feel equally blessed and cursed with my ability to remember in detail my early years. It's a beautiful thing to be able to recall some of my times as a toddler through to school age, but it can be tinged with lashings of melancholy. For me, it can be viewed through such an impenetrable thicket of emotion, that I wish sometimes I could screen wipe and escape it.

We were and still are a close family. Like most Irish families in the 1980s we all moved as one unit, shuffling and sliding across the arse-numbing wooden pews at Mass, with the constant landmines that were the kneeling bleachers. The genuflecting apparatus never failed to trip me up all the way along, no matter how fleet of foot I was. Having to listen to St Paul's paralysingly boring readings from Letters to the Corinthians had my mind wandering to dream waves and star systems beyond the death star. I used to think to myself, 'Who writes letters like that anyway?' Well, St Paul did. My youth was still an era of letter writing. Fair enough, not much had changed in 2,000 years since St Paul's times then. I felt the monthly letters I wrote were more exciting than anything in Scripture. My letters sounded something more like this: 'Dear Jim, could you please fix it for me to fly in a Spitfire and meet Darth Vader.'

If you grew up in Bundoran, swimming and jumping off Rougey Rocks was a rite of passage. As a family, we specialised in an all-at-once cliff dive off the top rocks, plunging us as one into the cold Atlantic 30 feet below. On one such synchronised jump, Frances missed the timing of her jump from the top rock, landing squarely on my brother's head as he hit the water first. The impact knocked him out cold. She immediately ducked under the water, lifting his head above the surface while she swam him in a cross-shoulder carry to the steps, hauling him out and bringing him back to consciousness. He had a mighty gash on his face and the scar is still visible today. We never told Mum what happened; it was our big secret. We instead concocted a story that he had tripped and fell on the way home, banging his face on the curb. If Mum had found out what really happened, she may have thought twice about our cliff-jumping escapades.

I was so light at the time that all the Fitzie kids hit the water long before I did. I practically floated down behind them, watching everyone else hit the water like little bombs going off.

Nobody in Bundoran had wetsuits back then. In summertime the water temperature increased dramatically. With a temperate climate that benefits massively from the full effect of the North Atlantic Drift in summer, it enabled us to stay in for hours. We kept swimming after school and weekends well into autumn. As winter's grip tightened, water temperatures dropped accordingly and it became much more an exercise of attrition. By the start of November, we would be so cold after 20 minutes in the sea that our skin would go pinky-red and we'd lose feeling all over. With purple knees, blue feet and hands that didn't work for good measure (we called the numbing hands granny fingers) and our ballooning skin swallowing up our wrists and ankles.

We had sibling fights of course, like all families, but they were never beyond the trivial. Squabbles were quickly resolved or quenched by an all-five effervesce for the sea and adventure. Frances had all the style in our family from my first memory of her to the last. She carried herself in all aspects of life with an unflappable ladylike conviction. In her younger years, she was above all a woman of the sea, a brilliant sea swimmer and Bundoran's first home-grown female surfer. She informed so much of my early development as a wee lad, nurturing my love of the sea. Frances inherited my mother's stoicism and she never suffered fools. She had no problem standing up for herself and what she felt was right. She wasn't uppity, but she had high standards for herself and expected the same in return. I remember her telling me at a young age to never leave the house looking dishevelled. 'Always turn your best side out, Richard,' she would say to me. It didn't matter whether it was for a simple trip to the shops or something more substantial. Always put your best foot forward. She once said to me, 'Richard, unless you are training or finished for the day don't go around in a tracksuit.' It's something I've carried with me since then, to never leave the house looking sloppy or sporting a tracksuit as regular attire. She encouraged me to 'stand on your own two feet to be your own man'. 'Your attitude will determine your altitude in everything you do,' was her advice for me. She wanted to set me on the right path in life, as Bundoran had a long list of vices available for youngsters growing up at that time. Frances wanted me to steer clear of all the pitfalls with a motherly rather than older sister approach. Having a boisterous mix of older sisters and a brother growing up served me well into the future, giving me that balanced outlook in life.

Frances had a steadfast love of Ireland's northwest. Her passion for the sea was infectious to us all. She hated to see the town and seafront strewn with rubbish and abused. One summer evening, when I was about five or six years old, the 'Famous Five' (as we saw ourselves) headed down to the beach for our usual evening swim. At the bottom of the steps there was a group of young skinheads, or boot boys as everyone called them back then, who were pissing and smashing bottles off the rocks and into the sand and sea. Unfortunately, this was a common sight in summer at weekends. Whatever snapped in her 16-year-old brain that evening set her on the warpath. She walked over to the group of lads after telling us four to stay where we were and passing me like a parcel to Annamarie. I remember what Frances said in her opening line to this jeering mob. She got right up in their faces and shouted, 'How would you like it if I pissed all over and smashed glass in your town?' She told them they were a disgrace and pushed a few of them forcefully, motioning them to leave the beach. She was brave and the rabble left, but not before a barrage of explicit insults that I thankfully didn't understand. I was frightened for my sister's safety; I was old enough to know she was outnumbered. My heart was crossways in my chest. She didn't exactly have the 'call in the cavalry' backup with us four if the group answered with their fists. I loved her bravery and flagrant disregard for her own safety to hammer home the point.

Even now, when we all get together for family meals, one particular event has passed into Fitzgerald family lore and gets retold with a lot of laughs. In September 1979, we were on a family holiday in New York. On the third morning, my dad decided to take us shopping to give my mum a bit of time to herself. My mother and father had very different styles of parenting. My mum was very much hands on and my dad was markedly hands off. My dad was at his most focused in music, but outside of that he could sometimes slip into deep space mode, detaching himself from the present reality. Maybe I've inherited that from him a bit. It wasn't born out of uncaring, it's just how he was; he was wired that way, as many men of his generation were. What seemed odd behaviour to everyone else was perfectly normal to him. So, off went the six of us to Fifth Avenue for a morning of shopping and donuts. We each had a wishlist of things we wanted. For me and my brother it was all about *Star Wars* figures and vehicles; nothing else mattered to kids in 1979 except *Star Wars*. We were both foaming at the mouth to get to FAO Schwarz's toys section. For my sisters it was rollerskates; the Astoria Ballroom in Bundoran had a weekly full-throttle roller disco set to the thumping soundtrack from *Saturday Night Fever* on repeat. White rollerskates with coloured polyurethane wheels were a must, and New York surely was the place to get them. New York of the late 1970s was a very different place than it is today. The city was much more dangerous, extremely run down in places, gritty, dirty with graffiti-covered walls and with sweaty heat in the subways that was at times unbearable.

Within 10 minutes of hitting Times Square we had become detached from our dad. He had one of his infamous mind farts and somehow lost us all in the Big Apple. We thankfully had stuck together, and as always, I was propped up on Frances's hip. We were all in that half-crying state of panic; everyone else in the city seemed to be twice our size and moving at pace on the busy pavements. New York, as all big cities do, seemed to completely ignore us. Looking back now, it was probably for the best that we went unnoticed. Frances as team leader took the bull by the horns and said, 'OK, we'll be alright, stop crying and no one start screaming, I know where our hotel is.' Luckily Mum had written down the hotel address and put it in Frances's bag just in case the worst-case scenario happened. We circled the wagons and had a family huddle in the doorway of a department store. Frances laid out the options for us. I think my vote didn't count anyway because I was too wee. I just wanted Han Solo, by hook or by crook, so I was in on anything that would get me the 3¾-inch plastic scoundrel smuggler. She said to us after we had calmed down, 'Right, we can get in a taxi back to the hotel or we can go get our toys and rollerskates ourselves.' She reassured us by saying everything would be fine. It was a pretty ballsy move for a teenaged girl from rural coastal Ireland to announce that plan of action in the centre of the world's most hectic metropolis.

We spent the next five hours or so shopping by ourselves in the sweltering heat of Manhattan. We rode the subway and walked endlessly in a quest for rollerskates and *Star Wars*. We bought our lunch at a 7-Eleven, eating turkey sandwiches and drinking chocolate milk on the Formica countertops facing out of the front window while peering out at the manic city just inches beyond the glass. We landed back at the hotel, exhausted and grimy, just before 2 p.m. like the final chapter in a Hardy Boys novel with bags full of *Star Wars* figures and rollerskates. In our minds, we had solved the mystery, proving the adults wrong. We were greeted by our mum, who was starting to lose her mind. She was in the process of gathering a search party of hotel staff and a New York cop from the sidewalk outside. My dad had only come back to the hotel 20 minutes before us, waiting until he returned before he raised the alarm by telling my mother he had lost us hours ago. Mum has often told us since how distressing that 20 minutes were when she realised we were alone in the city for most of the day. I'm sure she went through my dad like a hot knife through butter. He had spent the day doing his own thing in the city, whatever that was. I don't think my dad had fully registered the seriousness that he had lost his five kids in the city with the oldest being only 15 and youngest just five. On seeing us in the foyer of the hotel, he greeted us with a 'Well, sure, there you all are now, right, so emergency over.' He hadn't gone to the police or raised the alarm. The day ended well, but it could have easily been a not so happy ending. It was Frances again with her sangfroid ability to take charge in a crisis. To my five-year-old eyes, Frances was a big woman then and I felt no threat after the initial shock of our dad suddenly being lost in a sea of strange people. She made sure I got every *Star Wars* figure I wanted, and I was happy as Larry. Experiences like that lost day in New York helped to forge the identity and bond between us five siblings much more than any schooling or church ever could.

Nobel Prize-winning Irish playwright George Bernard Shaw has many famous literary attributes, not least his wisdom in timeless proverbs. Arguably his most quoted is: 'Youth is wasted on the young.' In the case of our family growing up, it didn't apply and couldn't have been further from the truth. As children and young adults, we embraced and experienced as much as we could. My mother encouraged us to give everything a go, which we did with various degrees of failure, success, happiness, defeat and sometimes inevitably sorrow. All this, my mum would say, was character building. She somehow knew on both an individual and collective level precisely the right amount of freedom and slack to give us. Nonetheless Mum was ever watchful and would haul us ashore whenever we needed it.

Almost all my early memories of surfing, sea swimming and beach adventures involve Frances in her capacity as family leader. I certainly wouldn't have evolved in surfing the way I did if it hadn't been for her and my brother. I felt safe with her in the water; she wouldn't let anything bad happen to me, and it gave me a confidence to spread my wings. I remember her pulling me out of a few situations where I'd managed to get caught in a rip or had gone way out of my depth in powerful waves. She would drag me back in with very little commotion, letting me catch my breath, then tell me to go at it again. By the time I hit secondary school as a teenager, my surfing had outgrown my brother-and-sister surfs with Frances. I had found my own circle of surf buddies, but I still swam and went to the beach almost every day with some family member. Even in the colder months, as our wetsuits got better we would have a surf or jump off the rocks on the Main Beach in sunshine or in hailstones. With the passing of a few decades since that time, I still look back at those years as the best days of my life.

At the age of 29, Frances was diagnosed with breast cancer. I was 19 at the time and it was a body blow to our family. It was the kind of hit that knocks the wind out of everything and resets what is most important in life. Of all the Fitzgerald siblings Frances was the healthiest: she was into healthy eating and exercise decades before it became commonplace. Of course, that's not how cancer works, but that's how I saw it. How could it happen to her of all people, a girl who was fit as a fiddle, who never smoked, barely drank and ate healthy food?

She had her operations with aggressive chemotherapy treatment that is horribly invasive on any cancer patient and those close to them. Her treatment seemed to go on for endless months. It was extremely hard on her physically and emotionally, but she put on a brave face at all times. If you didn't know she was sick, you wouldn't have guessed it if you met her, even with scarves and wigs she made them look on trend. She was eventually given the all-clear, to our collective relief. In the following years she got married and gave birth to her daughter, still working when she could, and was enjoying being a wife and mother more than anything in life.

Any cancer patient will tell you that being in remission carries the 'what if?' of uncertainty. What if it comes back hovering overhead like the malevolent dark cloud that it is? Frances didn't hold back, she lived life to its fullest, enjoying family, marriage, motherhood and of course her beloved time in the sea with renewed enthusiasm. When her cancer reared its ugly head again, it was much worse than before, accompanied with the dreaded line 'it has spread'. Her outlook was grim; even now it doesn't bear thinking about the day we received that news. We stayed positive as a family, despite the fact we all knew in the pit of our stomach it was bad, but none of us could comprehend the worst. We all went together on a family holiday to Tenerife in December 2002. My brother-in-law Liam Stewart, who is Annamarie's husband, was a local guard from Donegal Town.

He was into swimming, athletics and surfed a bit before he met my sister, so he had tucked right in with our family like another brother.

He was William Stewart on his driving licence, so we accused him of being an undercover Protestant trying to infiltrate our family. Liam had recently gone through hip surgery and was wheelchair bound for a few months and at best on crutches for that holiday. As we made our way through Belfast airport, our spirits were high as it was the first time in years we had gone away as a family. I was given the task of pushing Liam around in his wheelchair, which I accepted immediately knowing I had a week full of cheap gags at his expense. As I pushed him past security turning into WH Smith's newsagents and I jammed him up against the section with all the naughty lads' magazines. I locked the wheelchair in position so he couldn't budge. I spread a few choices of big-breasted magazine covers on his lap, telling him, 'Youse Protestants love that kind of stuff.' I walked away to sounds of him lowly cursing under his breath 'Richard, for feck sake ya bastard, yee let me outa here tee feck.' I turned around to see my mum and Frances doubled over with laughter at my toilet humour. It's one of the last images I have of Frances, laughing her heart out in Belfast airport while holding her daughter in her arms. She died in hospital three weeks later on 16 January 2003 at the age of 39. I couldn't bring myself to visit her in hospital; maybe it was a coward's way out for me but I wanted my last visual memory of her to be clear in my mind and how I always saw her: strong, beautiful, full of life, the leader of our pack.

I'm no stranger to recurring dreams. I have one about Frances that I love but hate at the same time. In my dream we are all in our old kitchen. My nieces and nephews, who were all children when Frances died, are all grown up now, young men and women with careers and their own lives. Frances is there, beautiful and smiling, my young-looking older sister forever frozen at age 39, as old as she will ever be. Everyone else ages in my dream. I am now 10 years older than she was when she died. I feel like an imposter in my own dream's memory of her. How will she recognise or know me as I'm 20 years older, a different brother now? I try to get to her, I have so much to say, but I can't. She is smiling at me, her face happy: content and sun-kissed, the way I remember her. I want to tell her how much we all miss her and love her. She has never known me as a married man, a father, she has never met my children. I want to tell her how much my daughter looks like her and reminds me of her with her strong personality and passion for the sea. I can't get the words out of my mouth; when I do, Frances doesn't hear me. I wake up feeling so euphoric at seeing her again; it felt so real, so close to me. Her image lingers with me for a few moments before I accept it's just my dream again.

Our family have never been the same since Frances passed. How could we be, as there is a gaping hole in all our hearts? I know I have been a different person since Frances died. It's said that time heals, but not for me I'm afraid. Over the 20 years since she passed away, I miss her more rather than less every day, and it cuts deep; that hollowness is impossible to quell. Especially when I surf, the memory of her is there every single time. The processes and stages of grief you go through to eventually finding acceptance still feel unattainable to me.

I couldn't accept Frances was gone. None of us could. It called into question my whole system of belief, mortality, morality and the purpose of what I now saw as a cruel life and world we live in. Anger is easier to accept than loss. I became angry more than any emotion: just a burning, searing anger. I became reactive, capricious and short-tempered, with zero tolerance for any windbaggery bullshit from anyone. It made me harder and more cynical of people and situations. In a contradiction, I gathered around good friends. I kept up an exterior veneer of being upbeat, pretending everything was alright, joking around, full of laughter. Keeping up appearances in effect, as if nothing had happened, while in reality you and your family are feeling crushed and vulnerable. It was a defence mechanism and deflected my true feelings, making it easier to deal with. Frances's funeral was a massive affair. She was a young mother very well liked locally, with scores of friends and relatives in attendance. I hated the process of the wake and funeral; it felt intrusive, like we were all exposed and up on a pedestal. It was no one's fault. It's a beautiful tradition we have in Ireland of the whole community coming out. It's just that at the funeral, after the umpteenth 'sorry for your troubles', I wanted to beam our family out of there and wrap a protective blanket around us all, shielding us from the outside.

On the drive home after, I felt incredulous looking out the car window at all the people going about their daily business. Didn't they know my sister had died? How could they be going to the supermarket, the pub, sharing a laugh with a friend on the street or filling their car up with petrol? Of course, the world goes on, but it seemed just so awful to me that it was.

Not a day goes by that Frances isn't in my memory many times. In my dreams of her, I can feel her picking me up as a child and slinging me on to her hip. I especially feel it when I surf; without fail she's on my mind as soon as I hit the water. It doesn't matter whether I'm giving a surf lesson, by myself or surfing with good mates, it's like a trigger. I can be a million miles away, but as soon as I put on my leash and hit the salt water, she pops right in there and a sadness washes over me, stinging like an open wound. Whatever shred of faith I had left in God or religion felt like it had evaporated when she died. I felt like lashing out, especially at God; he seemed like a good place to start. The hypocrite in me was looking for someone to blame. When I was out for a surf or a run at the end of the beach, I'd shake my fist at the sky like a madman in a fuck you God salute. If you believe Adam and Eve-style that God lives in a pearly palace just beyond the clouds, I was sending some bad-intentioned fist-shaking his way. It strangely felt good to vent. I was looking for someone to blame and he never answered back.

The year Frances died, my career was really starting to catch fire. Gabe and I were making big statements in the world of big-wave surfing by 2003, unlocking more secrets of Mullaghmore with each surf and getting some attention with the release of our first surf film together, *Eye of the Storm*, that year. It was what I had wanted, personal achievement in surfing, but I felt annihilated inside. I can't say that losing my sister gave me any extra ammunition or incentive to succeed. I couldn't imagine the alchemy of turning grief into success in that respect.

What losing Frances did do was to give me a 'I don't care, I'm not afraid of anything' attitude in the water. The bigger the better and bring it all on, as far as I was concerned. Courting danger in the sea didn't make me skip a beat. It was a strange, hardened emotional state to be in. When I reflect on that time now, I felt I was in a trance like an out-of-body experience. I didn't feel like me at all, my mind filled with numbness and anger. That mindset turned into a not-holding-back recklessness in big surf that I didn't quite have before. I was never one to go out for a punch-up in a pub to vent. For me, if I had built-up aggression pitting myself against massive waves alone or with Gabe, I would lighten that load and douse those aggressive flames fast. I lost any underlying fear of self-preservation. I was relishing the life-and-death situations often with an unhealthy sense of bravado.

I took off and rode some big, heavy waves over that period with a cavalier attitude. I remember taking an unnecessary hit on one brute of a wave. It administered a proper smack down and spin cycle, but I came up laughing from it. I have a very clear memory of that day. We were out by ourselves at big Mullaghmore in early spring. I copped just one beating that day near the end of the session. I had a douze-points perfect surf with a bag full of 20-foot waves. Very unusual for Mullaghmore, the wave conditions were almost glassy and smooth, with just a little disturbance on the wave face from the air-boils caused by the shallowness of the water underneath. The water was still winter cold, but with a beautiful thin blue sky and no wind it was dream conditions. It made for the easiest surfing I'd had ever experienced out there. On immaculate days like this, we would aim to come out of those sessions clean, with no wipe-outs if possible; because the cards were stacked in your favour, it was easier to be flawless. I had a clean sheet and felt very in sync with the waves and conditions that afternoon. Every wave I had was a winner. I was almost on cruise control, in an easy daze gliding along smooth as silk on the big chunks of North Atlantic power. Even on the biggest ones, it felt easy tucking in and out of their crystalline cylinders, meandering around big critical sections with self-assured and nuanced composure, not something I usually had while surfing Mullaghmore.

I remember having a mad moment and becoming unnecessarily unstuck from my board on one final set wave. Moments after detaching, I was deep down in the pandemonium of that wipe-out. I was in a rage, screaming expletives under the water while my head was racing, thinking, 'I'm glad I fell on this one. Is this it, is this all you've got? Pathetic. This is a piece of piss.'

One hundred per cent of my anger and rage was directed at God that day of course, who else? A God I might add that my logical head said didn't exist. How could he? The all grown-up, independent me believed in science. To me, any notion of creationist views was so absurd when measured against Darwinian realities. God and his lot had failed for starters on empirical grounds in my warped world of blame, just as a small, conflicted, compartmentalised chamber of my heart still said something to the contrary. Catholic guilt was striking me again, in the maelstrom of Mullaghmore of all places.

Gabe picked me up where the wave finally deposited me in a thick carpet of gurgling white foam near the end of the channel. I came up laughing and in a mad rage. Gabe said 'Are you alright, Rich?' 'I'm grand,' I said, 'I fecking loved every second of that beating', slapped the water and foam like a demented seal, looking every bit the deranged nutter to Gabe peering down from the jet ski. He replied, 'It looked like you jumped off on purpose on that one. Did you jump off intentionally, you mad bastard?' Who wipes out on a big wave on purpose?

He was right, I had jumped off a big but perfectly makeable wave. I hadn't jumped off for any safety or escape reason, but rather to put myself right in the line of fire. It was the inverse of big-wave surfing rationality. I just wanted to cop a massive beating by deliberately dismounting at the most critical moment, right at the bottom of a towering wave where I would get most axed as the wave discharged all its power. I didn't want to go back to shore with a clean record that day. I wanted the hit of ultra-violence associated with an enormous wipe-out. I wanted that loss of control and madness that becomes a precursor to a very single-minded thought, which is the clarity to survive a big wipe-out.

Gabe continued, 'I thought you were dead for sure after that hit. Rich, that was a fucking stupid thing to do, you were lucky to come out of that smiling.' I said, 'I know, I'm sorry about that, it was a daft thing to do but it had to be done.' We both burst out laughing with relief and the abnormality of what I'd just done more than anything. As I climbed onto the back of the jet ski, I felt a ping of guilt because I had put us both in harm's way on purpose, as Gabe had to come deep into the carpet of foam to get me. We were very in tune with each other's surfing; he could see that I hadn't tried to avoid taking a hit, performing no evasive manoeuvres. I had if anything teed myself up for it. It was a moment of lunacy. I had received the internal response I craved, conjuring whatever neurons fired in my brain's limbic system in those moments, even though I'm not quite sure what exactly that response really was. It felt good. I felt very alive: abolishing all fear and surviving, it felt liberating and victorious for me in my private war. That impetuousness became my philosophy for a while at least, with my mind a sealed environment, stubborn and impervious to outside influence.

My sister's influence on me and her loss to our family is incalculable. My mother stayed strong for us throughout, but it affected her the worst. It's the most unnatural thing in the world for a parent to bury any child, especially their first born. I only wish Frances had lived to see and do much more with her life and with her own family. A whole generation of surfers have since grown up in Bundoran not knowing her or that she even existed, never witnessing her prowess in the surf and her love and dedication to the sea, which is a real shame. She was taken far before her time, and in my own selfish way I wish she had been there to see some of my future successes. I think she would have enjoyed them, telling me to stay grounded and never to wear a tracksuit outside the front door.

# 25

# The Clare Revolution

It would be wrong to talk about big-wave surfing in Ireland without acknowledging the explosion in the big-wave surf scene in Co. Clare in the mid-2000s. It was something to behold. I can claim a fair few firsts in Irish big-wave surfing but I can never claim to be any part of the revolution down in Clare. I was an enthusiastic observer at best. I had my hands full on every big swell trying to untangle the puzzle of how to surf bigger at Mullaghmore without killing myself. I had heard rumours of a wave at the bottom of the Cliffs of Moher that was like nothing else. I was working in the USA at the time when Gavin Gallagher's short clip *And Then the Wind Died* broke out, featuring John McCarthy and a crew surfing waves and locations that just took my breath away. I sat at the computer screen in Florida and was just as gobsmacked as everyone else in the surfing world at the images I saw. If Mullaghmore was 'The Beast' then this wave in its Co. Clare fairy tale setting was surely 'The Beauty'.

When I got to surf this exposed reef break known as Aileen's shortly after seeing the clip, it was everything I had expected and more. The place sits at the bottom of the mighty Cliffs of Moher, one of Ireland's biggest tourist attractions, with over 1 million visitors a year. Dave Blount told me at the time that it was a crew of English bodyboarders who lived locally that blew the lid off the wave and surfed it first. They navigated the steep goat's trail down from the cliffs. One of them didn't fancy the 'one mistake and you're falling to your death off the cliff edge' trail, so he made the mega paddle out from Doolin Pier. Now there is a sea voyage story I'd like to hear in its entirety. I've surfed in some spectacularly beautiful places around the world, but for my money Aileen's is the most stunning setting I've ever seen or surfed anywhere. It's Celtic mysticism come to life. To most Irish people, the Cliffs of Moher are overfamiliar from above but transformative from the base of the cliffs looking up. It's a truism but a better description I can't think of as the whole scene resembles a fantasy seascape from a Peter Jackson *Lord of the Rings* film. If it had a soundtrack that morning it would have echoed to Clannad's haunting melodies in the sea mist, and when the wind quickened, clearing the sky, Davy Spillane joined in. That's what Aileen's conjured up for me on first impression.

I got to surf Aileen's with Gabe, Chris and Keith Malloy for that first time in 2006. We took jet skis out from Doolin and anchored them. We paddled the morning session and as the swell grew, we towed it in the afternoon and paddled again the next morning. That initial paddle session for me out there was an all-out attack on the senses. First, the absolute silence until the wave breaks, followed by a cacophony of calls from the thousands of puffins and other seabirds in the area, the noise like a stadium crowd with 700-foot cliffs in front holding onto and bouncing back much of the sound. That first time out, myself and Gabe were having a blast until I caught a rail on take-off and got a good hiding, the leash breaking on my 8-foot board. If I was to give Aileen's a comparison, it's something like Hawaii's Sunset Beach but much more prefect, hollower, bigger tubes, and it can hold more size without the lumps and bumps of Sunset. It was the embodiment of one of those dream waves I drew on my copy book in school. The funny thing about Aileen's for me was, although the wave has serious size I was good with that; it was the madness of surfing straight for the massive cliffs that went against every instinct I had. I never looked at the waves behind me after the wipe-out, just the cliffs ahead, and the rip pulls you back into the impact zone, not out into the channel. My board was free-running towards the boulders that look small from above, but some are car sized or bigger and covered in organic slime that makes navigating your way into and out of them very perilous, alongside the hulky mounds of white water smashing up against them constantly.

Chris Malloy saw my predicament and paddled over to the jet ski, started it up and came in to grab me from out of the water. We sat in the channel for a minute and Chris said, 'Are you going to get your board, Fitzie?' Now when Chris suggests it, you answer the call. I popped on some swim fins, he got me as close to the boulders as possible and off I dived, *Baywatch* style, to rescue my board. I made it in handy enough but regretted my decision immediately. Now I've seen plenty of broken boards in my day, snapped in two, three or even four pieces, but I watched as my board was hit by a wall of white water and exploded into smithereens against the boulders. If I had any doubt of the ferociousness of the place before, that moment sealed the deal. I had a nightmare on those boulders, which were a minefield for breaking your leg. I endured 15 cat-and-mouse minutes on the boulders, hiding behind big ones to avoid the hit of white water and then hanging on in an effort not to be pulled back through them. All the while Chris was zooming in and out of the impact zone to get as close as he could between sets. Eventually, I got a break in the set of the rising swell and swam like a madman out to Chris and was whipped out of there pronto. In the years since, those boulders have become the graveyard for many a jet ski and surfboard.

The leader of the pack in those years of discovery along the Clare coast was Mayo surfer Fergal Smith. Fergal moved to Clare with an ambition to surf waves like Aileen's to their limit. It's fair to say that Fergal went on to be Ireland's most recognised and best professional surfer of the era. To put a yardstick on Fergal's popularity and success in the years after, I remember one of the editors at *Carve* magazine telling me that Fergal was the most published and printed surfer in the European surf media for a sustained period of years rather than months. He outstripped most others in international publications outside of Europe too. Fergal never lost his Mayo roots, and is still one of the humblest, most down to earth surfers you will ever meet. The 2012 book *Cliffs of Insanity* by author Keith Duggan does a magnificent job recounting Fergal's journey, with insight into his fearless surfing that made him one of the most recognised surfers in the world at the time.

Aileen's has also since become globally recognised as a spectacular surf spot. Every hotshot pro has made the slippery trek down the cliff to surf its magic walls. As good as the travelling pros are, the local crew in Clare rule the roost, producing Aileen specialists and big-wave surfers who can surf it better than anyone.

# 26

# ISC and Florida

During the summer of 2005, I was approached by three surfer-businessman from Florida who had come over to Ireland on a fact-finding mission in the hope of getting me involved in their fledgling apparel company. They had taken one of the exhibitors' stands for the upcoming Florida Surf Expo in Orlando that September. The three Floridians had founded a company called Irish Surf Culture (ISC), producing Irish-themed surf wear predominantly for the Irish-American market. Come late September, off I went to Florida to check out what they had concocted. My then girlfriend now wife Briohny came along too for the weeklong trip to the Sunshine State.

I had been with Briohny for a while, long enough to know that she and I had something more. A couple of years prior she had pressed pause on her successful corporate marketing career in Australia for a year-long European adventure. Near the end of that year, she had found her way from the Continent to Ireland, initially to Greystones in Co. Wicklow, then followed her best mate to Bundoran for a summer of fun before returning to Australia. She meandered into our surf shop one summer's evening and before she opened her mouth, or I knew anything about her, I was smitten. I couldn't take my eyes off her; she was beautiful but wore her looks lightly. What a city-slicking Melbournian who didn't surf was doing in a surf shop in Bundoran I'll never know; you'd need her explanation on that one. We got talking and I found out she was working in town at a local Mediterranean restaurant called La Sabbia for the rest of the summer. She certainly didn't realise it then but before she left the shop, she had me hook, line and sinker. I made it my mission for the summer to ask her out, but first I had to become an annoying regular at the restaurant, dragging John McCarthy and Adam Wilson with me as back-up. It took me three months to gather up the courage up to ask her out. I had to outmanoeuvre all the other suitors baying for her attention. I found out quickly that Briohny had a fiery tenacity; she was incredibly driven, with a no-bullshit outlook on life, about as far removed from a needy girl as it was possible to get. Falling in love with a girl who had a strong character with a fierce independent streak shouldn't have surprised me too much, coming from a family like mine.

After Briohny sacrificed her blossoming career in Australia so we could be together, any thought of leaving her behind for a future life in Florida or beyond was not in my book, so we headed to the States together.

ISC and the three owners, Chris Wooton, Shaun Murphy and Richard Rosberg, were based in the city of Jacksonville on the northeast coast of Florida. We spent a few days there to meet their families and get a feel for their city and what they were all about. Chris and Shaun came from strong Irish-American surfing backgrounds, and Richard had been involved behind the scenes in sports like pro golf his whole life. They were all individually successful in their own professions, bringing different skill sets to the table. The trio had the necessary capital behind the brand to get it off the ground, coupled with a lot of enthusiasm to launch ISC.

They felt ISC needed my input and nod of approval as an Irish surfer, as they wanted their products and design to have some tie of authenticity to Ireland and its surfing culture. The Florida Surf Expo is held in the gigantic Orlando Convention Center and has thousands of exhibitors and displays from every surf and watersports company under the sun. Any company or product that is remotely water-based is in attendance. It was before the global financial crisis of 2008 when surf apparel brands could do no wrong and were on an unstoppable upward trajectory, with all associated living high on the hog. Surf, skate and snow companies like Quiksilver were fighting Nike and Adidas for the top two spots as the world's biggest lifestyle sporting brands.

At this stage, surf apparel was only second in sales to soccer apparel and jerseys on the global market. The ISC stand set-up was impressive, and over the Expo it attracted a serious amount of interest. On the second morning, we got a visit from a delightful middle-aged Floridian lady who popped onto the ISC stand. Her name tag announced her as 'Judy Moriarity Slater', suggesting the Slater family, of course. She told us she was Kelly Slater's mum, which was at the time and still probably is the best ice-breaking intro in the surfing world. She stayed for a long time chatting, and she loved the ISC stuff, telling us all about her proud Irish heritage and of course being a Moriarity by maiden name. Chris, Shaun and Richard hadn't put any pressure on me whatsoever, they just wanted me to observe and give them feedback over the Expo. As per usual, I had put undue pressure on myself to legitimise my inclusion beyond the symbolic. Deep down there is a salesman in me; retail is in my blood.

After a successful Expo, ISC asked me to come back later that year to spend a few months with them in design, marketing and sales. I agreed, as winter was our quiet season in Surfworld, and I was up for a new challenge. The urban seafront where we stayed was a collection of coastal communities collectively known as Jacksonville Beaches, or 'Jax Beach' in local parlance. It was interesting for me, as I had spent a lot of time in the USA but mostly only on holidays or surf contests. My father had been born in the States and my mum had worked there for so many years that she became a naturalised American citizen. So, our family had so many links to the States; it is a country and people for the most part that I have always liked, warts and all.

Over the next two years I worked with ISC in Florida for blocks of time, usually 2–3 months. I learned a lot about the inner workings of real American society, family life and, most importantly, business Stateside. Ways of doing business were very different to Ireland or anywhere in Europe, that's for sure. I worked on a whole new array of designs and concepts that would appeal to the US market but also to Ireland. Two very different markets, but we managed to get the balance right. I worked with a fantastic artist by the name of Michael Whitaker. Mike turned out one astoundingly original art piece after another that transferred fantastically to apparel. In my mind, he was one of the keys to the early initial success of ISC; he could put down perfectly in art form the concept I had in my head. He just got what I was trying to convey and understood how to bring it to life.

I was involved in every facet of the business, travelling from southern Florida up and down the east coast as far north as Cape Cod, promoting ISC through cold calling at potential retail outlets and surf shops. We were blitzing it where the brand was unknown. I really began to appreciate how massive the Irish diaspora is in the States, with up to 50 million Americans claiming Irish heritage. One of the best stops was in New York City. It was my first time back there since the terrorist attacks of 9/11 four years before. I have always felt modern New York is unlike any other city I've ever been to. The energy of the place visibly pulsates outwards; we were there in late summer, the zenith of activity. The weather was boiling hot with life squeezed into and bursting out of every crevice. It's not just the assault on what you see, it attacks all your senses. It's the smells – from putrid to delicious. And it's the taste of the street – the grit, fumes, the back of taxis, the subway – from which I could endlessly follow my nose around the city. Every time I'm in New York, I think of that line 'Live in New York once, but leave before it makes you hard.' It's true, I love cities for a day or two, but I don't think I could ever live in a metropolis like New York, no matter how vibrant and multicultural a melting pot it is.

We got to travel to the less obvious places like Savannah in Georgia and Tallahassee in Florida, where we attended every highland and Irish festival we could along the coast and its hinterland. We stopped at one southern barbecue roadside restaurant in deepest Georgia, Rabun County to be exact, where the movie *Deliverance* was filmed. The food in the restaurant was nothing but sensational, pulled pork before hipsters got hold of it and ruined it for the rednecks and the rest of us. It was melt in your mouth like you can only experience in the southern states. The restaurant's lack of sensitivities to political correctness was brazen. The décor of the restaurant had every Confederate American Civil War General adorned on the walls. The old patriarch proprietor of the establishment cut the look of a well-appointed but very elderly southern gentleman. He positioned himself just outside the door selling laminated A4 photos of himself in the foyer. In the photos he was dressed in a white suit with red cravat . He engaged me in conversation as I checked out his merchandise. He asked where I was from. 'Ireland,' I replied. I knew the cut of his jib so I followed it up without missing a beat by saying, 'Ulster sir, I am a proud son of Ulster.' He nearly fell off his seat with appreciation. He was all about the Antebellum Ulster Scots and hoisting up the 'stars and bars' for Old Dixie. With that off we went on a winding Ulster Scot-centric conversation. I didn't burst his bubble by telling him I was the wrong type of Ulsterman and the fact I was of the papist variety and not of plantation stock.

At $5 apiece for his laminated photos they were too good to leave behind, so I bought one of each and he signed them for me. I got him to write, 'To Richard, for God and Ulster' (minus my Catholic surname, which I didn't disclose) on both laminates. He wanted me to stay indefinitely, he said, but I knew if I took him up on his offer to stay even for a coffee and pie on the house, I'd blow my cover. He seemed almost to be in tears at my parting farewell when I told him I knew that the origins of 'rednecks' (due to the sun-burned white-skinned necks of manual working navvys) and 'hillbillies' (the male first-born of most emigrants were named William, after Mr Orange himself ) were both derogatory terms used to describe early Irish Ulster-Scot emigrants to the Appalachian Mountains. It got me thinking about my own 'Hills of Donegal'; maybe I should sell laminated photos of myself in the surf-shop signing them for Donegal and the Devil.

During my time on the east coast, I spoke to plenty of Americans who, when they found out I was Irish and lived near the border, looked on me with shock. I might as well have told them I was from Baghdad or Beirut. Their idea of Ireland was from reports on CNN and Fox during the troubles. To them, I came from a country with unbridled gun violence and worse.

I suppose it depends on the oxymoron perspective from which you view fighting violence with violence. I must confess that I was as quick to judge what's going on in the States as they were on the past and current situation in Ireland.

I went to a remarkably good music festival in Jacksonville called 'Springing the Blues'. We displayed and sold ISC at a small booth during the afternoon through to the evening. The festival was held on the 'Jax Beach' seafront overlooking the surf. It attracts tens of thousands of music lovers and some of the best blues, bluegrass and rock bands in the south. It was one of the strangest weekends: a heady mix of waves, blues and whiskey. Out surfing Jax Beach, you could hear and see the music from the water, popping in and out of the surf to catch musicians you wanted to see. Walking in and out of the festival to and from the ISC booth in board shorts with a board under my arm through the thousands of blues-centric crowds presented funny interactions all by itself.

One old black fella stood up from playing the harmonica when he saw me coming. He put his arms in a curved shape above his head, wiggling his fingers while advancing on me as quick as his old legs would take him. He said to me, 'Son, what am I?' Before I got a chance to answer him, he said, 'I'm a big wave and I'm coming to get you boy!' I burst out laughing, as did he and about five of his mates standing around. He gave me a hug and told me I was a 'crazy man', and he said he had come from Georgia for the festival. When I told him I'd come all the way from Ireland, he burst into a little Michael Flatley jig and said, 'Shit man, yer Irish, I fucking love the Irish, you motherfuckers are crazy, you drink, you fight and you hate the English.' I agreed with his four-point summation of our 15,000 years of post-Ice Age Irish culture, and said, 'You got it in one, mate.'

I'd surfed in Florida before but only briefly and mostly around

Central Florida and Cocoa Beach. The northern coast of Florida and south Georgia was new territory for me. Florida has repeatedly produced some of the world's best surfers, Kelly Slater being the most well-known and successful, but in terms of quality, consistent surf it's a minnow and not on many lists as a must-see surf trip destination. I did get some good surf in the winter months, especially around the surf breaks of the Poles and Dolphins Plaza, which straddle a big US Navy base that houses nuclear aircraft carriers. That was one surf break you were not permitted to walk down the beach to. As luck would have it, this beach was the best surf break in the area. Instead, you had to paddle down from further up the coast and back again après-surf. There were military sentries on the beach and you were not allowed to set foot on the sand as it was all naval property and you could face arrest. Thankfully, I never lost my board or snapped a leash prompting a swim to shore where you would get more than you bargained for.

I have always had a strong irrational fear of sharks that can morph into hysteria at the sight of any dorsal fin. I'm compromised though, because I am utterly fascinated by them. I know we are entering their realm when surfing, and if you spend half your life as I do in the briny sea you will eventually meet a man in a grey suit. I had up to this point a few minor sightings and scares with sharks surfing and diving in different countries, but nothing worth mentioning. The biggest shark I have ever seen was in Florida at the end of a winter's surfing in Dolphins Plaza, which has a punchy left-hander near the naval base.

Florida has the world's highest rate of shark attacks. The vast majority are non-fatal and caused by juvenile sharks chasing seasonally migrating bait fish mixing with beach users as they hug the coastline when travelling north or south. The coastlines of north Florida and south Georgia attract large numbers of calving whales into their relatively calm, shallow and warm waters. These waters at that time of year also attract large oceanic sharks that come to feed on vulnerable whale calves.

Chris Wooton and I were the only two out on a 3-foot messy but good day at Dolphins Plaza, when I saw what I thought was some floating kelp and seaweed only a few metres away. We get plenty of kelp in the water in Ireland and I'm used to seeing it float free after storms. Unattached kelp produces that visual trickery you can associate with clouds: it can take all different shapes floating in the water and changes constantly through the waves with its heaving silky bulk. I paid it no heed, perhaps ignorant or just blasé to the fact that floats of kelp are not found on this Florida coast. Chris and I were about 3 metres apart waiting for the set to come in, when a small swell passed between us. As it dropped bullseye centred between us, out emerged my kelp, except it wasn't my iodine-rich shape changer, it was a very big dorsal fin and the flash of a striped back. Shark experts say don't panic, keep calm, get your heart rate down and under control, and that's exactly how I didn't react. I freaked out and burst into panicked, shore-bound paddling mode. We both made dry land in record time. Chris was a solid lifelong local surfer who had been a beach lifeguard in his younger years. His business was in the fishing industry; they ran Safe Harbour, one of the biggest fisheries in the southeastern United States, so he was a real solid seafarer who knew how to handle himself.

Chris, like me, was out of breath, relieved and in a bit of shock. He reckoned it was the biggest shark he had ever seen, which was quite a statement. He was sure it was a tiger shark of about 14 feet plus, which is very formidable. To me it was gigantic, the stuff of legend, like my own personal Moby Dick. I hadn't time to get out my mental measuring tape as I immediately scampered like a scalded cat springing for shore. Chris seemed very certain but rightly pointed out that it was going against the current when it popped up between us and was probably stalking something else. I hadn't hung around to find out. As we made our way back to the car, we met two other surfers coming down to catch a few waves. Chris told them that he had just seen the biggest shark of his life hovering out there and it came so close that either of us could have touched it. They said, 'No way dude, that's sick, thanks man' and off they went towards the surf, telling us they'd keep an eye out. As I turned the corner to the car park, I saw them paddling out completely unfazed.

The USA is an easy country for other nations to throw dirt at; its connections to Ireland are deep in every facet of life, love, culture, society, history, art, business and politics. You name it, the Irish are tangled up in the history of America right the way to modern contemporary USA. I met a lot of really great Americans while working for ISC: funny, intelligent, surprisingly self-deprecating and understanding of subtle sarcasm, which goes against the American stereotype we are led to believe.

One morning Chris came down to tell me that the mayor of the city of Jax Beach wanted to meet me later that week if possible. 'Of course,' I said. The mayor had been a keen follower of Irish affairs and surfing, and he had admired the work my brother and I did with the school's cross-border initiative. He wanted to offer me the freedom of Jax Beach in recognition of my efforts. So, off I went to city hall slightly embarrassed. I've always struggled to take compliments or anything for free, it's not the way I operate. I have way too much Irish in me for that.

It was really a lovely heartfelt gesture; the mayor was most gracious and engaging, and I was more than honoured. I received the freedom of the city and a ceremonial key, which I still have. The mayor asked me to do a few talks in local primary schools, secondary schools and some third level colleges. By that stage in my life, I'd done enough TV and film work that I had a solid confidence in myself to stand up in front of any crowd and talk on a wide range of subjects. I could have easily declined, as there was no money involved, it was just a request followed by a handshake and a gentlemen's agreement. I saw it as a different challenge that would push me out of my comfort zone yet again.

I was asked to give a 30-minute overview on who I was, the growth of global surfing and of course politics in Ireland then open it up to questions from the floor. My delivery and content differed significantly from primary children to college students. Some settings were intimate in small classrooms and some in the colleges were held in big auditoriums through PA systems with many hundreds of students in attendance. All my talks were successful and went down well. I was always impressed by the level of intelligent questions I was asked, especially by the university students. I did almost no preparation for any talks back then. I'm not comfortable using bullet points, prompts or notes; it's all a bit too scripted so I never use them. I'd rather speak from the heart and give something different in each talk and see what direction it goes. Shortly after I had completed my mini-series of talks around the city, my time in the States was coming to an end as I was about to start the filming of *Waveriders* and I needed to be available for blocks of time over the course of the next year.

# 27

# Waveriders

The documentary surf film *Waveriders* (WR) was a slow burner from concept to completion. It had its roots in the late 1990s when I first met independent film-maker Joel Conroy. Joel and I collaborated on a few projects together and had developed a trusting working relationship. We had both bowed out of involvement in the rebel pro-tour. During 2002, together with Gabe we filmed *Eye of the Storm*, which was released in 2003. In 2001 and 2002 we had experimented with some different ways of shooting surfing. We tested pencil cameras strapped to a helmet with a weighty rig-transmitter and battery in a backpack on my back as I surfed. It wasn't practical: in one surf we broke two of the sensitive and expensive pencil cameras, which cost £300 each. We did manage to get a few good seconds of footage that got us chewing over future possibilities. It was a very early attempt at what GoPro cameras now offer action sports enthusiasts everywhere. *Eye of the Storm* was a dress rehearsal for everything we did five years later in *Waveriders* but on a much bigger scale. Gabe of course was there from the very start with his wife Lauren playing a critical role in writing and developing the project.

As an independent film, WR took many years to develop. Lining up all necessary elements, especially the funding, took many years. The film eventually got the green light and funding from the Irish Film Board, Screen Ireland and BBC NI. The premise of the film was a look at myself and Gabe, where we were at the time and the broader Irish surf scene with a deeper delve into the blossoming big-wave surfing scene in Mullaghmore and Aileen's. Of course, WR was never just a surf film. It needed a narrative arc to run in tandem with the big-wave journey. The emotional heartbeat of the film is the story of George Freeth, the turn-of-the-century American surfer/lifeguard. Freeth came from Irish emigrant parents: his father was a sea captain who moved from Ireland to California to Hawaii. Freeth grew up with a passion for the sea, especially safety at sea to prevent many drownings along the Californian and Hawaiian coasts in the late 1800s and early 1900s. He developed much of what we now consider modern beach lifeguarding techniques. Freeth was also a contemporary and predecessor in some ways of Hawaiian Olympic champion swimmer and father of modern surfing, Duke Kahanamoku. At the time, the ancient Polynesian sport of surfing had almost been eradicated in Hawaii due to European prudishness. Surfing was viewed as a scandalous and sacrilegious activity performed by almost naked natives.

Kahanamoku, with his three Olympic gold swimming medals and prowess on the waves, brought surfing back from the brink of extinction. With exhibitions of surfing on the US mainland and his sporting greatness, surfing was slowly accepted again to exist beside 'respectable society'. George Freeth's contribution in the history of the salvation and rebirth of modern surfing is widely overlooked. Some of this was his European heritage making him sit outside the Polynesian story. Freeth's early death at age 35 in 1919, from Spanish influenza, only added to the collective amnesia that surrounded his contributions. Freeth exhibited surfing outside of Hawaii and is the father of modern lifeguarding. In Freeth's life we had the narrative that would give WR depth. His story of heroism and tragedy was the perfect accompaniment to the more modern Irish surfing scene.

Joel had myself and Gabe already on board years in advance. We wanted the inclusion of many of Ireland's top surfers at the time, including Al Mennie, Andy Hill, Dave Blount, John McCarthy and Easkey Britton. (During the filming of WR, Easkey would cement her status as Ireland's first female big-wave surfer, catching some big waves at Aileen's with Gabe, myself and the Malloys.) Through Gabe we had Kelly Slater on board, and I had the Malloy brothers on side to explore the modern Irish-American surfers coming back to Ireland to surf some of the best waves of their lives.

We tested and prepared as much as possible. Although we were all involved, it was Joel who steered the ship, knocking WR into existence with his patience and persistence. He surrounded himself with a great crew of Irish operators, and in Derry's Margo Harkin he had a producer of quality. The crew was sprinkled with some New Zealanders, Aussies and Americans. The shoot for the film was to last most of 2007, as you can't force surfing and waves just don't turn up on demand. Several blocks of filming were set aside for surfing footage alone. The land-based pieces to camera are much easier to schedule. By and large, the surf showed up as and when we needed it. We had two blocks of filming in California and Hawaii. The filming of WR had so many high points: one of my favourite moments was when Gabe and I got to spend an afternoon in Waikiki chatting to legendary Hawaiian surfer Albert 'Rabbit' Kekai.

Rabbit had been born in 1920 and knew both Freeth and Kahanamoku in his youth. Rabbit passed away in 2016, but I felt honoured to have had the opportunity to spend a few hours in his company in 2007. It was truly a case of meeting Hawaiian surf royalty, and something that still lives with me.

We visited the memorial to Freeth in Redondo Beach, California. Afterwards we were invited back to the LA county lifeguard HQ, the real *Baywatch*. They showed us all their emergency response and rescue vehicles and equipment, giving us a grand tour and access to everything. Their reverence for Freeth was touching and their warmth for us and the story we were telling of Freeth was something I never expected.

I had told my wife a few years before that I knew the music star Jack Johnson, and in 2007 he was very much music's man of the moment. I had spent some time in Ireland with Jack 10 years before when he was just a college graduate working on one of the Malloys' films. I knew at the back of Briohny's mind was scepticism. She was thinking, 'Yea, right Rich, is he really your friend or have you just been surfing in the water at the same time as him?' We had a lay day while filming WR in Hawaii that coincided with the big contest final at Pipeline. I had met Jack a few days earlier when he had invited myself and Briohny to his house. He wanted to show me his studio and for us to have a barbecue with his friends and family while watching the Pipeline Masters final and the big showdown between Kelly Slater and Andy Irons. Jack had the perfect viewing vantage point from his front lawn overlooking Pipeline. Many years before, Briohny had famously camped out on the footpath in front of a Ticketmaster box office all night long to secure a ticket to Pearl Jam's Australian tour. As she sat on the Hawaiian lawn that afternoon between Jack and Pearl Jam frontman Eddie Vedder watching Slater and Irons go at it, I said to her, 'Well, do you believe me now?' which got a laugh out of everyone.

No project is frictionless, especially a film production. Gabe and I pushed the surfing side of things always. WR was shot on beautifully aesthetic but old tech 35 mm film cameras. For land-based shoots it gives an amazing rich quality on screen that you just don't often see in modern film-making. The problem with film cameras is that each roll of film is only a couple of minutes long and needs to be replaced. Replacing a can of film is a laborious, time-consuming process. Gabe and I appreciated that WR was much more than a surf movie, it was a documentary, soulful with an independent art house feel. In addition to the film camera, we pushed for a standard digital camera with an operator who knew how to shoot surfing and employed to film all the surfing sequences. As long as the battery gets replaced, a modern camera will miss nothing in the surf. With the rigmarole of changing the rolls in a film camera set against something as dynamic as surfing, the chances of missing good waves was highly likely.

As Gabe and I anticipated and red flagged from the start about missing surfing footage and memorable waves, it happened non-stop. It was no one's fault but surfing can be so unpredictable that more footage was lost than was shot. We pushed for an experienced surfing water photographer to be with us for all surfs to get that critical water footage, but with no full-time operator it was an opportunity lost. The waves were sensational one day, with a pod of spotted bottle-nosed dolphins breaching the waves as company. Alas, the whole footage was unusable, which was wildly frustrating.

As 2007 neared its end, the time and budget for WR was all but used up. We had captured some fantastic moments in and out of the surf. We had the beauty of Aileen's, the perfection of Bundoran's reefs, Californian sunshine and Hawaiian power in the bag. *Waveriders* had received a lot of support within the film and music industry in Ireland; Cillian Murphy leant his voice to narrate *Waveriders*, bands like U2 and the Undertones provided their music for the soundtrack. The only thing missing was that key big-wave sequence at Mullaghmore as the climax. We had a few sessions in the can at Mullaghmore, each with useable footage but nothing that shook the ground. We knew that we needed a special day to tie the whole film together to deliver the punch. As we were running out of time, at the eleventh hour just before Christmas a deep winter depression developed. It turned the whole North Atlantic into a rotating black hole on the synoptic charts. It was forecast to be massive, bigger than anything we had surfed before, bigger than anything we could have imagined surfing. We called Joel and told him that we were going to surf Mullaghmore when the swell hit. Joel could barely contain his excitement, telling us there was still enough time and money in the *Waveriders* budget for him and the crew to be there. The wheels were in motion with 72 hours to go.

## 28

# In the Eye of a Storm: Part 2

I turned the key in the ignition, once again kicking the van's engine back to life. Gabe and I had found our moment of solace that we had craved in each other. We didn't have to say much, mostly it was unspoken in our huddle of two. We had decided to set our course of action for the morning. That course was to go surfing plain and simple, the way it had always been between us. When facing into 50-foot waves, nothing is rational or logical about it. Self-preservation is out the window. We re-assured each other that camera crew or no camera crew we would still be here today. 'This is our day Rich, the one we have been waiting for,' Gabe insisted in his pep talk. We would get out what we had put in. We had put in a lot of hard yards surfing Mullaghmore dozens of times over the last 10 years. Now on this tempestuous December 2007 morning, as we slowly drove back to the harbour, a calmness descended on me as it usually did before going out into massive waves. The build-up was always the worst part. The days leading up to the big day, the night before of no sleep, waiting for daylight, tormenting myself with best and worst-case scenarios.

Once all that was behind me and we were on the run-in, I never failed to feel a calming confidence percolate up through me when Gabe was beside me in these situations. My trust in him was absolute, as I knew his was in me. In the distance, we could see the 50-foot storm surf with wave summits visibly peaking above the height of the cliffs before we dipped down in the road again. After our pow-wow, it all felt much less threatening to me than it was on the drive out at the start. The size and impact of the breaking waves were the same, and if anything, it had got bigger in the last 30 minutes since first light, with the swell forecast to be at its peak in the morning. The waves made for a furious sound and vision as they disembowelled themselves, slamming and then steamrolling with maximum impact off the coast. Waves of such untamed size and power made a mockery of most plans. But our minds were made up. Nothing could stop us now. We were going out as soon as we reached the harbour again, regardless of the day's obvious danger. I wanted no more discussion with anyone else, just to get suited up and go. The more you linger at the top of the bluff or at the slipway, it's easy for mind games to play out, letting in all the doubt and talking yourself round in circles and out of surfing.

As we reached the harbour, the full brightness of daylight had finally filled the early morning. I immediately saw a van I recognised in the harbour car park. The van belonged to Al Mennie, the Castlerock surfer who had been carving his own way in big-wave surfing. There were a few big-wave crews in Ireland at the time, but that morning there were just two takers for this forecast mega-storm. I was delighted to see Al with his jet ski hitched to the van. I would have expected nothing else from him. Al is reserved by nature with a quiet and at times introverted personality, but not in the surf. He is an absolute animal in big waves. By 2007, Al was an accomplished big-wave surfer and a brilliant driver and rescue operator on a jet ski. Teaming up with Al that morning was a UK-based South African surfer called Duncan Scott. Scott had relocated from South Africa to Europe to further his surfing career. He had plenty of South African big-wave experience. He had been coming over and back to Ireland in the couple of years beforehand. Although I had only surfed a few times with Duncan, I knew he and Al were as capable as anyone that morning. It was a thin layer of comfort. Now at least we had two jet skis in the water, with the four of us ready to go.

Back at the harbour, there was much activity within the production crew. There were even a few spectators turning up. Some stopping at the slipway but most just heading on past to the bluff. Word had spread of expected massive surf that morning. Most people were just curious to see if anyone was mad enough to go out. As we suited up, preparing our equipment, the jet skis checked and boards strapped down, I saw the health and safety officer for *Waveriders* coming over again, looking like she was about to have a heart attack. Some of the WR crew were specialised, but most, including her, had only worked on BBC TV shows and commercials before. There wasn't much health and safety attached to what we were about to do, and she knew it. I'm sure the whole situation made her job title feel impotent. She was up in my ear again regardless, something I didn't need at that moment. Her fear was that Gabe and I would be badly injured, or worse, and the production would be accountable. I assured her we would be doing this regardless of a production or not. I told her we would both sign a waiver if she needed us to before going out. I continued that we were going out there no matter what, on our own terms and on a timescale we felt was right, so just let us get on with it. If the production captured the waves and moments, that would be all the better.

In the end, I told her to bugger off just as Joel, the gentleman that he is, came over and calmly cleared her away. Joel knew us well enough to give us the space we needed. He had, without any fuss, captured a few moments (that are in the final film) as we arrived in the dark. After that, he took cameras out of the equation as we told him we would do our thing and he assured us he would do his thing and capture it on film.

I had driven a jet ski out of the snug safety of Mullaghmore harbour for the short journey to the fearsome headland count-less times. Even if the surf is 30 feet at the headland only a few hundred metres away, the harbour remains perfectly calm without a ripple because it's that sheltered. It's two different ocean worlds beside each other. That day there were head-high waves bending around the outer harbour wall with 2-foot waves breaking inside the inner walls. I'd never seen anything like it. As we cleared the harbour's protective arms, it was wild open ocean just a few metres beyond, with huge drifts of thick white and yellow foam in the channel being pushed out and down the coast by the wind. It's something to watch a 50-foot wave break from the front on the safety of land. It's a very different feast of fear for the eyes when you watch one break from a side view in the water. You get a real appreciation of the volume of water displacement in these waves. They are easily as thick as they are high, with hundreds of tonnes of water contained in each wave. As we watched the first set wave break, it reared but almost immediately bowed from the waist before breaking. It had a power beyond anything I had witnessed anywhere before. Waves like this suck and drain water off the reef in front as they slow down to break; often the water level in front can be several stories below the ocean level behind the back of wave. It looks like a trick of the eye, one of the optical abnormalities the ocean produces. This effect has a name in surfing: we say the wave is breaking below sea level and that's exactly what it was doing. The power of the wave is so great in those few seconds that it changes the level and depth in the sea, holding back a whole ocean for a few moments as it breaks. I'm no physicist, but the actions of huge waves over shallow reefs seem to fly in the face of natural laws. I never grow tired of watching that power to distort with brutal beauty.

There is no reward without risk, and with that in mind Gabe and I had decided to just watch one wave from the channel before we lined up out the back for a run-in on one. Sitting in the van, we had committed to a surf without any mistakes. A hard billing but a vital mindset, as you didn't want to make a mistake out here. If you want to psyche yourself out, you can achieve it almost immediately watching from the side, so enough of that. I loved the simplicity of those days, the black and white of it, no ifs and maybes, you either go or you don't. I latched onto the slack tow rope that became taut as Gabe pulled away, lifting me out of the water like a water skier. Gabe and I always laughed at the absurdity of the day; having a giggle in pressure situations was just our release. It was not the kind of situation many would find funny, but that's how it was for us.

Gabe took the jet ski way out before turning around. We picked the first big wave of the set and tracked it in, Gabe giving me the necessary speeded wipe-in before I let go. I could immediately feel the power and speed of the thing in front and behind me. The longer I stay on a wave, the more vertically steep and fast it becomes, until the wall goes beyond vertical and dredges itself into a giant cone shape. I go into a kind of trance in these situations, where moments feel like minutes and minutes feel like seconds. I will always have some gammy song in my head. It's as if my subconscious is breaking down the serious situation with some ridiculousness. That day in the water, when I wanted to have AC/DC's 'Thunderstruck' for company, I had the jingle from the old 1980s Fairy Liquid TV ad. Of all songs. If you have never heard the tune, you can google it. 'Now the hands that do dishes can feel soft as your face with mild green fairy liquid' was my internal soundtrack for the surf. It was blaring in my head. Catchy as it was, what on earth it was doing out there in 50-foot surf with me was a question only a psychologist could answer.

It's hard to get a measure of a huge wave once you are on it. It's not as if you can take out your measuring tape and have a look. A wave beyond 25 feet is hard to view any differently from say a 40-foot wave once you are on the face. What I mean is, your field of vision is the same. You don't all of sudden acquire an extra few degrees in your vision field. You certainly don't stop and look up or behind you. While surfing I could feel the extra size of the waves that day rather than see it. They were an extra 15 feet bigger than any other waves we had been out on. I surfed three waves with no mistakes and set my view to the end of the wave, heading for that exit every time. I still remember in each one the power, blur of speed, the critical moments, the point of no return when you commit. The movement of a massive curling wave is hard to draw a comparison to anything else. I knew if I fell off one of these monsters, I was in big trouble. But I made all three waves. On my second and third wave, I came perilously close to being knocked off by the exploding white water behind me. Getting caught by the avalanche of a 50-foot breaking wave and the rinse cycle aftermath was a situation that didn't bear thinking about.

We swapped over and I towed Gabe into three brutally big and powerful waves. He surfed fully committed and deep on each one, with no mistakes. We were picky and chose the bigger set waves; the smaller 20–30-foot in-between waves that on any normal day were the big ones just got gobbled up on this occasion by the bigger sets. It's a big playing field out at Mullaghmore: from take-off to where the wave ends can be several hundred metres. Considering the insanely vast amounts of water movement and wind, it makes those distances much bigger. In light of this, correcting our position was a constant. It always remained at the front of my mind: I didn't want to be caught out in the wrong position by a rogue wave. Nobody wanted to get wiped out. Luckily, that day none of us did. We had a system going with Al and Duncan that we picked off waves in the same set. We spread apart so as not to get in each other's way but close enough that we could back each other up. Al and Duncan were cool, professional and committed, both catching some incredible waves.

We had been in the water for two hours and had miraculously all come out of the surf clean. No near misses, broken bones, lost boards, rescues or lost jet skis. I motored back towards the harbour, all the while being tossed around by the ever-vexed sea. Squinting and blinded by the driving wind and hail, I navigated the short distance by dead reckoning; I couldn't see land or the harbour, but I knew which direction it was. As soon as we got to the lee of the harbour's inside wall, I took my hand off the accelerator and the jet ski rocked to a stop. I turned and gave Gabe the biggest hug I could manage. 'Thank fuck for that,' he said. In that moment we had answered our own question of are we good enough. The answer was a resounding yes. We knew it had been a day's surfing like no other.

Back in the harbour, a surge of elation tinged with a lot of relief swept through the crew as our two jet skis reached the slipway. I was delighted to see the health and safety officer hadn't suffered from a bout of spontaneous combustion while we were out tackling the waves beyond the headland. She and I shared a wee hug with a smile on her face, our mini verbal altercation two hours earlier forgiven and forgotten in an instant. Joel came down and said, 'That's a wrap boys,' which got a laugh. Joel and the crew may not have captured every single moment or all the waves during that session, but they had more than enough for the dramatic climax to *Waveriders* that we wanted. Chris Malloy had uncannily predicted on camera a few months earlier that some time soon 'the biggest waves of the year would be surfed in Ireland'. His prediction had come true quicker than any of us thought it would. Very few swells anywhere in the world that year compared to the size and ferocity of Mullaghmore that day. The waves we tackled were the biggest ever surfed on the Continent. A record that stood for years until Nazaré came on the scene and changed everything in the big-wave surfing world again.

~

When *Waveriders* opened in cinemas in Ireland in August 2008, it received much critical acclaim and was a commercial success. Gabe and I had a fun-filled week-long promotional tour around the country. Starting in Cork we visited what felt like every radio station, with print media and TV appointments along the way. We had stops in Galway, Sligo, Limerick and a final one in Dublin for a two-day stint. It was a week I'll always remember that was highlighted for me when we were chat show guests of Ryan Tubridy on RTÉ. We also attended a few opening nights overseas in the months that followed. There was one night for the great and good in the south of France. I attended a rooftop screening in the middle of Melbourne city. *Waveriders* also played to a packed opening night in southern California.

I attended a special screening at Cineworld on Parnell Street with all my family, with my mum by my side, which was a special moment for me. It was a warm August evening in Dublin. As we were waiting for the pedestrian light to go green before crossing the road to the cinema, a big double-decker bus came rumbling past. I looked up to see my image staring back at me from the artwork all over the bus. It proclaimed many superlatives about *Waveriders*. 'Breathtaking' is the one that stood out. I'd seen plenty of buses around the city that day, but this one was up close. I nudged my mum. 'Now that's not something you see every day, is it? I could get used to this.'

# 29

# Prowlers 2009

By the mid-2000s, a few more crews in Ireland had invested in a jet ski and equipment for scouring the coast for big-wave locations yet to be surfed. Fergal Smith, Tom Harrison, John McCarthy and Dave Blount formed the core of an ever-expanding big-wave scene in Clare. Paul O'Kane and Mikey Hamilton in Sligo had put their years of expertise in surfing and surf rescue to good use in the pursuit of big waves along the coast. Al Mennie from Castlerock in Co. Antrim had developed himself into a formidable waterman. Al and his brother Andrew had already established themselves in the top flight of Irish surfing. Now Al had partnered up with Devon surfer Andrew 'Cotty' Cotton, forming one of the most important partnerships in big-wave surfing. Within a few years there would be swarms of big-wave crews from all over Ireland and a constant stream from overseas coming to Mullaghmore, Aileen's and beyond.

Irish and UK-based surfers who cut their big-wave teeth in Ireland, like Al and Cotty, would be instrumental in opening up Nazaré in Portugal as early pioneers. It started to come full circle as Irish or Irish-based surfers began to influence what happened in big-wave stops around the world, especially in places like Nazaré. Cotty in 2022 is still one of the most respected big-wave surfers in the world. He is an original and long-term stalwart in Nazaré. In 2021, he was one of the heavily featured surfers in HBO's series *100-Foot Wave*. I surfed quite a bit with Al and Cotty from 2005 to 2012. One of my fondest memories of surfing with them as a crew was in 2009. Driving between Bundoran and Sligo town was one of my most trodden paths. As soon as I could drive, I was on the road south to Easkey or Strandhill for waves. At about the midway point to Sligo, the coast scoops down, revealing an open ocean stretch. For decades on any big swell, I would slow down and pull in to watch a few big-wave breaks on an outer reef off the coast. The surrounding townland is called Moneygold, sounding like a snappy name from an Enid Blyton adventure. Ironically, its name comes from an event not a million miles from an adventure storyline.

The wave I was looking at breaks way offshore in the middle of the ocean. It's a sea mount, an undersea mini-mountain whose summit sits just below the water's surface. It's so far out to sea that it picks up and is exposed to every swell going. The downside of this is that it is also open to every wind, cross rip and current imaginable. It gets plenty of swell, as I'd observed over the years. Where it gets tricky is the wind: even favourable offshores can rip it apart. For it to be surfable, there needs to be a big low-pressure swell with light winds, a combination that only comes together once in a blue moon. This is the same stretch of coast that sank the Spanish Armada in 1588 during a September storm. The small towns and townlands are steeped in Spanish Armada history. Moneygold derived its name from all the Spanish shipwreck treasure that washed up here after the Armada, or so local folklore has it. It's a rugged, serrated stretch of coast with some gorgeous beaches, but under the influence of a heavy swell or storm it's easy to see why and how dangerous exposed reefs, massive waves, rocks and currents could easily sink a flotilla of ships that got too close.

By 2009, I was well versed in big waves and what it took logistically to make it happen off the coast in Moneygold. There was a small crew of myself, Al, Cotty, Neil Britton and Paul O'Kane, along with a Sligo-based Aussie surf photographer, who were keen as mustard to get out there. It was just a waiting game, for the first swell had to have the magic combination of slack winds and 20-foot-plus surf to make it really break at its best. The photographer and I had talked and fantasised about what it would be like out there, as no one had surfed it yet. In winter 2009, we got our green light with a clean swell ranging between 20 and 30 feet and light winds. We met at Mullaghmore harbour, launched the jet skis and motored straight past our usual big-wave spot at the headland. It was tough going and took about 40 minutes of traversing open-ocean lines of massive swell. We arrived at the spot, which had that same eerie quiet that I'd experienced at Aileen's a few years earlier. It was lying flat in-between sets. So it was impossible to judge anything out there, with no point of reference and deep water all around; no jutting-out headland on the flank or waves hitting beaches down the coast that could indicate an approaching set.

We sat in where we deduced the safe channel was. Surfing a wave way out to sea is a very different challenge, needing a whole other level of awareness than any wave, big or small, that breaks near the shore. The flow of water all around us suggested that we had just missed a big set. Looking at the spot where we thought the wave should break, we saw a big deep-blue triangular mound of water rear up from nowhere. The water was so deep around the waves that you couldn't see swell coming; even the biggest sets were hidden in the depths until the last moment before they lurch up to break. The first wave had risen up from below sea level with no warning and unloaded immediately on the sea mount with tremendous, untamed power. In the silence of sea, with just the slack wind for company, we watched the first wave break with a thunderous clap, breaking the silence. It pitched so fast and so steep before it curled off the sea mount, perfectly as thick as it was high. An incredible 30-foot wave waiting for aeons to be surfed, as far as we were concerned. Our jaws dropped and everyone scrambled to get their boards unhooked. Cotty was fastest out of the traps, towing into the next set and riding a perfect wave that dwarfed him. I was up next and repeated what Cotty had done; the wave was colossal but mechanically perfect at 30 feet, with wide-open gigantic tubes on offer. The lip and curtain of the barrelling wave hit with a fury and power matching anything I had surfed. I caught a basket full of waves that day of deep take-offs, committed lines and bottom turns with a few room-sized tube rides that dissolved into the channel.

It's often said that amateurs talk about tactics and professionals talk about logistics. That day we had a great crew of experienced big-wave surfers. We had tactics and logistics down pat but also the experience and individual flair to surf the waves to their maximum. It was a day in my big-wave surf career I will always savour: a new wave I'd looked at for most of my life, and now we had launched and succeeded in surfing it for the first time. By 2009, I had a truckload of big-wave experience under my belt not only on the waves but driving the jet ski in critically dangerous sea conditions. You never relax, but experience gives you confidence. I felt calm and equally confident with the ability of the small band of surfers out there that day. My equipment, along with the jet ski I had at the time, were more than fit for purpose. Looking back, I relish that day more than almost any other. It was the perfect big-wave surfing experience into the unknown.

After a few hours of surfing incredible waves, Al and Cotty pulled their jet ski alongside mine. Al said, 'Rich, what do you think? Should we call it a day?' He continued, 'We have all had waves of a lifetime, nobody has wiped out, no jet skis lost, no boards broken and no injuries.' I said good plan, let's call it a day then and head in. I hadn't realised it, but Al was right. It was a perfect surf from start to finish: no wipe-outs, no rescue, a rare day indeed in big-wave surfing. No one held back, everyone was taking off behind the peak to maximise the wave, getting as deep as possible, even though these incredible waves had the power to cut you in half. It was a real statement of how far Irish big-wave surfing had come that we could have a home-grown crew surf a wave like that where everyone was so committed, professional and surfing right on the edge. Days like that don't come around that often.

Before we left and headed for the bumpy ride back to the harbour, the boys said to me over the noise of the four jet ski engines that I should be the one to name this new wave. As the 'local' boy I had been harping on about this wave for years, about how on certain conditions I thought it was well surfable. I shouted to him over the racket, 'I think we should call it Growlers.' All through the surf, once the waves broke after the initial sound-spitting clap it made, it continued with an unearthly guttural sound as it rumbled on like a beast growling. I'd never heard another wave make that kind of noise before, so that's what it sounded like to me and I thought Growlers sounded perfect as a name. Al couldn't hear me properly through all the noise. 'What did you say, Fitzie? Did you say Prowlers?' I imme-diately thought that sounded even better: the wave prowls around below the surface in the cold dark depths and comes up to hunt you down. I shouted back, 'Yea, that's what I said: Prowlers.' So, Prowlers it became, and the name stuck.

In the days and weeks following that surf at Prowlers, the photographer's photos and story made the rounds through the European and international surf magazines' online sites. Even the *Irish Times* and Joe.ie got in on the story, publishing interviews and photos. Our mission to Prowlers caused quite a stir at home but more so overseas in surfing circles. The images of the waves we had surfed were up there with any of the world's best big-wave spots. To many, it seemed unbelievable that in 2009 there were still waves of that quality unsurfed in western Europe.

## 30

# Euro Surf 2011

To better or match our surfing lives after the success of *Waveriders* and the record-breaking waves of December 2007 was always going to be a hard thing to do. For Gabe and I, in many ways it would be the high point in almost two decades of surfing, pioneering and adventuring together. We didn't just suddenly stop surfing big waves or Mullaghmore after that day. If anything, it pushed us into the spotlight like never before to continue. With the afterglow of *Waveriders* still burning as the film rolled out on DVD, in cinemas and TV across the world, it kept us in demand for the next couple of years. I would receive constant messages from friends everywhere saying, 'Hi Rich, just wanted to let you know I've just seen *Waveriders* on our flight to Dubai', or as part of a film festival in Sydney, that kind of thing. Gabe and I kept going back out to Mullaghmore, but occasionally, like that day at Prowlers in 2009, I surfed big stuff without him. If Gabe couldn't make it over from France, there was now an established and growing community of experienced big-wave riders in Ireland who I could hook up with.

Individually, my professional career as a big-wave surfer

couldn't have been stronger. I was on mouth-watering professional contracts with wetsuit, apparel and skate shoe companies (even though I couldn't skate the length of myself). In the non-surfing industry, 3G and Volkswagen had signed me up. I was like a billboard; I had barely any real-estate left on my surfboards for another sponsor's logo. Turning down offers from conflicting sponsors more than I could accept was the new norm for me. I had expanded my surf business to three surf shops and two surf schools. In addition to the surf school in Bundoran, I had seen an opportunity to open the first surf/ stand-up paddleboarding (SUP) venture in Brittas Bay to capture the Dublin crowds in the summer. As a silent partner in one and an investor in an another, I had two surf apparel companies on the go. Stepping back from surfing was the furthest thing from my mind; I just needed some re-adjustment and to evolve in time. Standing still never suited me. Our surf school in Bundoran took up most of my time now. We kept our surf school as customer-based and as personal as possible, avoiding going too big. It had become busier and more successful than I or the staff could handle most days. There was a limit to how many we could safely give lessons to each day. We constantly maxed out at 150 newcomers a day, all keen first-time surfers. The other surf schools in Bundoran dwarfed us with their daily numbers. I enjoyed the energy and fun of bigger groups but my heart and soul were still in the more intimate one-to-one lessons. I did as many of those as I could fit in per week. Most of the time they were a financial loss-leader and not worth doing. However, I enjoyed those one-to-one sessions, which gave me a chance to chat, give time to and get to know customers.

At the start of 2009, I heard through the ISA that Ireland and Bundoran in particular had been chosen to be the location for the 2011 European Championships in two years' time. It would be the third time the town hosted the event. I was immediately struck by the possibility of competing in it. I hadn't surfed in a regular surfing contest at any level since 1997. I had been focused on big-wave surfing since missing the last home Europeans in '97 due to illness. When 2011 came around, it would be 14 years between competitions for me. I knew I would need to surf the whole season of qualifiers in 2010 and 2011 to make the Irish team. So much had changed in Irish competitive surfing since 1997; the standard was unrecognisably high from when I remembered. Watching the Irish Open division, the surfing was as good as any WQS event. Surfers like Cain Kilcullen, Fergal Smith and Stephen Kilfeather were at the level of any pro-surfers in Europe. Cain had toppled tour surfers like French Pipeline Masters champion Jérémy Florès in the past.

My body shape had changed. I had more muscle mass and bulk from years of strength conditioning for big waves. I was still flexible and in great shape, but nowhere close to where I wanted to be to compete. In contest surfing you need to be quick, light and responsive. I put myself on a mega-strict regime of training for the following year, working at it every day as an obsession until I was leaner, stronger and more flexible than I had ever been. I set myself a few targets again: modest ones, but targets, nonetheless. Aware that there is more to competitive surfing than fitness, I was still rusty on the tactics, mind games and aggro of competitive surfing. I wanted to make the Irish team by first setting my goal to be in the master's division at the Europeans. I thought if I could make the team and just get through even one heat at European level at home in front of a home crowd, it would be vindication for the heartbreak of missing out 14 years before. I owed it to myself, and at age 36 by the time the event came around, it would be my last realistic chance. I was already way too old in many respects for contest surfing, but I felt better than ever in the water and my regular surfing was sharper than it had ever been.

When the contest season started in earnest, I was ready and chomping at the bit to get a contest jersey on. The qualifiers were split between five events starting in autumn of 2010 and concluding late spring of 2011. I was like a caged animal to get going. All the disappointment of missing the home event in 1997 came back as motivation for me. As the championships were being held in Ireland, competition for places was as fierce as I'd ever witnessed. I got off to a flyer in Easkey, winning the event in sunny weather and 4-foot surf. I continued on a roll, winning the next three events against some quality Irish and overseas competition. I qualified with four event wins and enough points to make the team. The last event was a dead rubber for me, so I was shrewd for perhaps the first time in my competitive life in letting that event go, and I stayed at home the last weekend. Four back-to-back wins was the best run I had ever had in domestic contests. The Europeans were scheduled for September, and before kick-off I attended all training camps and team meet-ups. On the side I asked my mate, two-time European champion Grant Robinson, to knock me into shape for the psychology of contest surfing. We trained in the evenings throughout the summer, running over every heat scenario until I was blue in the face, so that by August I knew everything backwards. My good friend and local board shaper Gavin McCrea came on with me to help me with prep and boards during the event. With the experience and expertise of Grant and Gavin, I had surrounded myself with a good team. When the Europeans kicked off it was blessed with mild sunny weather and good waves for the whole 10 days. Bundoran had changed dramatically as a town, the place and people fully embracing the event at every level. The whole thing felt and looked like a late-summer surfing event in California. My nieces and nephews were given time off school to come and watch my heats and the whole event had a festival atmosphere.

Surfing in a heat is like a fight, it takes place far away from the judges and crowd in comparison to other sports, with lots of verbal nasties, paddling over boards and argy-bargy going on. I've done a bit of boxing and martial arts over the years. Surfing a heat has similarities. You can deliver a knockout blow from the buzzer. It can more likely be a cagey affair with a bit of shadow boxing and sizing everything up. Eventually, you must go on the offensive, hunting down waves and at times your competitor with as much guile and skill as force. I was ready for it all, even the sword play. During the event, I did have a bit of wetsuit grabbing, taking a buck by the scuff of the neck in a heat out of sight of the judging tower. One of the French surfers and I clashed more than once. I never backed down, refusing to be intimidated on my own patch. I was as prepared as I could be for my first heat with a packed town full of local and travelling spectators. I blitzed my opening heat in shifty, heavy 5-foot waves at Tullan Strand. As the contest was in my hometown, I elected to stay at home rather than the team hotel. Briohny was pregnant with our first child, and I wanted to be there always. I attended every team meeting and training, but for the first time at a big international event I put myself before everything else. I was laser focused to do what was necessary to go far in the contest. I won my first few heats and by the end of the week I had landed myself in the quarter-final, winning that too. It was what I had always dreamed of from a contest, to be winning heats and still in the mix at finals weekend at a European Championships. This was more like it, I was on a high.

I had a brilliant start to the semi-final with a massive cheering crowd watching on. I led the heat from the start until the final few moments. There were three other top surfers in my heat, each more than capable of winning it. I was pipped at the end of the heat, failing to make the final at the death. I wasn't disappointed. I was on a cloud of happiness that I had had a chance at redemption after 14 years. With such a gap in years since my last competition, I had gone much farther than I dared dream at the start. Finishing fifth in a European Championships in my hometown: I would have bitten your hand off at the start of the week for that. I felt I had surfed the best heats of my life at any international event. While I had been preparing for my second heat earlier in the week, I had checked the heat sheet that morning and saw that I was up against a surfer who was competing for a lesser European nation. I recognised his name instantly, a South African World Pro Tour veteran. He had only recently come off the world tour. I managed to beat him that day and later put another World Championship tour pro-surfer to the sword before the end of the week. It was another one of those events where half the competitors weren't European. For example, the Australian pro-surfing champion, James Woods, surfed in the event for a European team. He didn't manage to make the Open finals, such was the high standard of the contest.

That season of 2011–12 had a few more good times in store for me. Paul O'Kane had been the driving force in organising the first big-wave event at Mullaghmore. It was to be sponsored by Billabong, and there was a growing hype about the event. With a waiting period over autumn–winter, there was a good window of time to wait for exceptional conditions to run it in. Mullaghmore didn't disappoint and produced a perfect long-range 20–25-foot day with sun and light waves to green light the event. I was in Australia at the time for a few weeks, visiting Briohny's family in Melbourne. When I got the message, I flew straight home, as the event was given the all-clear for the following weekend.

The running order was invitational for 20 two-man teams taking part: the best in the UK and Ireland with a host of Europe's best and mix of US, Brazilian and Aussie surfers too. The mild winter weather and a weekend guaranteed a huge crowd of thousands of spectators and media all along the coast. Driving up to Mullaghmore Head at first light that Saturday morning, the place was already overflowing with people, cameras, cars, vans and contest infrastructure. I thought to myself how times had changed since our first days of nobody watching bar sheep and seagulls. Gabe and I had received an invite, but I immediately stipulated I only wanted to compete alongside Gabe. I'd forfeit my place rather than go with someone else.

I put no pressure on Gabe, but when I had a chat with him before leaving Australia he was eager for us to partner up again for the event. Two teams were sent out for each heat, both surfers in each team being scored on their best wave. The highest combined score at the end of the day won the event. Gabe and I surfed what I'd say was our best, a perfect heat and one of our most assured sessions ever at Mullaghmore. The waves were big but not giant. We were the most experienced team out there and the veterans of Mullaghmore. Everything went like clockwork for us, no fear, no holding back, it all just flowed. After so many years together, we could finish each other's sentences in surfing terms. Every transition was smooth, controlled with big perfect tube rides under the blazing winter sun and blue sky. It was a special day and dreamland stuff for us.

I came in from my heat to be greeted by a teary Kevin Tobin, my childhood surfing hero. I hadn't seen him in over 10 years, but he had travelled down for this event. He gave me a big hug and said to me how proud he was at the way Gabe and I were surfing. He was taken by the waves we caught, telling us our waves and surfing was out of this world. It was a huge moment for me. I still think KT is the coolest thing in surfing. In the end, Gabe and I made the top three teams that were separated by less than one point. Gabe won wave of the event with an incredible tube ride, and the prize-giving was full of humour and friendship.

The whole weekend was a triumph for Irish big-wave surfing and camaraderie between all the competitors. I didn't realise it then, but that weekend was our swansong and the last time Gabe and I would surf Mullaghmore together or separately for that matter. It's been over 10 years since I surfed Mullaghmore.

Before the year was out, I was voted 'Donegal Sports Star of the Year'. An honour for me above any, it surpassed my national team representation. The best was saved until last. My daughter Ella decided that the night of the presentation was a good night to make her entrance into the world. I missed the gala presentation but in the wee small hours of the night I had in my arms the most precious thing I had ever held: my newborn daughter.

# Epilogue

# The Future

For the last five years, since 2017, I've been living in Australia sharing my time between Ireland and the Victoria coast. It was all good until the Covid-19 pandemic hit, with Melbourne enduring one of the world's longest lockdowns. I hadn't been home to Ireland for over two and half years. If there was any silver lining in the nightmare of the world suffering under Covid-19, it was that it forced my hand. What I mean is I would have never written this book if it wasn't for lockdowns. Writing a book wasn't even on my radar.

Like all families we had a good innings on streaming services over lockdowns. Ella discovered the film *Soul Surfer* on Netflix. The movie tells the dramatic life story of the early years of inspirational Hawaiian surfer Bethany Hamilton. My Ella is now aged 10 and has become a handy wee surfer in her own right. Our house, except for the garage, is about the least typical surfer's house you have ever seen. We never watch surfing online or any surf films. You are more likely to find us watching *The Mandalorian*, football or rugby on TV. So, I was surprised to find Ella watching *Soul Surfer* one rainy evening and even more so when she announced it was her new favourite film.

I've never told Ella or my son Kai anything about my past life in surfing, nor have they ever seen any of my surf films on screen or any surf photos. Seizing the moment, I piped up to Ella and announced, 'Did you know your dad has met Bethany Hamilton and her family a few times and she has been in daddy's surf shop in Bundoran as well?' I produced a few photos of Bethany and I to back up my big claim. Ella was genuinely amazed. 'Daddy, how and why are you standing beside her?!' I pumped it up even further with 'I bet Harry Styles can't say that!'

As my kids surf they are getting a bit more curious hearing bits and pieces from their mum about the surfing exploits of their previously cool dad. I recently overheard both of them boasting to one of their friends, 'My dad used to be a big-wave pro-surfer, you know.' If they stay the course and get hooked on surfing like I did, well then, I'll be all in. I don't push either of them when it comes to surfing. In saying that, the two of them are much better surfers and are more confident in the water than their age suggests. For now, I'm more than happy for them to explore all activities from reading books to bashing the keys on our piano, ballet, football or whatever else they want to have a shot at.

Watching my children being born instantly altered something in my DNA. I was filled with pure love and a feeling so strong to nurture and protect them. Those feelings of parenthood have stayed just as strong in me since. As all children do, my two have taken my focus off myself, which is necessary and healthy. Ella was born a few months after that last surf with Gabe at Mullaghmore. I knew that night in the maternity ward at Sligo General Hospital that it had all changed for me. Over the winter, when Ella was just a newborn baby, I'd see big storm systems heading for the west coast, a time that usually got me giddy with big-wave excitement. Previously, I had my fingers crossed that the wind would stay favourable; now I had my fingers crossed that the wind would blow horribly onshore, rendering the big swell no good for surfing. It was a complete mind shift for me. I knew it signalled the end. You have got to want big waves 100 per cent. It's too dangerous to go out their half-cocked. Now all I wanted was to be there for Ella 100 per cent.

Back in 2012, when I turned 37, I was still on significant money from professional contracts. It was nothing to be sneezed at, equating to a full year's wages. I was doing good, but when contract negotiations came around again, I knew in my heart I was done. I thanked every sponsor who had supported me for years. One sponsor I had been with for the last 15 years. I didn't ask for any new deals, telling them all my time was up. It felt it was the right move for me, although cutting away that money stream did sting. It probably seemed like folly to anyone looking in, as I had just had the best year of my life in contests. I'd also surfed the big-wave event of our dreams with Gabe, my daughter was born, and I was awarded Sports Star of the Year. A successful year for me like no other. But as a good friend and ex-top 16 pro-surfer said to me after he retired, 'It's always good to go out on your own terms bowing out on top.' So that's what I did.

It's impossible to turn off that tap completely. Of course, there were times in the last 10 years when I watched all the action and how much it's progressed at Mullaghmore, Aileen's and beyond. I'm not immune to getting pangs of wanting to be out there again. I'd never say never. One thing is for sure, if it ever happens again, I wouldn't do it without Gabe. For a few years after 2012, I'd still get media requests to do all kinds of stuff.

Some I did, most I didn't. Among others I turned down a guest spot on a TV3 chat show and a well-paying gig when Samsung wanted me to be the new face for their latest mobile phone TV advert. Turning it down sounds mad, it was easy money, but my head or heart wasn't in it. I didn't feel it was right for me at the time. If you turn down too much, eventually your phone stops ringing. I did cherry pick a few things that I liked the sound of. I was cast in a Jägermeister ad for TV and cinema across Europe. It was a week-long big-budget shoot in Iceland in November 2014. I knew the other four surfers who were cast. Dave Blount was one of them, the other three were UK-based. The production crew in Iceland were the same company who shot *Game of Thrones* when they filmed in Iceland. We were in good hands. I was delighted to be cast; it was all new to me, and surfing in Iceland with a few mates for a week was a great experience. A highlight was surfing in a blizzard way up in the coastal wilderness in the northwest of the country. The water temperature was 1–2 degrees above freezing, with a minus-20 wind chill factor. I loved every second of it. Later in 2015, I coached the Irish junior team at the European Championships in the Azores: another Euros which was hectic, but I loved it. It gave me an understanding from the other side of the fence at what Roci and Brian Britton had endured coaching us as kids all those years before. The Irish junior surfers in 2015 were much better behaved and more mature than we ever were in the 1980s and '90s.

Since 2016, even though we have a prominent surf business in Bundoran, I have personally stepped much further back from surfing than I ever imagined I would. The surf shop keeps me in touch with what's going on, so I have a finger on the pulse at least. Recently though, in the last year particularly, as my children have grown a little older and my bad back is starting to feel less like a corset, I've re-engaged with surfing much more. I haven't ruled anything out for the future if my desire to be in the water increases. I still feel I have a chapter or two left in my surfing journey. The last 10 years have been a long pause.

~

To try and sum up where Irish surfing is now in 2022 into a neat line or two would be impossible. One thing I can say with certainty is that it has changed utterly and beyond all recognition in my lifetime: from something niche and local in Ireland to something mainstream and nationwide with a broad domestic and international appeal. I still find myself doing double-takes as surfing is so much more in the public consciousness in Ireland, when you hear a Dublin-based 2FM DJ casually talking about heading out west for a weekend of surfing, mulling to himself on air whether the waves will be better in Lahinch or Achill Island.

The one thing for me above all is that I love to see Irish people continue to take to the waves. Irish surfing is now so much bigger than one area, organisation, any surf school or surf shop, any one wave, or any one person to effect change. Surfing in Ireland is diverse, and it's still full of character and colour if you know where to look. We all now have a healthier awareness and growing respect of our coastal environment, with participation in surfing widespread throughout the country both on and off the coast. The future is bright too, with Irish big-wave surfers leading the pack at home and now influencing international big-wave surfing too. To me that's just incredible, as I remember when and where it all started. In Gearoid McDaid we have an incredible talent leading from the front with one big result after another overseas. The under-age level of Irish surfing in 2022 is frighteningly good, and the next few years will be telling. There are surf and SUP schools everywhere that cater to everyone. You'll see plenty of people on Grafton Street or any town centre decked out head to toe in surf wear, even though the likelihood is that most of them have never stood on a surfboard in their lives. Even in the most remote part of west Connemara, if the waves are up on the intricately stunning Galway beaches, you'll be guaranteed to see someone surfing. Surfing as a sport has developed in Ireland along many lines. Its development is imperfect and fractured in places. But the waves stay the same and are the real talking point. I know most of the younger generation involved in the private and national growth of Irish surfing. In most cases, no matter what coastal town you live in, there is a safe pair of hands involved.

I'm proud of everything I achieved in surfing; even the mistakes were worth making. At the time, I certainly wasn't thinking about what legacy I'd leave behind in my wake or some claptrap about only doing it for the love of the sport and to inspire the next generation of kids. I was a kid myself at the time. Those feel-good statements would ring hollow if I started to attach them to myself. If I transport my mind back, I surfed because I grew up on the beach and had my brother and sister take me by the hand and push me into waves. Later on came the full realisation of how good Irish waves were, and we as a family opened the first surf shop out of necessity. Gabe and I had no idea how far and globally reaching big-wave surfing in Ireland would become. We pushed ourselves to surf bigger and bigger waves at Mullaghmore because we wanted to. We never for a second considered how it would look in 20 years' time or how it might influence any surfer in that future. Most of the crew surfing Mullaghmore now were just starting primary school when Gabe and I went out there on our maiden voyages. It would be up to someone else to talk about legacy and contributions. For me, seeing the new generation of Irish surfers surfing our big-wave spots with more confidence, skill and on much larger waves than I could imagine is just pure satisfaction. I feel a sense of pride in Irish surfing more than anything as I watch from afar at the yearly progress. It's the natural way of things: change, evolution, improvement, new faces and moving forward on what has gone before is a good thing. I'd be gutted if that wasn't the case.

In 2020, Bundoran boy Conor Maguire surfed a 60-foot dreadnought of a wave at Mullaghmore. It caused a sensation everywhere in surfdom and mainstream outlets. To many surfing observers, me included, it was the global wave of the year. Conor's stock has risen dramatically since, as he continues to set the surfing world on fire with his approach to multi-storey-sized waves. He is now one of the most respected, in demand and recognised big-wave surfers in the world. Not bad for a Bundoran boy. I've known Conor since he was a child; his granny's house was just across the road from mine. He would be in and out of my house after school as a wee surfer boy. I can't claim any real link to Conor's astonishing ability in gigantic surf or his success. I had stopped surfing Mullaghmore many years before he took to its cavernous waves. He is a self-made, very humble and impeccably well-mannered fella following his own path. After his monumental wave, I received a private communication from Conor that sums up his character:

'Thanks for having time for me when I was an annoying wee cub running about the surf shop. Growing up watching what you were doing inspired me to want a career as a professional surfer. You laid the path that I followed, Thanks for everything, Rich.'

It was a touching message from an incredibly down-to-earth young man. If I have inspired, well that can't be a bad thing, and maybe I have added a few more bricks in the vast story wall of Irish surfing? If so, then I'll take that all day long.

# Acknowledgements

For my Mum, thank you for everything. My brother Joe, my sisters Annamarie and Karen, this story is yours as much as it is mine. To Mum, my sister Frances and my Dad, I only wish you were still with us so I could put this book in your hands. To my friend and author Mark Mc Meniman for being in my corner from the earliest iterations of this book. I can't express how much your invaluable insights and encouragement helped me along the way. Gabe Davies, my brother in arms, thank you for saving my skin on so many occasions. You are my other half in surfing and we are long overdue a reunion in the sea. To The Irish Surfing Association, Irish Surf Teams and our local surfing community through the years, thank you for all the good times and memories.

To Bundoran past and present, the place and people I love; you will always be home for me. Thanks to my main man Patrick Timoney for your loyalty to me in keeping the ship afloat. My good friend Chris McHale for keeping the light side in check. Po O'Donnell and Adam Wilson for your constant and unwavering friendship. Colm Hamrouge for always being at the end of the line for a much-needed conversation of pure lunacy. Amber and Todd Cousens, Lee Jones and Shane Holman, the 'Latte Lads', for your companionship over the bumpy years of lockdowns as this book was taking shape.

Jeff Walley and Joel Conroy for early draft reading and your vote of confidence in what I was writing. Mark Geagan for giving me an early opportunity to flex my writing wings.

Thank you Catherine Gough, Kerri Ward, Tom Whiting and all the team at HarperCollins for your belief and hard work in making this book a published reality for me.

Lastly my wife Briohny, this book exists because of you. You seeded this book in me. With no fuss you gave me the time, space and confidence to write it. When I so often threw my hat at it in doubt and frustration you gave me a well-placed nudge and you were always the calming presence to get me and it back on track. I truly couldn't and wouldn't have written this without you.